RETRIBUTION ROYALE

The Untold Truth Behind the 1946 Windsor Jewels Heist

RETRIBUTION ROYALE

H L LEAVEY

Granddaughter of infamous cat burglar Leslie Holmes

First published in Great Britain by **Paraiba Publishing**

eBook ISBN: 978-1-9193670-1-9
Paperback ISBN: 978-1-9193670-0-2

This book is a work based on true events. Certain names, places, and identifying details have been changed to protect the privacy of individuals.

About the book

Although written as a tale, this is a true story.

I have tried to keep as close to the truth as possible in my interpretation of events. Main events and characters are based on fact; a few have been created for the flow. Real quotes are marked in double quotation marks, the rest of the dialogue is fictitious. All press articles are exact.

I wish to warn the reader there are some scenes that are sensitive in nature.

It's time to tell the truth, whatever the outcome.
I dedicate this book to my mother, for she wishes her father's side of the story to be told; something he couldn't do whilst alive.

Chapter One

Wormwood Scrubs Prison, London.
February 28th, 1947.
The night of the storm.

The rough hand pushed Leslie Holmes back into the stark cold cell and slammed the heavy metal door with a resounding clunk. The sound seemed to reverberate around the unforgiving room. At the same time the wind picked up and howled at the tiny, barred window. It seemed to mirror his heart's cry of anguish. He'd had a hard time. They'd been pressing him to reveal the whereabouts of the jewels again; but all he could think of was Judge D's sour face as he almost doubled Leslie's sentence with no reason or added evidence. The court had nothing on him; no clues, nothing; and that was all they were going to get: Nothing. Not after the judge sentenced his life away, breaking it into little pieces. Five years is enough for anyone, but too long for his lovely fragile wife, Gwen, to survive without him.

Les leaned back on the hard mattress and laid his head down on the damp pillow; the pillow that smelt of other men's fears, other men's fevered anguish. He had to get his head round this sentence, even though he knew it should be much more. He'd talked with the chaplain, and yes, they could lengthen the sentence for no apparent reason: it seemed they could do what they want. The chaplain's head had also hung low, hardly able to look Les in the eye, he carried the blame himself as he was the one who'd pushed Les to go to appeal. 'I'm so sorry, Les. I just don't know what to say or do now. I've never heard of anything like it. It's outrageous behaviour by the judge.'

That statement almost seemed ironic: the judge behaving badly. Nevertheless, it didn't change anything. Les was in for the long-haul and he had to get used to it.

The wind seemed to scream again as his heart cried with guilt and sorrow as he imagined his family trying to survive without him. It was a freezing night, and the cold had penetrated straight to his heart, stabbing him with the pain of conscience. Thoughts whirled round, and round, in his mind. Why had he risked everything? Why hadn't he thought about the consequences? Where would the children be sleeping now? Would they be together? Would they be warm? He couldn't even bear to think of his beautiful but delicate wife being brutally sectioned, admitted into a mental hospital, vulnerable and afraid.

His mind so restless with memories flooding back, he desperately tried to make sense of his situation; make sense of how it was that he was lying in this cell, on this foul mattress, alone. This had not been what he'd planned for, all those nights at war with only Gwen's face keeping him going. However, he knew better than anybody life never went as planned: if it did, they'd be together right now, curled up in each other's arms.

Then his thoughts turned to the 'ex-King and his mistress' as he called Edward VIII and Wallis Simpson. They were the real reason behind all this. Looking back, their lives had been intrinsically linked for a long time. Leslie's sister, Eva, had worked at Fort Belvedere for many years, sometimes giving secret snippets of royal gossip. So, he'd known all about the royal couple, hearing inside information on their Nazi sympathies, their traitorous movements driving him to despair while he fought for his country. Questioning whether it had been their actions that had tipped him over the edge, to the irrational behaviour he knew he would suffer from for the rest of his life.

Rain lashed the prison window, pummelling the glass. The rhythmic sound suddenly reminding him of marching on with his troops in the pouring rain; wet, starving and weak; but so determined. His flashbacks of war, of fighting the Nazi's were harsh: it had been torturous, but he knew, necessary. He'd fought hard for the freedom of his country, put his very soul into protecting his officers and fellow soldiers, only to survive all that, for this: to be locked away -incarcerated- for stealing.

Since he'd been back from the war, circumstances had become so difficult, it was literally steal to survive, or watch his family starve: he'd decided to provide for his family. Of-course, there was the matter of the Royal Robbery...but that was something else altogether. They'd have to prove that first. He lay there, deep in thought, searching for understanding as to why he'd lost it, why on earth he'd risked everything he held most dear. So, he decided he had to go back to the beginning, hoping he'd find the answer to his actions, and to his burning question.

Chapter Two

London,
Spring, 1938.

Leslie was from a band of brothers from Surrey; Tom, himself, and Sam. They were all handsome, though Sam really was striking and if anyone had to be the most handsome of the three, it would be he. They were men of a strong lean physique, with thick jet-black hair and dark piercing eyes that had a spiritual potency. They were sexually electric and exciting men. There was, without doubt, a touch of rivalry between them.

Not adverse to hard work, Leslie enjoyed working as a roofer-builder. His physique made this easy and his hands sensitive to a fine understanding of craftsmanship. Tom and Sam had a lucky break and found jobs as stewards on the cruise liners, taking them away from the London grind and opening their horizons.

Gwendolen was a magnetic redhead. It was 1938 and London was so exciting. The fashions, the music, and the possibility of work making it the epicentre of the country.

So, there she was at the dancehall in Piccadilly one night. She was wearing a simple, angle cut, black and tan deco dress. It clung to her in just the right places, being perfectly proportioned. She wasn't showing any flesh, but she didn't need to. People throughout the room knew exactly where she was. There was just something about her, as if her spirit oozed into the ether and touched everyone's soul.

To pin down just what it was she had would be impossible. She was just a normal girl of average height and not an outstanding beauty; but her spirit, her fire, magnetism, sensuality, and not forgetting her fragility, made her captivating. So, in this way, Gwen swept into Leslie's life and bowled him over. He couldn't take his eyes off her.

Gwen looked over in Leslie's direction, whether she knew subconsciously she was being watched or just felt the power of his stares, it doesn't matter, as at that moment they locked eyes.

He strode confidently towards her. Les was turned out immaculately, the fit of his clothes showed his lean cat like masculinity to perfection.

'Would you like to dance?' he purred.

So many relationships have started with an innocent dance. However, dance is anything but innocent, being the chance to enter someone's aura, feel the rhythm of their heart, and look deep into their eyes, their soul.

Gwen said nothing, looked at Les, and took his hand. The way she took his hand endeared her to him forever. It was such a delicate, frail, beautiful hand and so tenderly placed, asking nothing of him, but to guide her to the dance floor. He knew from that moment he'd do anything for her, absolutely anything.

The band seemed to pick up on the couple's energy and the music became more intense. People filed onto the dance floor and the band kicked into a hit. It was a favourite of the time and there was gaiety all around. They found themselves being pushed closer together.

'Sorry about this! Everybody loves this one. Do you like it? I'm Leslie by the way.' As he spoke, he looked deep into her, with his dark exciting eyes. He showed he was capable of anything, like a raven full of magic.

He sensed there was something about her. An edge that no other girl had, something intransient, inexplicable, and elusive; but there all the same.

'Hello, Leslie,' she said calmly in her soft voice, well aware of the wild prey she had in close proximity; the look from his eyes was unnervingly powerful, and the scent of his maleness mingling with his aftershave was affecting her. The brooding sensation of desire was awakening. The clarinet humped its wild sensual abandon, and their bodies followed suit. It was two different people that emerged from the dance floor as the band wound down.

'Let me buy you a drink," he said, not letting go of her hand. "You never told me your name!'

'I don't know if I should - you seem like trouble to me,' she said, breaking her gaze from the power of his.

'Listen to me, the only one here that's trouble is you! You're something special," he said purposefully, 'I'm going to get you a drink. Then if you wish, you can tell me your name, or I'll just crown you 'my queenie'!"

Life had been hard, whereas he was making it all seem such fun, and instinctively she felt safe with him.

"Queenie' will be just fine for now!' she replied cheekily.

Chapter Three

Cannes, south of France,
Summer, 1928.

At the turn of the 19th century Wallis Simpson was then known as Bessie Warfield. She was born the illegitimate child of a sickly sibling of a 'well-to-do' Baltimore family. The Warfield's denied her father the right to marry his love, or even to baptise the 'bastard daughter'. They were aware that his consumption would soon get the better of him and didn't care for the financial responsibility: believing that he'd chosen well below his social status.

Tuberculosis finally took Bessie's father, and her mother found herself in financial difficulties. Bessie strategically charmed her way into her grandmother's heart; with her precocious attitude and Warfield looks, the grandmother couldn't deny that this headstrong girl was one of their own. Wallis soon dropped the familiar term of Bessie, believing it to be derogatory, explaining: "it's something one would name their cow", demanding to be addressed by her name, 'Wallis'.

Wallis had quickly worked out the power of money and status - or her lack of it, and was not ashamed to ask for wealthy Uncle Sol's hand-outs, even demanding the best education one could buy. She'd realised the importance of improving her social standing, for she was determined to climb up the rungs, financially and socially. She had set her violet eyes on the best, being the best, and being with the best. Girls in her class explained that Wallis had said she was going to be top of the class, and top she was, stopping at nothing, becoming quite calculating. She was not necessarily attractive; however, she became determined to make the most of what she had.

Alberto da Zara, one of her many exciting lovers, summed her up well: "although she's not beautiful, she was extremely attractive, and had very refined and cultivated tastes. Her conversation was brilliant; she had the capacity of bringing up the right subject of conversation with anyone with whom she came into contact."

By 1928 Wallis was contemplating her second marriage, to Ernest Simpson, an Anglo- American shipping executive and former captain in the Coldstream guards. He was broad and strong with blue eyes and incredibly well 'turned-out'.

Her letter to her mother, expressing how she: "really felt so tired of fighting the world all alone and with no money" helped to understand how she could have started an affair with Ernest, then still a married man. A man she didn't really love. They'd met at Christmas and their relationship deepened over roaring fires, golden whisky and poker. Nevertheless, Ernest wouldn't think of divorcing his wife.

Wallis herself was technically still married to Win Spencer, a naval officer, quite a character, but an abusive alcoholic and bi-sexual adulterer. Once her divorce from Win was settled, she was free to pursue Ernest Simpson, in so doing, bettering her social position.

Wallis obviously got her way. Ernest did divorce his hospitalised wife. During the divorce proceedings Wallis cunningly stepped out of the firing line, accepting an invitation to stay with her friends Katherine and Herman Rodgers in Cannes.

The Roger's had a beautiful house on the Riviera, Villa Lou Viei, an ancient French villa dating back to the Middle Ages, beautifully elegant in its surroundings.

Wallis opened the window to the guest bedroom and the balmy scent of late-night jasmine and frangipani mixing with the sea air relaxed her very essence.

It was a glorious night. She'd been quite stressed with everything back in America, and realised how she'd needed a break, to get away and just relax.

Katherine, Hermann and Wallis had been out dancing in Nice at the Palm Beach Club, and the night before they'd been gambling at Casino Partouche. Wallis loved being swept up in the glamorous and cushioned lifestyle of the wealthy; all playing at being incredibly beautiful and outrageously raucous.

Hermann, now back at Villa Lou Viei, shouted up to her,

'Wallis Darling, it's just so beautiful tonight. We can't go to bed now, so Katherine and I are having rather large nightcaps on the terrace. Get yourself down here and join us, will you? The moon looks wonderful on the water...' He added as a teaser, 'There's a 90-yr old brandy here, just opened, if that'll sway you!'

'You make it so difficult for me to resist! But I warn you, I'm dressed for bed!'

They laughed, enjoying the ease of their relationship. The past difficulties of the 'ménage a trois' had passed, and they were left with a deep fondness for each other.

As she wafted down the stairs, her blue silk Chinese pyjamas looking splendid on her boyish figure, her mind turned to her pressing romantic situation.

'Now then you two, we've got something rather serious to turn our heads to tonight,' she announced.

Katherine looked up, concerned. She'd known there'd been something eating away at her friend. Hermann joked,

'What's that, Wally? How much of the bottle we drink tonight?'

'Herman, be serious for once! You can see this is important to Wallis.' Turning her attention to Wallis, Katherine asked, 'What is it, Sweetie? What's been eating at you? You know I can tell. I've heard you pacing in your room at night.' She looked at Wallis with kind eyes.

'I bet it's a man!' said Herman.

'You win!' Wallis replied, reaching over and chinking Herman's glass. The crystal glass caught the moonlight and the liquid within suddenly looked like an elixir of life. She took a sip.

'What is this? Eau de vie? Does it have magical properties?' she asked. It may as well have had, as she suddenly felt relieved, her head seemed clearer than it had in a long while. She took a deep breath, soaking up the therapeutic air and sighed deeply, all her worries escaping from her body.

'It's about this situation I'm in with Ernest Simpson. It's all rather messy, but now we are both free, he's asked to marry me. It's just...Oh, I don't know,' she said, shaking her head in despair.

'I can see from the way you speak you're not, shall I say, 'passionate' about him, Dear.'

'Well, I suppose I am fond of him, but not 'in love' with him, not like I felt for Win, or any of the excitement that I had for Felipe Espil, or Prince Caetani.' She sighed, and took another sip, 'I mean these men were a challenge, a whirl of excitement, but also incredibly unstable. And look what they did for my reputation! I have my future to think about. What do I do?'

Katherine carefully picked her words and said, 'I don't want you to make important decisions on the basis of what Hermann and I think, but Darling, you have yourself to consider. We worry for you and want to see you more settled. This Ernest fellow, he really does adore you, I do feel he would be good for you. These passionate relationships are not necessarily good for a lifestyle. Look at Hermann and I...'

'What are you saying, Sweets? I drive you wild! You told me so!' Hermann laughed.

'Yes, my tiger! But what really drives me wild is the reassurance in the security of your love. I feel safe and treasured, Sweetie, and that in itself is enough to turn on any gal!' Katherine said, while affectionately patting his leg.

'And anyhow...' Hermann guffawed as he almost gargled the brandy, 'there's always an affair if you want the risk!'

Katherine poked him in the ribs affectionately, 'Just you dare!' she quipped.

They all laughed, Wallis could see it all now, 'He's not so bad, and I certainly would be able to get on with life.' She paused, swirling her drink, then added, 'We do get on.'

'That's most important, the rest falls into place,' Hermann said, his tone finally wise and considerate.

'Yes, and I can't carry on like this anymore, I mean, I'm absolutely penniless! It's embarrassing drooling over this season's fashions with no funds!' Wallis said jovially, more upbeat in herself now, seeing a way out of her predicament.

'I understand. Just think if you send that cable of acceptance tomorrow, we could go shopping straight away! You'll be needing a whole new wardrobe for London; that's where you said you'd be living, isn't it?'

'Katherine, you are so practical!'

'Yes, Honey, and so close! You'd only be a train journey away. The Orient Express is truly wonderful.'

So, they all raised their glasses to 'Mrs Simpson', and the future was decided.

Chapter Four

Virginia Water,
Late spring, 1938.

Les had arranged to meet Gwen on Sunday. He'd become intoxicated, unable to stop thinking about her. His workmates had been laughing at him all week as they re-tiled a roof,

'Les what's with you? You're walking around in a dream. It's been lunch for ten minutes and you've not come down. You look like you're up with the clouds. Be careful, this is dangerous work to have your mind elsewhere.'

He looked and smiled; it wasn't he that was elsewhere; it was she that was with him. Something magical had happened when they'd danced that night. He felt a sense of purpose like never before.

As for being on the roof, he was made for this work; like the Moa Hawk Indians building the skyscrapers of New York without any safety, totally unafraid of heights: so was he. He became cat like and so agile his feet never seemed to land on the ground, guided like an eagle on the wind.

So, as he dressed carefully in his Sunday best, his shaving immaculate, he combed back his jet-black hair with just a slick of cream to give him that movie star look; his dapper, gentlemanly side able to come out. He knew this was no ordinary date.

Gwen made her way to the park at Virginia Water. She was wearing a deep-green pencil skirt and matching short-waisted jacket, showing her figure and complementing her auburn hair. She finished the outfit with a jaunty beret on the side with a feather. She looked cracking; nothing special but put together in such a way it signalled her out from the rest.

She was also thinking back to their meeting and how powerful it had been. How since that moment her stomach had not settled, but it wasn't just that, there was an edge of fear. Her sensuality was something she couldn't quite understand. She'd been able to keep it in check, but it had already got her into difficult situations with men becoming so persistent, almost dangerous.

Gwen longed to be with someone, but he needed to have the same edge and magic to life for her to know he'd understand her. She felt she'd seen that in Leslie's eyes, along with a feeling of security and kindness so rare in a man.

She quickened her step as the anticipation to see him rose within, giving herself a hug of reassurance to step forth and not to think or worry about the past or the future. She wasn't sure how she could explain, or when to explain, that things were not all as they seem, or should she even tell him at all? These thoughts had burdened her nights.

She walked through the gates of the park at Virginia Water and was hit by how beautiful and serene it was. Nature took her in and caressed away her fears as the birds sang away her dark doubts, filling her with positivity. The rhododendrons were out in abundance; love was in the air.

They'd arranged to meet at the totem pole. She wasn't exactly sure where, but he'd promised her it was easy to find. As she walked through, her easy gliding rhythm was having its effect; totally unaware of the men staring at her. As she approached the totem pole a group of men had turned and were pointing at her; she spotted them and that feeling of being out of one's comfort zone welled up again. Trying to keep it together she looked around for Les.

She turned and there he was, walking towards her. He looked so handsome, his step seemed to sing, and his eyes were so reassuring that any worries she'd had melted away.

He'd spotted her, and the men leering at her, so he walked purposely towards her as if claiming his prize. There she was: so beautiful. He swept her up like a bird and spun her whirling round, mesmerised in her golden world as the sun shone iridescent shafts of fire through her hair and lit their passion; he was mingling with her spirit again. Her eyes sparkled and her infectious laughter filled his world.

'I missed you, Queenie.'

His sure, sexy voice had a powerful effect on Gwen, almost hypnotising. She looked at him as he lowered her back down and their lips accidentally brushed so close together, he'd touched her lips with his. It was only the lightest of kisses, but the energy fusion was zinging. They stood back and looked at each other. No words needed, they both laughed. He tucked her hand in his close to his chest and they turned towards the water's edge, laughing and teasing as they went. The day disappeared so quickly; like ice in a glass, it melted into being just a memory.

Chapter Five

Wormwood Scrubs
28th Feb 1947
The night of the storm,

Thunder cracked over the prison roof once more, the sound reverberating dark fearful emotions bringing Les starkly back to reality, back to his prison cell and away from his memories of Gwen. How wonderful, how innocent it all had been at the beginning. He was so grateful for those times with no cares in the world, but how things changed. Life had certainly dealt them a rough hand.

The night was to be a long one, he just knew it, with the storm tormenting the impenetrable stone building; but the real storm was the one in his head with restless, righteous but guilt-ridden reason riding his back.

He saw flashes of the newspaper headlines before him and remembered guiltily how he'd secretly relished reading the exploits of the police as they'd desperately run around in a helpless goose-chase, snatching any hope of a lead, however false. He'd literally watched events unfold, as the Metropolitan CID launched a world-wide search, for something that he knew was right under their very nose.

On Friday October $18^{th,}$ 1946, literally just after the robbery had taken place, the Daily Mail led with the article:

"Europe Combed for Windsor Gems Gang. A manhunt extending the whole of Europe has been put into operation for the thieves who stole jewellery, valued at "not more than £20,000," belonging to the Duke and Duchess of Windsor."

He'd had to follow the papers to find out the moves of the police and the way their thinking was leaning. He'd not wanted to enjoy them, but it was a vicarious pleasure that he couldn't help; feeling he was wise enough to dupe the top minds of Britain, then France and America.

The first few articles seemed more engrossed with assessing the correct amount the jewellery was worth. The initial amount (probably most accurate) was quoted to be between £200,000 and £500,000. The Duke, panicking, realised his recent pleas of poverty wouldn't hold with such statements, along with being immediately reprimanded by his brother, the King, for languishing such monies on Wallis while the country was absolutely broke and rationed up to their eyeballs, so he consequently made continual statements at how annoyed he was: "There is absolutely no truth in the published statement that the value of the jewellery was £250,000. Its value was not more than £20,000, and you can say that I said so!"

Les had to laugh, he knew, just looking at the gems, they were definitely worth more than the £20,000 the Duke wanted the world to believe, and there were also gems declared as stolen that he'd *not* seen there that night. Things were not adding up.

The Daily Mail went on: "it is known that the burglary was the work of a clever 'cat burglar." They'd at least got something right.

"Scotland Yard, continuing their enquiries into the burglary, have visited scores of the known haunts of thieves in London, frequenting east and west London Pubs and drinking houses... Scotland Yard is also in continual contact with the Surete General in Paris. Hundreds of French detectives are today checking the movements of all known French and Continental criminals and tracking down all known jewel thieves.

Members of the Special Branch at Scotland Yard are investigating movements of all known criminals from abroad who have entered this country during the past few weeks. Ports and airfields are being closely watched.

The most important clue at the moment is the description given by several people living near Ednam Lodge of a large military car seen in the vicinity of the house on two or three nights during the week. The police are convinced that the robbery was carefully planned over a long period and that crooks from the continent are involved."

He lay there, well aware all this was his fault. Nevertheless, it infuriated him the police were missing the point, they'd not cracked the most important part: *the reason for the robbery in the first place;* and they certainly hadn't a clue as to where the jewels were.

The cell suddenly lit up in a flash of lightning, silvery shadows of the barred window loomed over him, reminding him where he was. His penance being paid by torturous days and nights fretting about Gwen, his children, and his utter helplessness. He pictured Gwen's beautiful face before him, her eyes wide with love and total trust. It broke his heart to think of her now in an asylum, alone, with no one to protect her. The mental decline in her when he'd come back from the war had been apparent, but he'd hoped his love and stability would have helped her get better, but he'd only made matters far worse and now there was absolutely nothing he could do. Then another ominous roar of a thunderclap broke overhead as if to verify his fears: things were not well on the outside. All he could do to stop himself from losing it, was to try and take his mind back to the good times, the moments he cherished. However, these were tainted with the extreme guilt he now felt. Then came the anger, the burning anger towards *that* woman, now the Duchess of Windsor. With her, he felt no remorse, only the immediate need to decide what he was going to do about the royal gems.

Chapter Six

London,
Autumn, 1929.

Wallis left the balmy Mediterranean and flew to London, just in time for the summer society season. Ernest and herself were married, a very low-key affair, on the 21st of July 1928.

A year later, Wallis had to travel to New York to visit her ailing mother. Ernest didn't accompany her on this trans-Atlantic crossing, so she was probably 'in the thick of it' on-board the Olympic. She had all the opportunity to mingle and further increase her social standing (using her wit and sexual dominance) that a woman like Wallis could have possibly hoped for. One never quite knew who one would meet on these crossings and there was always the air of excitement pervading the cabins. Wallis was probably quite relaxed about things: having got rid of her troublesome first husband Win (not before she learnt some sexual 'tricks' during their posting in China), and now, in a better financial and social position married to Ernest. Just the worry of her mother's health pressing on her mind.

As she dressed for dinner, she used her sense of style and slender form to its absolute. Wallis was most definitely clothed in the height of fashion: her armour to captivate whomsoever she wished. Like a snake, the way they can shed their skin, hypnotise their prey, consume them whole, breaking down and digesting every live energetic morsel, leaving no trace of their prey's very existence whatsoever: Utterly fascinating.

So, as she sprayed her heady perfume around her, using any ploy she could to make herself more alluring, she looked herself in the mirror with that self-belief and determination that she was to become famous for and walked along the starry deck. She heard the bands playing and cocktails chinking; she might well have thought everything was going her way.

'Hey Wallis! Please do come and join us, we're having gin-slings!'

Wallis surveyed the room for who exactly was the most opportune for her to speak with; nothing was ever accidental with this calculated woman. Deciding to follow the invitation, she slithered through the crowds, heading for the people at the bar.

'Good evening, Daaarlings,' she said, as she approached the most affluent group of beautiful, successful people in the room, asking, 'What are we up to this evening?'

'Well, Squidgy here, and Dotty, are in the doldrums, and so we're all trying to keep their spirits up as there's nothing worse than sad at sea!' Gerard explained. 'So 'bottoms up' as they say!'

'Why? What on earth could make them so gloomy? They were just fine when I saw them at lunch,' Wallis asked, not really liking this tender confiding of emotions.

'Haven't you heard? They got news this afternoon; it's all going crazy back in New York. Squidgy, as you know, doesn't like to talk about it, but has always been top dollar and had piles of stocks, and is a really successful chap - until now, it seems. He's lost nearly all of it. I just thank God that I'm from good old British stock,' he said, shaking his head. 'Hopefully, I won't be affected by all this. I don't think I could take the strain.'

Wallis's face drained of any colour it had. At that moment, what she'd built up and stood for, her most important assets, drained away in the crash. It wasn't a lot, but she'd clung to it as a safety line throughout her life. She lost almost all her inheritance from the Warfield estate, her investors couldn't sell the shares in time, and to make matters worse, Ernest's stateside holdings were also wiped out.

This was devastating: everything she held important had gone. From this moment on, she was determined she'd do all she could to make sure she was never in such a position again. Her materialistic want for wealth and prestige became obsessive. Her need was never satiated, the fear it could be taken away always lingering. Jewellery became her ideal, a commodity turned into a beautiful display of assets; assets she could see, feel, and flaunt.

Wallis suddenly needed to know she was in control of something; needing the feeling of power and domination she could only find in the bedroom. She had to prove she was still alive as she contemplated dragging an innocent by-stander back to her cabin for a night of fornication. She wasn't averse to extra-curricular activities.

Chapter Seven

Birmingham,
Spring, 1938.

Gwen had to break away from Les that day in the park, as she felt overwhelmed. She needed time to think. There was only one person who could understand and give her advice and that was her mother. Her mother was 'up -country', in Birmingham. Gwen reckoned she could be up and back in a day if she caught the early train.

'Hello Ma!' she said, as she approached the elegant but frail lady sitting by the window. The light was playing on the lady's faded auburn hair; it was obvious they were mother and daughter. Her mother stood and turned towards her, her face lit up with joy, the light in her eyes so vivid.

'My darling girl! Come here and give me one of your best hugs.'

They laughed and chatted, holding hands all the while, as she described her London life. Then Gwen looked down and knew she had to discuss Leslie.

'Ma, I don't know what to do. I've met someone and I'm all in a muddle.'

The knowing voice of her mother replied with deep concern for her beautiful daughter,

'Well, my dearest, you've always known my opinion on this. I've been worried that your idea to 'avoid a relationship' will only lead you to a sad and lonely life. Life is to be lived, and you are to be loved, my dear. Please don't cut yourself off from life; it breaks my heart. Especially for something that may never happen: your fears may be unjustified.'

Gwen was so strong in spirit; however, at that moment close to her mother she broke, and let out her aching continual fear. Maybe letting go of it would help it never to return.

'But Ma, they say it can possibly be made worse by having children, or by stirring one's emotions as love does. Look what happened to Grandma. I can't put that on Leslie.'

'Listen,' her mother said, purposefully, 'I know life has been tough; unpredictable to say the least; but we must try not to waste a precious moment. I had you, and I'd never take that away. We've shared some great times, haven't we?'

Gwen looked into her mother's eyes and saw such love, such joie de vie; today, anything was possible. However, she also remembered only too well the smell of fear, the screams of pain mingled with the acrid smell of cleaning solutions and the feel of the cold tiled room on her skin. These elusive and sickening memories were still hurting. The memory of the wild caged animal her ma had become in certain phases of her life; screaming for her freedom, for her sanity, for her life, was still with her.

To have psychological problems as a woman in the early twentieth century was no laughing matter. Schizophrenia was not understood: the victims were treated like vermin; degraded, abused, drugged, and left in the most hideous institutions. Their spirit withering away with every minute.

Gwen and her mother were both ok at this time, unfortunately her grandma had died in one of these horrific institutions. Neither of them could ever forget the haunting images. Gwen had only had one episode: a short while, in her teens when the stress of losing her mother to one of these places, knowing how she was suffering, was enough to drive anyone over the edge. However, her mother was home right now, and things looked rosy, and so they were.

As her mother wrapped a beautiful embroidered tasselled Spanish shawl round her elegant shoulders and poured another cup of tea, Gwen knew she was to follow her destiny; not run from it anymore. No fear: just joy.

Chapter Eight

London,
Winter, 1929.

Wallis was back in London, in residence with Ernest. The black cloud had finally started to lift. The loss of her mother, on top of the financial losses, had been a lot to bear. Nevertheless, she decided she'd do whatever it took to pick herself up and was starting to enjoy London: not the weather, but the atmosphere; the buzz of the city and its people. When, later, she stated how she abhorrently hated the place, she'd obviously forgotten these years of frivolous fun. She was climbing the social circuit like only she knew how, and their life was busy with parties and more parties. This was how she thrived.

They had bought and moved into a slightly less grand situation than the one they had been renting from Lady Chesham, but it served their purpose perfectly. 5 Bryanston Court was a wonderfully large flat in Mayfair that came with plenty of staff and room for entertaining: things were swinging.

Admittedly she'd found it hard at first, missing her American social circuit, and found the weather damp (often suffering from colds and feeling low), but her perseverance and the arrival of American acquaintances to the 'London set' pulled it all together. Her friend Consuelo, and sister Thelma were here from the States, with their smouldering Latin good looks and party attitude they made all the difference.

'Ernest Darling, I've arranged for Consuelo, Thelma and a few others to come for drinks Tuesday. I feel it's important for us to do this.'

'Sweetheart, I'm hard pushed at the moment. I have a meeting Tuesday, you know that. Haven't we got engagements every night this week?'

'Look, it's hard for me here. Don't you understand that? Or are you so inept at feeling that you can't see what's important to your wife?'

This comment was a bit harsh as Ernest was incredibly considerate of Wallis's needs, knowing she'd been under the weather again and was always crotchety when so.

'Don't say such things, Wallis, you know what you mean to me, and Darling,' he said, taking a breath, with a tinge of sadness in his voice, 'I do understand what I've put on you, expecting you to just nestle right in here. Carry on, if that's what you wish. Invite the whole of London - anything! Consuelo is a great gal. Have you met her sister, Lady Furness, yet? It's all quite exciting as she is rumoured to be The Mistress!'

'How fascinating! But to be honest I do find this entire 'royalty lark' such a bore, don't you?' she replied, pretending not to be interested. Coldly, trying not to look at him with such contempt. 'You idiot,' she thought to herself, 'why do you think I'm going to all this effort to casually fling us all together?'

Everything Wallis ever did was pre-planned with meticulous forethought. Wallis had been obsessed about Prince Edward since a little girl (with a picture of him even then), and she was still fuming that her first husband had been such an embarrassment to the navy that they weren't allowed 'on-board' when His Royal Highness visited San Diego; leading to her missing out on meeting him, when all her peers were on board. This was a mistake she made sure would never happen again. Here, in London, her secret comfort and escape from it all was curling up reading the gossip rags and the Court Circular in The Times, devouring every morsel of the Prince's comings and goings; what he was doing, wearing and who he was seeing. What woman, or come to think of it, man, at that time didn't have a slight crush on this beautiful golden physically perfect specimen of a 'dream boat prince'? But, of course, the papers didn't include his humaneness -his faults- private as they were.

She got up out of her chair, turning away from her husband and reaching for the tortoise-shell cigarette box. As she bent over to reach for a light, her lean almost androgynous body showed off a perfectly cut suit. She didn't want her husband to see the secret glimmer in her eyes as the beginning of a challenge to take on all challenges was starting to unfold in her eggless nest. London was fun, but she was bored and looking for the next thrill and she thought she'd just found it. The snake had found her egg.

'I'll arrange it then,' she said flippantly. 'We've a busy weekend ahead. Don't forget the Rodgers are coming over from France as there's that Mosley rally we've all been invited to. Oh, and I've promised them the theatre! Do be a dear and sort something out,' she requested.

He stretched to touch her as she passed, however, somehow couldn't. She was deliberately just out of arms-reach: not into the displays of affection he kept trying to bestow. Ernest, not too affected, reached instead further and turned on the wireless.

Chapter Nine

Windsor,
Summer, 1938.

It all happened rather quickly. Les was a determined type of guy. Once he'd made up his mind that was it. He worked every hour he could. He had an aim - the ring.

He knew Gwen wasn't showy, or that she thought such things important. She put more on making the moment special with love and laughter than ever any materialistic object. That's one of the reasons why he loved her and so he wanted to get her something special. She was his diamond, shining happiness into his life and he wanted it to be right.

He had been walking past the jewellers in Windsor and there it was: a second-hand, beautifully worked art nouveau, pavé and baguette diamond ring. It was perfect: artistic, unusual, and the tiny diamonds seemed to sing. Les felt so pleased, it was as if made for her.

'Gwen, be my queen, make it real, let me be your king, your love, and marry me. I understand how the king could have abdicated for love, for I would go to the moon for you.'

'Les! You know you already rule my world, you soppy so and so! Yes! I'd love to marry you. Oh, but I just ...I have to tell you something first. I've been meaning to talk to you, to find the right time but I couldn't.' She choked on her words, stammering, trying to find a way to explain, 'I don't wish to bring you any pain, Leslie. I don't think you realise what you're taking on. I'm frail... mentally. I cannot take too much stress. It can affect me in a way I'd never wish for you to see. My mother and grandmother you see, we ...'

He kissed her lips, stopping her speech, and looked into her eyes, saying,

'I know you are delicate. I know you are special. I love you because of these things and I promise to do all I can to make our lives smooth and joyful, my dearest. I won't let anything hurt you.'

'I know, Leslie, but please, let me tell you. I must warn you. You must know so you can make sure you really want to marry me.'

'Nothing will change my mind.'

'But you must understand. For if I ever become ill -God forbid- you see... there is a chance I could. No-one really understands it,' she admitted, as tears started to roll down her cheek. 'Oh, I just don't know the future.'

'I do,' he said reassuring her, 'you are mine. Marry me.'

With that she replied, 'Yes! Yes! Yes!' whilst kissing his face through the tears of joy and relief for having told him. Kissing him again and again, till the salt of the tears dried and their love was secure.

The wedding day came. It was a glorious summer's day. The smell of the flowers and lush leaves were in the air, and the birds sang in celebration. The gentle breeze swaying the branches caused the leaves to reveal bursts of sun, shimmering dancing patterns all around. He stood there waiting, the anticipation was almost too much to bear, and then the car pulled up. He saw her father get out and extend a hand and he knew it was to be.

She wore white silk; it fell over her body like a waterfall of water frozen over her skin, falling all the way to the ground. Her auburn sun-kissed hair was worn up with tendrils hanging down making her look irresistible. She had little crystals delicately placed in her hair, catching the light through the white lace veil. She shone love: he never looked so proud. They were an incredibly handsome couple it had to be said, standing there together: she in white, he in black.

The family were happy for them and the love they'd found. However, there were one or two who had their doubts: 'something's not quite right' was whispered. There are always doubters. They were wary of Gwen as she was quite a well-to-do city girl from a decent family in Birmingham, and they were country folk from Surrey.

'She can't even boil an egg, you know!' went round the congregation.

Nevertheless, it was a superb night. They danced and drank all they could. Les pulled Gwen closer as the saxophone droned its latently sexy sound. Pulling tighter together, their desire for each other reminded them they had unfinished business to attend to, so they slipped away.

Closing the door to their room, already undressing and giggling while throwing their clothes off with wild abandon. Suddenly Leslie stopped,

'No, Darling, I don't want to rush this. I need to savour every minute.' He took the last of her clothes off carefully, with such love, and with heavy desire he laid her down on the bed, kissing her softly and laid his naked body next to hers: the feeling of skin to skin was electric. She arched her beautiful body towards him, begging for him to give her what she needed. She knew that he would calm this longing, this aching she'd had for him. With his tender kisses to her body she was just going wild,

'Please, oh please, make love to me,' she murmured.

As he entered her, as his muscles rippled, the whole strength of his body took over hers. She wrapped herself around him and they rocked together in absolute bliss. In this moment it was all as it should be: life was demanding its destiny -whatever the price. The pleasure went on and on: they were finally one. All night they made love. She wanted more, as if making up for the years of desire laid aside.

Chapter Ten

London,
Winter, 1931.

The Simpson's residence was finally finished with all the redecorating and was immaculate, so up to date. Wallis had wanted the best, of course. Touches of Chippendale, a mahogany table with her Chinese vase from Peking, a regency mirror, silk covered sofa and chairs, and finally the look was complete.

The London set were highly impressed with the decor as they piled round that Tuesday night. Most of their places were old money and ancestral steeds that hadn't been changed in years; or rented pads from other aristocrats, so Wallis's house was an exciting breath of fresh air.

Consuelo's sister Thelma (Lady Furness, the prince's mistress), had special attention paid to her that night. Wallis beamed in, focusing all her efforts and charming her with all her power: this one was important to Wallis. She was delighted at the thought of hearing first-hand snippets about the prince's private, intimate life: the life not told or 'revealed' in the papers.

They became friends -who wouldn't- as Wallis was so good in a social setting, so knowledgeable, entertaining and slightly edgy.

'Sweetie, let's meet for lunch at the Ritz. Just you and I! That way we can catch up on all the American gossip!' Thelma announced. This became a regular event.

Before Wallis knew it, she and Ernest were being invited to all the exclusive parties. Being 'friends' of the sisters had really opened London society doors: all wanting to bask in the closeness of connections to HRH. It was only a matter of time before they received the invitation she'd been scheming for.

Benny and Consuelo Thaw invited the Simpsons to join them for the weekend, at the Furness's country-pile at Melton Mowbray, in Leicestershire. Lady Thelma Furness would be there (her husband Lord Furness conveniently away on safari in Africa), and the 'pièce de résistance'... both Prince Edward and his brother Prince George would be 'in-residence' for the weekend, up for the hunt. Wallis must have been beside herself: the realisation that after all this time it was going to happen, all those years of fantasizing and dreaming of him, following his movements and now... the moment was drawing close, the finest moment: when a dream is about to be realised.

'What do I do? What do I wear? Phone my hairdressers! I need a full makeover!' A slight edge of panic was in her voice as she realised all the 'dos and don'ts' involved in the protocol of meeting a royal.

Wallis was a nervous wreck by the time they were on the train. Ill with a cold, probably exacerbated by her fretting as her endless meticulousness to social etiquette didn't stop there, suddenly realising,

'What on earth do I call him? Aren't we meant to address them in a certain way?' She didn't want to be let down now by something she hadn't taken into consideration. She was well aware she wasn't of the highest aristocracy, or from a British family of industry, or some particular political standing. Wallis had faced this outcast feeling all her life, being the 'poor cousin' of the Warfield's. So, in a way, she'd had all her life to pull on her reserves of character, wit, and social etiquette to cover up, or smooth-over this annoying little inconvenience.

Sneezing and shivering in their compartment, Wallis went on, swearing about the "damn English weather", as the thick fog outside stole the view of the British countryside. Not that she was even considering the countryside as her mind raced on.

'Ernest! Bertie! That's it! I can't go. Stop the train!'

'What is it, Darling?' Ernest asked.

'Well!' she huffed, 'what with me sneezing all over the Royals for a start, you've forgotten something- I can't curtsy, God-damn it!'

They all fell about laughing at the surreal moment they found themselves in.

'Oh. look here, Gal, that's easily rectified, if only all problems were so simple,' said Bertie.

'But how, Bertie? How? We're arriving in three hours, and I've never curtsied in my life!'

At which, he gallantly stood up as the train rocked unsteadily from side to side and performed a perfect (if a little masculine) curtsy; nearly falling over, sent off balance by the rocking of the train his arm unfurled like a fern, almost scraping the floor with his hand, he rose elegantly and gave them such a cheeky grin, then a wink; at which point they all broke into squeals of hysterics and just couldn't contain themselves. He'd brought them back to reality and made it all a giggle, taking the stress out of the pomposity of protocol and throwing it away.

Her shoulders relaxed and she jumped up, ignoring her raging cold and said, 'Again Bertie! Again! This time slowly. Slowly! Teach me!'

For the full three-hour journey, she practiced again and again, till perfect.

There she was, on that fateful night, of the 10th of January 1931, standing in front of Prince Edward as he took her hand and said, 'Good evening'. Wallis curtseyed, and looked deep into Edward's beautiful blue eyes, deep into the sad and tormented soul that was bound by royal patronage; seeing the pain of his insecurities and the deep loneliness that high positions often come with.

She'd worked him out, in that instant. The snake had centred on its prey. She could see his fear of inadequacy in his eyes, in his nervous twitching of the hand, and felt her instincts told her what he wanted; to be dominated, controlled, both in life and in the bedroom. Her years in China frequenting the singsong houses (elaborate and decadent brothels), learning the arts of fornication, the perverse sexual acts and the sexual powers of the art of Fang Chung all helped now, and were to become incredibly important to their relationship.

Dinner was a bore for her, she was too far away from him, and the topic of conversation had been hunting. Wallis hated hunting. To her, there was nothing more tedious, and her flu was raging, so she went to bed rather let down by it all. She couldn't help sulking, angry at the anti-climax of the evening.

At lunch the next day Wallis had her chance to strike. There was an empty seat next to Prince Edward and she just walked right up with that self-assurance of hers and sat down. His Royal Highness started to politely ask if she missed American central heating, she turned to him and to everyone's shock and horror, laid into the Prince, telling him off for such a boring topic of conversation. She looked right at him, with a look of utter distain making him feel worthless, saying:

"I am sorry, Sir, but you have disappointed me."

Entrapped, he asked in what way, to which she famously replied:

"Every American woman that comes to England is asked the same thing. I had hoped for something more original from the Prince of Wales!"

Everybody was stunned; a look of 'the audacity of the woman' was thrown round the room. Wallis had set the dye of their relationship there and then. The net had been cast.

Chapter Eleven

Winter 1938
Birmingham.

The newlyweds moved to Birmingham. The work was good for Leslie, and Gwen could be close to her ma. They had a fabulous flat, with a spacious and light living room and she had a knack of making a place so lovely. Her use of colours and Bohemian textiles made the place glow. They laughed and teased each other all the time and the house always had music playing. Gwen was so happy. Les said she was his 'glass of champagne', always bubbling and effervescent, always lifting his spirits.

Les came home one night. It was early December, and he'd been working all he could till the light of the day had faded and become too dark to work. Christmas was coming and he'd seen to it they'd had enough to treat themselves. He opened the door and saw her there, approaching her he placed his freezing hands on her face.

'Oh my! Is it really that bitter outside? You must be frozen.' Gwen looked at him with wide eyes.

'Yes, I suppose it is, but it's warm in here, and even warmer in bed.'

Laughing, she kissed him and went into the kitchen.

'Well, you'd better eat all I put on your plate. You're going to need all your strength!' throwing him a wink. 'There's a letter on the table for you. Maybe you could read it once you've cleaned those hands -and that mind of yours- ready for dinner.'

He pulled up the chair and sat down, letting out a deep sigh. He sighed the sort of calming breath only possible after a hard day's work; having achieved a great deal, coming home to the exciting love of his Gwen and the smell of a good stew pervading the flat. He picked up the letter, it had a London postmark.

'It's from my folks.'

'Yes, clever clogs! Even I'd worked that one out! What does it say? Any news?'

He read it as she dished out his stew. She knew he loved a stew. He came rushing over to her, taking the ladle out of her hands and taking her hands in his he proceeded to dance, almost dragging her around the room, whooping with delight and breaking into song.

'What? What! Les, tell me what!'

'It's my brothers, you know. Well, I suppose you don't! They're back for a bit and are coming to visit. They'll be here for the weekend. Oh, we'll have a ball. You'll see!'

She'd not yet met Tom and Sam; what with them being away at sea. She could see how excited Les was at the thought of seeing his brothers and it was time for them to let their hair down and celebrate. Everything was going so well.

Gwen spent the next few days baking and preparing what she could: a tart lemon drizzle cake, beef and Guinness stew, a quiche Lorraine, and she found the sherry her father had given them for a housewarming present. All in all, she'd done pretty well for a girl that couldn't even boil an egg when they got married. With preparing all that and sorting out the bedding, she was a bit pushed come Friday evening,

'Les, I really would like to get myself together and refreshed before your brothers arrive. I don't want to meet them like this, like a regular housewife! What will they think! They won't understand why you've dragged yourself all the way up to live here in Birmingham!'

'Hey, don't knock it. I love it up 'ere',' he said, clowning around using a heavy Brummy accent. 'Look I'll tell you what, I'll meet them off the train and take them to the pub for a swift one, then we'll come back here in a couple of hours. How's that?'

'Wonderful. You are wonderful,' she sighed.

He slicked back his hair, picked up his trilby, and winked at her as he closed the door behind him.

Gwen was a little apprehensive, not that she ever gave a damn what people thought of her. She had a wonderful sense of self that no one could ever knock. Nevertheless, this was family, and she wanted to be and look her best. First impressions counted to her, and anyway she hadn't really had a reason to put on a frock in a while, and this was as good as any. She didn't know why, but she had a slight 'butterfly flyby' going on in her belly, so poured herself a sherry, lit a cigarette and took a moment to herself. She knew that with the band of brothers together for the weekend, this was her last moment of peace for a while; not that she didn't love frivolity. She loved to get dressed up properly, enjoying the calm art in piecing together an outfit, and she was brilliant at it. She'd easily found work in dress shops as she was always immaculately turned out, never going anywhere without matching hats and gloves. Her figure, almost too thin from her kinetic energy on overcharge all the time, enabled her to wear the style of the moment well. She thought she'd slip on her navy crepe dress tonight, nothing too much as it was only dinner at home; the navy was so good for her skin tone and set her auburn hair alight at night. Her hair, loosened from being set in the curlers to give her that movie star hairdo, looked elegant. She kept it all minimal; even so, she couldn't hide her internal beauty and happiness.

The men piled back. She could hear the laughter rising up the stairs, rushing around straightening the pillows she started to tremble slightly.

The door opened and in they walked. Never having seen the brothers all together, this was quite a sight for a young lady, almost overwhelming; but the moment Sam stepped round the door she froze. The sparks filled the room. Everyone must have noticed. It was as if Clark Gable had just walked in.

Gwen threw the cushion down, she'd been holding it to her, almost hiding behind it for protection from her feelings, but she couldn't pretend it hadn't happened. But she could ignore it, for now.

'So, this is your queenie!' said Tom.

They were introduced and all shook hands along with the usual formalities and pleasantries. She handed round a sherry to each of them. She could feel their eyes on her, devouring her, and she -for once- quite liked it.

When she handed Sam his sherry, he looked straight at her, penetrating deep with such a sexy glance. She could feel his thoughts, they were wild, however, her love for Les was strong and true.

She served the meal and the talk was amazing. The brothers talked deep into the night, explaining their travels, describing the countries they'd been to. Thoughts of Egypt and the pyramids, the dust of the desert, India and the yogic gurus, America and the Red Indians, New York and the skyscrapers, all filled their minds. That night Gwen's horizons were broadened as they sat talking about all these different cultures, comparing it to their own philosophies of life.

The brothers had bought a wedding present for Les and Gwen, a Benin fertility carving, brought back from the depths of Africa. It was meant to be a sort of joke, as they didn't think there were any problems on that respect, but the statue had a deep effect on Gwen. The two primitive bodies carved out of mahogany were, it looked like, in the throes of orgasm, bound round together; where they started and ended was unsure, what part belonged to which was unsure; all she knew was it was so unnervingly sexual. It sat there on the table, commanding an audience, as if still under the power of the chief witch doctor, demanding obeisance to its desire of carnal bonding. It was as if the drums were beating, hypnotising one's senses, putting one's blood into a frenzy for the act of joining together: the power of creating one from two, the atomic fusion of souls in the fire of passion; right there on her kitchen table.

She had to get up from the table, break the spell somehow, so she went over to the gramophone and put on the nearest record without thinking, hoping the change in atmosphere would do it -would bring her back to reality. It was Billie Holiday's sultry, raspy voice that spoke back to her amongst the sweet saxophone, "from the moment we met...I see your face...It's just the thought of you, the very thought of you, my love..." She turned, pensively and sat back down. They all lit a cigarette, and silence fell as they stared into space, letting Billie's dulcet tones wash over them. It was late and bed was calling.

They planned to go out the next evening. Tom and Sam hadn't been out in their own country for a while and wanted to see what the scene was like at that moment. Things had been changing swiftly with the times, and they wanted to catch up. There was a dance on at The Grand. A Dixie band was in town, and they were all looking forward to it, everyone loved music.

The joking and banter had started, and they were gearing up to have a fun night. As the men had an aperitif and sorted themselves out, combing their hair slick as was the fashion at the time, and splashing on the aftershave Tom had brought back from the States, they joked about their childhood together. Laughing as to whom first saw Jenny's knickers!

Gwen was desperately deciding what to wear, the red one, or this or that, but then decided on her old favourite that always made her feel so good. As she slipped it on over her head the black satin brushed her skin, and she felt like a million dollars. It was just a classic black tulip sleeved, figure hugging dress with a touch of French lace around the neck; but what it did for her was something else. She was the movie star in this: it was deadly. Her figure, slender with rounded breasts, shimmering in the satin, made her look irresistible. She tousled her hair and went to join the men.

As she entered the room, they fell silent and just stared at her. Les pulled himself together and went over to her, kissing her cheek and saying,

'My dear queenie... I don't know if The Grand is grand enough for you!'

'Don't be silly. I can't wait! Are you ready boys?'

'Well, I suppose we'd be honoured to have you with us; but you'll have to put a sack over your head or something -coming out with us looking like that!' Tom said jokingly. They all laughed, except for Sam, who said nothing, just stared.

They stepped out into the cold night air making their way to the gig. They'd linked arms and were striding up the street with such confidence and camaraderie; it was obvious to anyone to see this was one of those good moments in life, when everything was wonderful. Life was fun and exciting and there to be enjoyed.

As they walked, they passed a load of people all in black shirts, all riled up and angry. It was the straggling end of a Fascist march that had been taking place. It had been broken up before too much trouble started, but the undercurrent feeling was still in the air.

'What on earth is all that about?' Tom said, questioning his brother.

'Oh blimey, don't ask. There's a lot going on that makes me wonder what's happening to our country, Tom.' Les paused, sighed, then added, 'You're best off out of it; keep to the ships if I were you. People are getting these ideas: communism, fascism, talks of that German guy 'Hitler'... I don't like it, I just don't.'

No more was said, but they all realised how serious it was. They turned the corner and approached the hotel; it had been recently refurbished in the fashionable style, and it now looked something special. The art-deco features reeked sleek success. Everything had been thought of, from the most wonderful heavy brass leaf-patterned doors, the geometric jungle carpet, the long black marble pillars in the entrance area, exotic plants and even the modern shell up-lighting; but this was nothing to the stunning stained-glass window that separated the bar level from the lower dancehall. It shone glimpses of another world: an angled geometric jungle scene, big leaves in vibrant greens, deep orange tropical flowers and among it all a black sleek panther looking as if he's about to roar. The light filtering through the stained glass and the blurred movement of people behind it all helped to make the stained-glass scene appear to come alive.

They took off their coats and entered the bar.

'Gin's all round?' asked Sam. People were turning to look at them. They looked a striking group, the four of them.

'What a good idea, make mine a double. I think I'm going to like it here!' Tom replied.

The brothers loved to be in the thick of it and this place was humming, packed out. It was a wonder they didn't get their eyes poked out by all the cigarettes held up high in holders as they made their way to the bar. The band started up, the wonderful, capped trumpets and brushed symbols rhythmically calling them down the stairs to the dance floor. The stained glass was directly above the band, and the glass shone a glow over the whole darkened room giving it an exotic feel. People were swinging, the band was fantastic, and these musicians were the real deal.

They danced and danced; Les was such a good dancer and Gwen loved to let him guide her. Then Sam came up, asking if he could have a dance with 'your beautiful wife.'

'Yeh - just not too close! I know your tricks!' Les quipped. He was well aware of Sam's reputation as a womaniser.

Sam took her hand and led her deep into the crowd, the music turned softer and more sensuous, and they looked at each other as they moved together with such ease.

'You've been ignoring me,' he said.

'No, I haven't,' she snapped back, maybe a little too fast and her voice a little too high.

'Look I know I shouldn't do this but...'

'Then don't,' she said, almost pleading for him not to voice what they felt.

'No, here me out, Beautiful one. I have to say it.'

'No, you don't.'

'I do and I will. We both know that there's something incredible between us. I feel it, and I want you to know that if I'd been there that night at the dance when you met my brother, things would be very different.'

Being up close, and the scent of him, was intoxicating; she needed to breathe and keep her head, but every time his eyes caressed her, she fell a little more. Snapping out of it, she replied,

'Well, you weren't, and they aren't. Things are as they are, and if that's the case its best we just steer clear of each other.' She brushed a loose tendril of hair from her eyes. 'I'm happily married to your brother or hadn't you noticed.' But she knew he was right.

'Well, that's what I mean. Gwen, I just had to talk to you, let you know how I feel so that we can find a way to keep it all together. Les would just go crazy, but I'm going to have to live with these feelings I have for you forever. They're not going to go away, just up and leave. I'll be lucky to get you off my mind for a minute.'

'Oh, Sam, don't be crazy.'

There was nothing she could say, nothing to say. They just clung to each other in the only moment he could claim as theirs, and then as the song wound down they returned to the others.

She was relieved to be back, next to Les; she loved him so much, trusted him so deeply. He was so good to her, she loved him for that; these wild untamed emotions Sam stirred were not what she wanted.

They carried on as if nothing had been said, but the others must have noticed the difference in the atmosphere.

Chapter Twelve

London,
Spring, 1931,

When Wallis returned after that fateful weekend meeting Prince Edward, she realised her life had changed. It had just stepped up a gear, and so, she felt everything else around her had to step up to the mark -or go.

'Ernest, Darling, I think there are some members of staff not suitable for our position, now that we're, well, you know, friends of the Prince.'

Ernest laughed, 'Well I wouldn't exactly call us that, Honey!' However, looking at her, he could see how deadly serious she was, so he humoured her, 'Are you sure, Darling? I was glad to get back home, and the staff are a pleasant enough group to come back to. The house seems to tick along very well.' Pausing and looking at her thunderous expression he added, 'These matters do concern you, I know. Who were you thinking of, exactly?' he asked sheepishly, knowing how Wallis could be.

'Well, that chauffeur has to go!' she said, dragging out the 'has' in her guttural Baltimore drawl. 'Did you hear his tone of voice to you today when you remarked on the traffic? Utterly contemptuous and totally unacceptable! I mean, just imagine if he had that attitude in front of Prince Edward!'

'Wooooow now, pretty lady! Hold your horses!' Ernest said in his softer American drawl. 'Wait a minute. He's not exactly likely to be rocking up here is 'He'!'

'Well Ernest! That's just your problem isn't it, Sweetie! You don't have any desire to better yourself. I know you are comfortable in your sense of self, but life is to be pushed to the max! That's what I'm here for, Dearest.' Her tone heavily sarcastic on the term of endearment. 'You can't deny we are good friends with Bertie and Consuelo. Her sister has already come here and who exactly is she entangled with? Hmmm?' Wallis gave him that school mistress look making him feel like he had all his sums wrong. 'All I'm saying is you just never know, and we must be prepared.'

'Ok Kiddo,' he said, as he went over to the drink's cabinet, poured himself a whisky and took out a fat cigar: anything for an easy life.

'Ernest, do you have to smoke that now? You know how I hate smelling like an ashtray,' she said, whilst waving the smoke away from her. 'Anyhow, I've not finished, I can't stand the vulgar London accent of my maid, what do they call it -Cockney! I won't listen to it another minute longer. And, while we're at it, the cook really hasn't the insight I need for entertaining, and keeping the standards of fine dining that I require. She'd be ok for a regular British family I guess, but our tastes are so much more refined and continental. I'm sure that was the first time she'd prepared avocado the other evening!' she quipped, 'I'm giving her a month's notice.'

Ernest took a sip of the fine malt whisky, as the bitter-sweet nectar hit the back of his throat, he swallowed, not only the whisky but his words, summing his patience.

Things did change: Wallis became more neurotic about the perfection of arrangements, menus and guests, who to sit next to whom. She, it had to be said, was good at entertaining, and the evenings always worked well. However, Wallis was becoming overly fastidious; neurotic to the point of not sleeping, and she kept having bouts of flu, making her more determined to carry on regardless, not wanting to miss a chance.

The problem for dear Ernest was the expense of entertaining: it had shot right up. He could only stand by and watch as she recklessly spent his hard-earned dough.

Chapter Thirteen

Birmingham,
Autumn, 1939,

It was only a year on from when Les and Gwen had married, but all had changed. It was now a different world: the world was at war.

The preparations for war had been going on for some while before it was declared: gas mask fittings, corrugated steel Anderson shelters delivered to people with gardens, blackouts prepared, sirens installed and tested, and the factories were busy working rotating shifts throughout the days and nights.

Gwen was heavily pregnant and the Birmingham maternity Clinic she went to requested that they were evacuated out of the city, to Stratford upon Avon. She was one of the many: up to 13,000 pregnant women evacuated out of the big cities to the 'safety' of the countryside.

It had all been quite traumatic. Her pregnancy was not void of problems due to her being so thin. They'd also been really sad to leave their flat, their first love-nest, only to be then moved to an area they didn't know. Many people were in the same boat, change was all around, and one just had to get on with it. Les, in his wonderfully resourceful way had found a little terraced cottage with a garden to rent, and there was so much work available they felt they'd be able to manage.

There they were on that momentous day, a beautiful September morning; the sun singing in the sky and the flowers still in their last full, fluffy blooms of summer.

It was 11 o'clock on the 3rd of September 1939. They were sitting over a cup of tea as the wireless broadcast spilled the terrible words coming from the voice of Neville Chamberlain, the Prime Minister at the time. No one really had an inkling of the harrowing events that were to unfold, or the hardships people would have to endure for such a long time. The atmosphere was positive, people were determined not to let that 'Living Devil Incarnate' Hitler, bully or threaten their country, and would do whatever it took to put him in his place.

A few weeks later, as Gwen was putting up the blackout blinds, she felt a piercing agony and had to sit down. Les was still out at work and wouldn't be home for a while. She couldn't carry on with the blinds, she couldn't move, water rushed down her legs. There was a knock at the door. It was the Air raid Precautions Warden, coming round to check that no light was visible. He started knocking louder at the door.

'Hello? Anybody home?'

'Yes. Hello George, please come in, the doors open.'

He entered the kitchen, familiar with the house and Gwen, as he'd helped show them the ropes and given them advice since they'd arrived. Standing there he looked really quite official with his tin helmet with the big white 'W' on it, and his cardboard box with his gas mask in, strapped over his shoulder, torch in hand.

'Hello Mrs Holmes, what's going on here then? You're not prepared for the blackout? This sort of behaviour can't go on, you'll let us down!' Then he looked at her and saw her terribly white face and the look of pain in her eyes.

'I'm sorry, Love, are you alright?'

'No, I don't think so. I think my contractions have started, and Les isn't home for another hour. I've got to get myself to the maternity unit.'

'Now, don't you worry yourself,' seeing the look of panic in her eyes. 'My Gina has had six little'uns and she just popped them out! They are very good, the people here, you're in safe hands on that front. What we have to do is find a way to get you to the maternity unit, then all will be fine. I must carry on with my blackout duty. Can't be letting the country down can we! But I'll just pop along to Mr Henderson; I know he'd drive you- a pretty lady like yourself, a 'damsel in distress' and all that. Just sit tight and do your breathing.'

'Thank you, you are such a dear man.' Even when she was in distress she turned a man into a puppy, just with one smile.

'Right you are,' he said with a slight blush.

He was right, and all went well. Les and Gwen gave birth to a baby girl. She was a chubby cheeked adorable, red curly locked, scrumptious, little fidget bottom! They were over the moon,

'Queenie you are incredible! I just don't know how you made this little one. Look at you -you're nothing more than a sparrow as it is! I love every morsel of you, and of my little girl - my very own daughter!'

Things went along, gradually getting harder and harder. The war that people had thought would be over quickly, and 'our boys back for Christmas', was showing no signs of abating a year later. More and more boys and men were signing up or being called up.

The informative war posters were popping up everywhere. The famous 'Your King Needs You!' pointing accusingly at the viewer, calling for men, and 'Look Out in the Blackout' warning people of the dangers of the dark, as so many accidents were happening; from burning oneself to a dramatically high rise in car crashes (leading to the white lines being painted on the roads to show the way). 'Lend a Hand on the Land' was plastered everywhere, expressing the serious need for growing one's own vegetables and the country to supply our own food. Parks and golf courses were ploughed up and seeded for crops. Potatoes were a lifesaver.

The wireless was becoming such an important feature in the home. They'd sit in the evening and listen with bated breath to what was unfolding. Les was doing all he could, from digging work, to helping secure the air raid shelters for the town, and Gwen had been helping doing sewing as she was adept with a needle.

They were exhausted that night as they snuck into bed, it was a cold November night and all they were wishing for was an unbroken night's sleep, snuggled together in their bed. They'd had four nights in the past week that the sirens had given the terrifying alert call. The piercing alarm sounded again into the night, rising and falling like the breath of war, warning of the possible approach of the terroriser. They'd had to scramble down to the shelter at the end of the road and make do. The harsh cold floor would be covered with some blankets and pillows, but sleep would be broken, if any at all. The stories were starting to filter through about 'so and so's husband' in France, or the person's son that was 'lost in action.' These were horrific bedtime stories, not really what was needed to put one in a restful state; nevertheless, they'd always end on a positive note, saying how, 'We'll get them, we'll win.' After the stories were displays of caring and charity among them all, and songs sung to sooth the children.

But that night they just didn't want to believe it as the sound pierced the silence of the night. The siren built up strength, then fell, again, and again, whining, resonating all around, calling the people to safety.

'Les, please, do we have to go tonight? Couldn't we just stay here, Pattie is fast asleep. I've been worrying she's not getting enough rest,' Gwen pleaded.

'I know, Darling. I've noticed, and this worrying isn't going to do you any good either.'

'They've not struck here at all, have they? The last few nights nothing happened after the sirens.'

'I'm aware. Nevertheless, it's been best to be on the safe side. Just look what's been happening to London. The reports are shocking. There won't be anything left of our capital at this rate. God bless those Londoners, they've got it real bad. They've had these raids every night since September. They must be cracking up down there.'

He pulled her closer to him, and wrapped his arms tight around her, wanting with all his heart to protect her from all this. She felt as safe as she could, knowing she was with Les. He was her soldier, he always came through and straightened things out for her, she hadn't dared contemplate what she'd do without him, how she'd survive if he wasn't by her side; she'd really come to rely on her wonderful warrior.

They lay there together, with each other's warmth comforting and soothing away the fears in the minds, but then, the terrifying sound started to approach. They'd heard the odd few aircraft before, but this was different, it was a deep drone of many heavy aircraft. It sounded so ominous, riding death through the night. You knew each plane was going to bring destruction, it was just a matter of where. It seemed to go on forever, like a continual blanket of aircraft.

Gwen started to shake and her voice so soft and trembling, she started rambling,

'I wonder where they are heading. It doesn't seem they're coming for us, but they'll get someone that's for sure. Oh Les, this is all so wrong. Why do people want to hurt each other so?' she ranted on and on, 'There's so much love to live, and tonight so many are going to die. Why? Where are they going? Flying overhead like that? You don't think they're heading for Birmingham do you?'

Les, for once, couldn't kiss her and make everything better, he didn't know where the planes were heading, and he didn't want to fob her off with 'everything will be alright'; they were always so honest with each other. She needed reassurance; not lies. What could he say?

'Petal, we've been very lucky, we've been spared. I don't want to think what will be happening tonight. We can only deal with the aftermath and help wherever we can.' He sighed, and said deep in contemplation, 'It seems this war is stepping up a pace. I'm going to do all I can to make sure you are as safe as possible. We must always go to the shelter in the future, however tired.' He stroked her brow then said, 'You promise me?'

'I understand. I do, but it's just such a strain, so many faces. That old gentleman keeps coughing all night, dear of him, but I just can't sleep with the noise. I suppose it does give a certain sense of reassurance, us all together like that doesn't it? But I'm so glad for this moment, with you, facing this just you and I tonight. We are troopers, aren't we.'

Les was deep in thought; this was all getting serious. He was going to have to think of something. As she lay there, he calmed her down, the trembling eventually subsided, and they drifted into sleep. Suddenly, she woke-up, they must have only been asleep an hour or so, but now she was sitting bolt upright, looking at him.

'But ...oh Les... I've a terrible feeling, something awful is happening, I can't stop it. What about Ma? She's all on her own, she'll be scared.' Gwen was shaking with worry, 'The planes were heading her way. Oh, she will be safe, wont' she? She has to be.'

They didn't really sleep after that, just drifted in and out, the nightmares playing out in their minds, but finally the long continuous reassuring sound of the 'all clear' came, and they could finally sleep safely. It was nearly 5am and Les was able to get a few hours before he had to be up for work at 8 o' clock. People still had to be up and out to work, whatever the night had been like, however traumatic or sleepless in the air raid shelters.

That night had been the 20th of November 1940.

She was right: the planes had been on their way to Birmingham and heavily bombed the city. Total devastation reigned. Along with many other buildings, the BSA munitions factory had been hit, successfully, collapsing every floor onto each other; 81 out of 83 night workers died in the shelter, in the cellar. One of those lucky two had been pulled from the wreckage with no harm to him whatsoever, when all around him everyone had been crushed to death. A kink in the RSJ steel girder had saved his life. That was one lucky fellow. Many others around the city weren't so lucky. The air attack had been brutal.

The next day Gwen listened furiously to the wireless. The news didn't really say much about the Midlands, as it had been a terrible night all over England and she must have missed the bit on Birmingham. She kept listening, again, and again; but nothing.

The next day one of the neighbours had heard through a friend the seriousness of that night for Birmingham. Gwen was beside herself with worry. She couldn't eat what food they had and couldn't seem to settle the baby. Les came back that night and took over, singing softly to gurgling little Pattie, letting her squeeze his finger with delight. He looked over at Gwen,

'Honey, you are going to have to eat, otherwise I'm going to have to force-feed you like this sweet baby of ours.'

'Les, I'm worried sick. There's no word coming through from Ma, and I know it's been awful bad in Birmingham. Mrs Kentish was telling me terrible things.'

'Look the only way to stop this fretting is to go there. Tomorrow's Saturday and I know Patrick always drives up to the market and then pops in to check on his aunt. I'll go and ask him if we can catch a lift.'

They drove up that Saturday, and as they approached it was clear how bad that night had been. Streets and buildings were decimated; people were wandering around still shell shocked. Men were sifting through the rubble, hoping to find the few last surviving people. The roads were getting worse as Patrick picked the car through the rubble. They drove along New Street, the devastation everywhere, their mouths dropping in disbelief; the Lyons tea shop where they'd often gone was a pile of rubble, Marshalls was flattened, even the Dolcis shoe shop was gone. It was scary how something could be thriving and so full of the bustle of everyday life one minute, and then like a ghost town that had been long gone the next.

As they passed their old flat, they noticed the roof of the building was no longer. Then they turned round the bend and The Grand, the fantastic hotel with all that beautiful stained glass had taken a hit: the whole of one side of the building was no more. The haunting thought of that wonderful night they'd all had now just a memory, as the venue had vanished. Gwen was finding all this hard to take as she'd grown up on these streets. As they turned into her parent's street, it was obvious that it wasn't going to be good news.

'Stop, please. Stop the car! I must get out!'

Gwen already had the door half open and was on her way out. She ran screaming up to where her parents' house had been, her body wracked with hurt, she doubled up and fell to the pavement: the house was no longer. It, and three others next to it, had been obliterated, then fire had finished what the bomb had started. Someone came out of a house up the road and spoke with her, they obviously knew each other. Gwen pulled it together, but then at something the lady said, she just fell into her arms, her body sobbing. Her father was not at home; he'd been staying and working at a factory near the Malvern's, helping with the design of engineering parts for the war. Her mother had been at home and had been killed; but they reckon on impact: so, no suffering. They'd found her body before the fire really took hold.

Nothing was left; no possibility of rummaging for any of what had been her inheritance -not that she cared- but it was her ma's memories she would have liked, her beautiful Spanish shawl, the jewellery that would have been hers, and the furniture, all gone. And with it, a part of Gwen's resilience went as well.

They stayed in town for two days, doing all they could to help. Les set to, helping shift rubble and Gwen helped the people in the street. It comforted her to be near these people who had known her mother, helping to soothe the pain of her loss. But they had to get back, they were shattered, and their little Pattie had been left with Mrs Kentish.

There were more air raids, and that week in the air raid shelter they learnt of the devastation in Coventry. They weren't to know the figures, but that November 4,330 homes in Coventry alone had been destroyed. Coventry was only 19 miles from Stratford-upon-Avon. Les then found out (who knows how -but he did) that the War Cabinet had been moved to Hindlipp House in Worcester, 25 miles from Stratford-upon-Avon, and Parliament was moved to Stratford-upon-Avon itself. This was all too close to home for his liking. He wasn't afraid of anything, and he was to do his bit yet, but like any man with his family, he wanted to know Gwen would be as safe as possible. The air raids and the loss of her mother had made a noticeable impact on her. She was staring off into space more than usual and becoming more animated when in discussion. He thought this was merely normal and everyone was a bit like this, considering. Things had been difficult; it was only natural for there to be some emotional fallout from events.

Chapter Fourteen

London,
Summer, 1931.

There was no reckoning with Wallis now, this group she was with were the 'high rollers', and she was loving every minute of it.

'Darling, are you able to sit here with me for a while? There's something I wish to talk to you about,' Ernest said one afternoon.

'Well, perfect timing my dear,' Wallis butted in, 'I'm so excited. I have to discuss something with you. You know how Consuelo, Thelma, Gloria and my cousin all had their official presentation at court? Well, I want to be presented...'

'But Wallis, I don't mean to interrupt or upset you,' Ernest said cautiously, 'but you are divorced. I don't think it's possible, Darling.'

She glared at him coldly, 'We can get round this little set back, I know we can! The law has changed now, Darling, didn't you know? A divorcée may be presented as long as the fault of the divorce lay with the husband... Win owes me.' She leant forward and kissed him softly. Ernest looked deep into those violet eyes, trying to see a clue as to what his wife was really up to. She was getting carried away on this royal lark, but it seemed to make her happy, and he loved it when she flashed those eyes at him.

He knew she'd found settling into the way of things in London difficult. She'd been quite ill and depressed, on and off, but this had really lifted her out of the doldrums.

'Ok then, what's the harm in a little bending of the truth. I suppose.'

She kissed him again and started to tell him of her ideas for the night. His reason to talk to her would just have to wait. Financial worries would not go down well right now and he didn't want to ruin the moment: she was in one of her rare affectionate moods, curled up on the sofa with him like a contented cat, purring over the finer details.

'Do you think Lester would lend us his touring car? I bet he would, he likes you. Will you ask? Oh, and Thelma still has her feathers...' she continued, planning.

Wallis spent many a sleepless night worrying whether the documents would pass the royal boards scrutiny, but her worries were unfounded, and she was on her way.

'Ernest are you sure we aren't late?'

'No, Honey, as long as we leave right now, and I mean NOW!'

'Ok, ok, I'm ready. What do you think? Fit for a king?' Wallis turned, she grinned, wide with anticipation and excitement. Ernest thought she seemed like a vulnerable, young girl going on a first date. She, of course, looked immaculate.

'It really was an effort pulling it all together, but I do believe it's come off rather well. Don't you?'

'Yes, Darling, you look like a princess,' he said admiringly.

'Are you sure the dress doesn't look too loose? Consuelo is so kind to have lent it to me, but her bust is bigger than mine -the bitch!'

'It's perfect, Honey.' He paused, then looked at his watch. 'We've got to go, if we want to be ahead of the crowds.'

'Alright then, let's do it!' she said, sweeping up the white satin dress in her hands and heading for the stairs.

It had to be a white dress, with three white ostrich feathers, worn as the symbol of the Prince of Wales. Luckily, she'd been able to borrow Thelma's feathers and train. So, what with her friends help, and a new aquamarine and crystal necklace she'd bought especially, her look was achieved.

The wealthy American, Lester, did lend them his carriage (the touring car), and so they set off to Buckingham Palace.

Wallis was ecstatic as she entered the inner sanctum of the palace. Never in her wildest dreams had she thought she would be here, being presented to King George.

The sumptuous red carpet, the guards in their finest Elizabethan liveries, and the chandeliers twinkling, made it seem unreal. She took it all in; the paintings, the decor, the incredible Throne Dias that the King and Queen were sitting under; she'd never seen anything so majestic.

Then she set eyes on Queen Mary's jewellery. Her Royal Highness was wearing a diamond and pearl choker, along with other pieces that evening. The large old-cut diamonds were glistening and shimmering their powers, hypnotizing Wallis.

'Ernest, just look at Queen Mary's diamonds! Oh my lordy, what I'd do for just one of those rocks!'

'I'd hate to think!' Ernest replied, and they both laughed.

The event ran its course, Wallis was presented, and all went well. After a while Thelma came up to them, 'Hey Sweets! Don't you both look splendid! What did you think of it all? Impressive, huh? Well, we've tired of it all now, you've done your curtsy Wallis; like a pro, I've gotta say!'

'Thanks Thelma, you look fine too,' Wallis replied.

Then Thelma said, as if an afterthought, 'Hey, we're all piling back to mine for a bit of a 'shindig', we'd love you guys to tag along. David's just gotta wrap up some finalities then we're away. Ok?'

Wallis was beside herself; it couldn't have finished on a better note. As she walked around the grand room, soaking it all in one last time, she came into earshot of the Prince talking to his father; hearing a snippet of a private conversation. He was complaining how the lighting was rather unflattering for the women. She laughed to herself and stored this information for later.

Once they were back at Thelma's, and David was near (David was the name Prince Edward liked to be called by his close friends), she brought up the subject of how she heard him say all the ladies looked 'ugly', and snubbed him after that, leaving him speechless. This was all new to him, being treated like this; he was rather taken with the down to earth, 'you 'aint somebody special' routine.

Wallis was secretly jumping with excitement when he offered to drive them home,

'But we've our own chauffeur outside, Honey,' said Ernest.

'And? So? Send him home! We can't turn His Royal Highness down, can we?'

So, they ended the night in style, asking the Prince up for a nightcap as if he was a long-lost friend; he declined.

Their lives carried on at such a pace, spiralling with late nights, parties and events all linked with HRH. They were haemorrhaging money and Ernest was finding it impossible to keep up, not only financially, but he was exhausted. He seemed to be the only one who had to get up at eight in the morning, get on the tube (they'd had to sell the car and dismiss the chauffeur -to Wallis's dismay) and go to work.

It came to a particular night when Wallis laid her trump card and secured herself firmly in the Prince's sights. She'd been on hot coals waiting for some official invitation from His Royal Highness and it finally arrived. She had to have some sign that her efforts snaring him obliquely were paying off, and this was perfect.

Wallis and Ernest were invited to Fort Belvedere, for the weekend, in late January. They were to be part of a group gathering at his abode, nestled on the outskirts of the Windsor Great Park. It was his private hide-away from it all, with deer roaming wild and the ancient trees sheltering him from the public eye. He'd been lavishly re-decorating it with a Turkish bath, new furnishings and 'central heating'; all with the guidance of Thelma's American influence.

Wallis came down for the evening. She entered the room and decided she was really going to leave a lasting impression on him tonight; the challenge she had set herself was heating up and she was stimulated by the whole situation. She'd persuaded herself that if she'd been able to win the incredibly sought after Felipe Espil, when every woman in Washington had wanted him, then why not this 'David'?

Wallis stood out as this sleek, streamlined, headstrong woman in the room. The other women were beautiful, but feminine and fluttery. The dashing Prince Edward, reliably bored by all this, made his way over to the 'cougar' in the room.

She looked at him with a look of distain as if he was in her way; he looked around, but no, she was looking at him.

'So, Your Royal Highness, there's always a lot of fuss made about just one 'little you' isn't there (playing on Thelma's nickname for him, 'the little man'; possibly in reference to his manhood). It must tire you so! Tell me something interesting this time,' she crooned, as if she, the royalty, and he, the subject. Prince Edward was taken aback, for he was adored wherever he went, replied,

'Well... I feel the most interesting thing in this room is you. You are the most fascinating woman I've ever met.'

'You're not going to bore me with flattery now, are you?' Wallis snapped back.

Edward stood dumbfounded. He couldn't believe her outrageous behaviour, her cutting wit enthralled him, and at the same time deeply excited him. Her refreshing arrogance to his position made him feel like himself in a way like never before: feeling momentarily freed from his shackles of royalty. They danced and danced. Wallis thought, 'It was working! He does like me; he's hardly danced with Thelma all night!'

Wallis found him incredibly skilled on his feet, and he couldn't stop pulling her close. Edward felt subconsciously reassured by her androgynous figure: not such a threat to his masculinity as a curvaceous woman.

It's all down to timing. He'd never met anyone so domineering, self-confident, and sexually sure as her and he was smitten. Everyone else in his life had been slightly sycophantic up until then, but Wallis really gave the impression that she wasn't all that impressed. Wallis liked a sexual challenge, that was no secret, and for her, his title of 'Most Eligible Bachelor in the World' probably seemed more of a thrill than the fact he had the title Prince Edward, and was destined to become the King of England.

Chapter Fifteen

Stratford-upon-Avon,
Summer, 1940.

Les and Gwen had been happy until the bombings but now had growing concerns as to the future. Les thought it was time.

'Listen Queenie, I've been thinking long and hard about this; hear me out.'

'Les, you've got that serious look you get!'

'It is serious, sweetheart. I know we have settled in here...'

'Yes?' Gwen said, questioning him with her eyes.

'And the people have been really good to us...'

'Yes...' she acknowledged.

'But we've got to think what the best thing to do is. You've little Pattie to look after and if we're going to have another little one, one day...' he looked at her lovingly, 'I want you to know you've got family near if for any reason you need help.'

'What are you trying to say?'

'Well, I've been in touch with my family back in Surrey, and my sister Eva says she will let us stay with her till I can sort something out.'

'Move again, right now? And be at the mercy of your family? I know they aren't too keen on me - are you sure?'

'Yes. I wouldn't have put it to you if I didn't think it was our only option. It'll be good to know that you'd have other people around you that care. I know what you think, but you are wrong. Eva is lovely, we have always been close, and believe it or not she does like you,' he pressed.

'I know, she's a kind woman.'

'I want to know you'd have family around you, if I have to go and work away from home. I know we've not dared talk about it, but it's only a matter of time before I get called up. If it doesn't happen, I'm going to have to enlist anyway, as these Germans need to be stopped.' The determination in his voice was frightening.

'Les, what are you saying?' she said, with the look of shock in her eyes. She had to face the fact that Les was going to have to go and fight, along with the awful reality of losing her mother: everything suddenly came flooding in.

'Well, we'd better make the most of these times.' Gwen went to the gramophone and put on a record, poured a whisky for each of them, loosened her beautiful auburn hair and turned around looking incredibly seductive,

'Let's dance. Take me to that wonderful place we go when we dance together; take me there and don't let me come back.'

His breath was taken away, she mesmerised him and for that night they forgot all the worries of war, rations, bombings, everything. They were back in that magical dance hall, where they met, with the knowing bond of true love pulling them tighter as they whirled round and round. They made deep passionate love, right there in the living room; she needed the reassurance of his maleness, the safety of his smell, the escape of orgasm.

Days after, they packed up, again, and with little Pattie playing hide and seek, crawling among the bedding and boxes, giggling so contentedly, oblivious to the upheaval; they awaited Eva's husband. He had been able to borrow a van and together they'd pooled their petrol rations (Les somehow had got hold of a few extra with no questions asked), and made their way south. Les and Gwen were in high spirits, they had a way of always being full of hope, even in the face of adversity.

They stayed in the house with Eva, her husband Albert and the children. It was a squeeze, admittedly, but Les had been right, and the feeling that they were 'all in it together' seemed to be good for everybody. The women were getting to know each other better, sharing the chores and helping each other with the children. They had some fun times, all together, but both Les and Gwen knew they needed to find their own place.

Les spotted a little cottage, opposite open heathland, it was run down and looked derelict; everything else was occupied or the rents were too steep. This would be perfect, with all that feeling of space and countryside, as if in the middle of nowhere, and still just a short walk into Sunningdale. They also wouldn't be too far from Eva's, so he asked around. It turned out to be property of the Sunningdale Golf Club, backing onto the golf course, as it did. He approached the club with the proposition that, as he was a builder, if he was to work on the house and get it fixed up, maybe they could live there on reduced rates. Les had a way about him and the golf club agreed. In the circumstances it seemed that the golf club couldn't refuse; everyone had to show willing to 'do their bit' for the war effort, and housing was just one way.

They set about getting the house into a habitable state. Les did the work gradually, as he could find materials. There was plenty needed to be done, but they just did what was immediately necessary for them to be able to move in.

They scrubbed the house from top to bottom with Jeyes Fluid to get rid of the mould that had crept into the building while it had been empty. One of the windows was smashed and Les went asking about and found a piece that would cut to size.

It was all coming together so well and before long he went over the heath foraging for wood to burn. He soon gathered a healthy wood pile stacked in the lean-to off the side of the house, a comforting sight on these cold winter days. The stench of Jeyes Fluid had finally faded, the place now whitewashed was ready for Gwen to bring it to life. Eva had come to help her and together they measured the fabrics to the windows; before long the bohemian materials that made it her home were fitted to size, and suddenly the house became a home.

Eva and her husband Albert lent them some chairs, and Les had found an old table in the lean-to shed that when cleaned up was a gorgeous piece of oak. The table must have been really old, with a lovely deep grain pattern and age smoothed top, giving a richness to the room and a feeling of many times gone by.

Looking round, with a wonderful sense of achievement, it was time to move in. They would be in for Christmas, not believing their luck at how things had worked out, they decided to have a moving in party to celebrate and thank everyone for all their help.

That first night together in the house was filled with such excitement they were like a couple of school children exploring it all over again, this time as their own home.

'You know, I've got a good feeling about this, we're going to do just fine all things considered.'

They had the electricity turned on and were trying to plug in the gramophone, as until they'd heard their favourite songs and held each other close the house was still not quite theirs. As they started to lay down their own memories, the cosy cottage warmed towards them.

Les had lit the fire, checking it'd draw; it drew well. The smoke raced up the chimney pulling the licking flames higher and higher, the crackling of the wood eased with the heat and the pungent smell of pine sweetened the room.

Gwen looked at Les and her eyes shone with happiness, her beauty never more so as that night. Her hair was picking up the light of the fire and glowing with the warm golden flickering heat. She leant forward as if an angel sent to bless him and kissed his forehead as he sat mesmerised by her.

'You were right, again, my lovely Les. Moving us here was a good idea; although we didn't know it would turn out quite so well did we!' Gwen mused. Memories still so fresh of the death and dust of Birmingham, then standing there on the pavement, in Stratford-upon-Avon, with their lives packed into a van.

'Didn't I tell you to stick with me, and I'd be able to make the impossible possible,' he laughed proudly. 'Things have been tough the last few months,' he admitted, soberly looking back, 'and I'm not going to say they'll get much better, but being here is a step in the right direction. The garden is fabulous. I'll get out there as soon as possible and prepare the soil for planting all we need. I'll be able to feed the five thousand with that garden -just you see if I don't! Have you seen the apple trees? It's good to know we've all this around us. Come here and sit with me,' he said, tapping the chair.

'What about this gathering? Christmas Eve you said?' Gwen questioned. 'You do realise that's in four days! You'd better prove you really are a magician and pull that rabbit out of that hat, as I don't understand where on earth we're going to get the money. We gave our ration slips to Eva for letting us stay and feed us, remember!'

'Do you really think I want you to be worrying yourself? Leave it to me. I've not let you down yet, have I? You just prepare everything the best you can.' He then added, reassuringly, 'Anyway, everyone is bringing something over to contribute. Eva is bringing her wonderful stewed apple and raisin crumble and Tom said he's got some great Bourbon that he brought back from the States for us to try. Can you imagine that!' he said, with a glint in his eye. 'I think he's bringing a girl for us to meet- that'll be interesting!' He winked. 'I even think Sam's coming over. The people next door are going to pop their heads round for a bit as well.'

'They're a strange lot, they were staring at me yesterday as if I was a gypsy moving in - not neighbourly really,' she said, laughing.

'Yes,' he said, chortling, 'I'm sure they are only coming round to see if we really have improved it here. They think this place is a write-off, but we'll show them!'

Les, while asking around, had found work and was starting the next day; it would help keep the wolf from the door, but the problem was the rations.

It turned out that where he'd been sent to work was a farm over the heath, about 4 miles from their home. He rose early and got himself together in the dark, not wanting to disturb Gwen. He put his work boots on and headed off in the direction, hoping to get a lift. The dawn was breaking late as it was the winter solstice. The days were so short with the sun reluctant to rise; even so, it was a beautiful sight that morning as the damp mist rose from the heathland, revealing the burnt colours of heathers bathing in the warm pinks of the sunrise. The air was crisp, and he seemed so light on his step, full of positivity as he marched on.

The farm was a beautiful old place with some wonderful big old barns. Two were full with straw and hay for the winter feed, the other was to be a shelter for the pigs if the weather got too bad. There was a lot of land ploughed, and chickens were everywhere. What with the war, the farmer decided he needed to add a bit onto the barns so the workers could live on the farm; the government would subsidise the work. The farm had a friendly atmosphere, helpers had been sent in, even some 'land girls' from London. There was a good feeling in the air, they were all providing however they could for their country.

It was to be just him and another fellow, Freddy, to do the building work. Freddy seemed fine, but a bit quiet, shy maybe, thought Les. There were plenty of old stones left in a far field from the ruins of a little old farm cottage, so their work was cut out lugging the stones back over the uneven fields with a wheelbarrow before they could start building. Les loved a bit of hard work, whistling as he went.

The next days passed so quickly and when it came to the 24th he was called over by the farmer, Ronald. He was a big old chap, seen some work in his time, and his large hands looked like they had the earth of the fields engrained into his very skin.

They got on like a house on fire since the first time they'd met, and had been bantering back and forth, giving each other friendly insults whenever they passed one another. Ronald felt that Les was good to have around. There were quite a few people he'd taken in, having lost his regular workers to the 'call-up', but he felt good knowing Les was among them. He needed someone to help with a particular job and didn't want everyone to know and thought Les was just the man. Ronald had been able to hide a pig from the authority, up in a little coppice between the fields and hadn't been able to deal with it till now. He really wanted to give everyone a good meal and something to comfort them for the fact that they weren't with their family and loved ones this Christmas; there was nothing more comforting than roast pork and crackling.

Les couldn't believe his ears as Ronald took him to one side and explained the situation. He laughed out loud, looking at this great big old guy, 'Who'd a thought it! He's a one!'

Everyone was starting to do things like this, to get through the hard times. So, Ronald and Les made their way to the coppice; walking with purpose; their mouths almost salivating as they pictured that plate of tasty food. Then, the reality was in front of them; this sweet looking pink pig came up to Ronald, snuffling and snorting affectionately into his hand looking for apples or any treats that he'd been bringing him. The dark eyes looked straight at Les and Ronald, questioningly. Ronald said a little prayer, a little ditty more pagan than Christian, thanking the earth and its gifts. Then he set to in a way only a farmer could, with his instinctive knowledge of how to deal with animals. The problem had been how to keep the noise down as the wind could blow the sounds of a screaming, squealing pig a long way, and the local pub wasn't too far; let alone the fact that the police constable's cottage was only over the field. They had to act quickly before the fat friendly thing worked out what his fate was. Pigs are so quick and intelligent, and his eyes seemed to pierce right into their thoughts and see the truth. Les had to keep his mind away from the killing and just do the job.

Les and Ronald got round the back of the pig, the hind, and Ronald put his legs astride him, straddling him, speaking soothingly all the time, stroking his head whilst he unsheathed the knife. The blade suddenly caught a ray of sunshine and glistened its shiny, sharp, deadly purpose. The look of sheer panic pierced the pig's beady eyes, and it swung round nearly toppling Les. The pig was hellish heavy, being a strong mass of muscle. The squeal rang through the air, so high and desperate, but that was his last, as the blade sliced cleanly through, garrotting efficiently, and the job was done. The sound hadn't really been able to get strength behind it before the wind was taken out of his sails, so to speak, and one squeal wouldn't have carried far. Mission accomplished, they set to, dealing with the carcass there and then.

Ronald jointed up the carcass so professionally you'd think he was a butcher, but then this was what his life was all about, raising stock for food. They piled the meat into the wheelbarrows, covered it with branches and dug the earth over to hide any signs of blood.

Ronald insisted Les took a lovely bit of pork home with him, for helping, as well as some wages; though Les swapped most of the wages for potatoes, turnip and swede.

'You enjoy that!' said Ronald jovially. 'Your help was invaluable, and somehow I know I can trust you, Les. Go home and fatten yourself up, will you! I don't know where you get your strength from, you're so lean. Oh, and just be careful who you share that with,' he said, with a glint in his eye, 'as I'll not be responsible for anything if you know what I mean!'

'Ronald, you've been a Godsend. You'll never know how much this means to me and my family. I have to say you are the fattest, dirtiest, smelliest looking angel I ever saw! Merry Christmas to you!' Said as he threw the bag over his shoulder.

Ronald replied, 'Give my regards to your wife, Merry Christmas!'

Les turned round in the direction of home and couldn't get back quick enough; firstly, if he was to be found with this meat there'd be trouble, and secondly, he couldn't wait to see the reaction on Gwen's face.

He burst through the door, he could see the look of concern in her eyes as it was already dark, and people would be arriving soon. She still had nothing to prepare, but she had got the stove hot and ready to cook on, just hoping for something, and also to warm the kitchen as the temperature had dropped; not that Les had noticed with all his excitement.

'You're never going to guess what I've got in my sack!'

'Rocks for all I care!' she replied. Gwen was agitated with him; leaving her this close to the gathering that he'd arranged, with nothing, literally nothing, to prepare. 'They'll be here in an hour.'

Sweeping her up, he kissed her as his infectious good mood made her laugh.

'Go on then! What is it? What have you got in your sack?'

He put her down, went to his bag and poured the contents on the table: potatoes spilling out everywhere, swede rolling around, then as he shook the bag, a heavy thud, as the pork landed onto the surface.

'What is that?' Gwen exclaimed.

Then as she un-wrapped it, 'It can't be, tell me... its meat! Is it a joint of pork? How on earth did you get hold of this?' She squealed with delight, 'It's fantastic! Les, just fantastic. Do you know how long it's been since we've eaten like this?'

He looked at her and beamed with satisfaction,

'Let's just say it's a job well done! Look I'll give you a hand -we can have it all ready in a minute. There are still some apples on the roof of the shed that look vaguely edible, I'll go and check.'

They rushed around and before long it was all prepared, the old black-grated range turned out to be a godsend and cooked like a dream. The pork was in, and the potatoes were nestled up around the joint, all roasting beautifully, the swede was bubbling away, and the apple sauce was just enough to stretch. They'd had to cut a lot of bad away from the apples but luckily had plenty to choose from.

Gwen slipped away to get changed and it was only at this moment, slipping into her faithful blue dress, that she thought of the last time she wore it: when she met Sam. Suddenly her back froze as she remembered Les saying that Sam may even come. She hadn't taken it in before, but the thought of seeing Sam made everything seem very complicated. She just wanted to relax and get to know Les's family better, but knowing Sam was in the room would add a difficult angle to it all. She decided to change into her deep rust-red dress that had a pleated swing in the skirt, and justified it with the fact it was a more Christmassy colour.

Les came in to change as she was straightening her stockings. He came over to her and turned her around. Looking right at her he said,

'I love you, Queenie. I only hope you know how much.'

She replied with all her heart, 'Les, you're the best. I love you too.'

They kissed falling onto the bed, and he teasingly saying,

'Now, let me help you with your stockings!' As she flung her legs high up in the air. She had lovely slender legs, as they laughed and passionately tousled around they heard knocking at the door.

'Bugger! They're here already. I was hoping I could take those stockings off you...' he said in a deep sexy voice.

'Hellloooooo!' came from the door.

'Come in! The door's open.'

It was Les's sister Eva, her husband Albert, their little ones, and Tom and his date, a dark-haired beauty in blue, with deep blue eyes, but no real spark.

'Here's that bourbon we were talking about! Crack it open Les, I've been dying to try it!'

'Yes! Tom how on earth have you saved it till now!' Les cracked back.

'Well, I needed some good company to ramble on at, and you seemed just the person! So, let's get cracking and start rambling! This is my friend, Caroline. Everyone, meet Caroline!'

He took the glasses from Les and poured out a shot for everyone. He proceeded to down his straight and poured another.

'Come on, keep up, little brother!'

'Enough of the little! I'm sure I'm half an inch taller than you.'

'No, that's just your hair, you dandy!'

With that they all laughed, clinking glasses and cheered the Christmas in. They settled the babies and children in the bedroom with Christmas stories and humming carols, soon the little ones were out like a light. The neighbours knocked at the door,

'Hello, do come in,' Gwen said, as she opened the door, wanting to let these people know she was no gypsy. She couldn't have looked more elegant if she tried in her softly pleated dress, with the rust colour highlighting her auburn hair. That was the only part of her that could have been gypsy.

The neighbours entered reluctantly, as if walking into a contaminated building, explaining,

'We thought it was only right to pop round as you had invited us - what with it being Christmas and all.'

'Well, I'm sure it will be a pleasure to make your acquaintance, as we are to be so close to one another, in such times as these. We can only make sure we enjoy today even more: for the troops away from home on such a day.'

With that the neighbours softened with a touch of humility and were then handed a Bourbon.

'Would you like a dash of soda?' Les offered.

'What is this?' Staring at the drink as if poison.

'Good Bourbon straight from America, brought it over myself,' said Tom. The neighbours looked at each other as if they'd been handed cyanide to drink.

'It won't kill you!' Les joked.

The talk turned to the war and how it was that Les and Gwen had moved house. The smell of pork was wafting through the house,

'Is that pork I smell?' said the lady from next door.

Les looked at Tom, 'Yes, it is.'

'Where did you get something like that? There's not been any pork in the butchers for ages. We've had to kill our chicken for tomorrow,' the neighbour said almost accusingly.

'Well, it does seem rare, but Eva here works at 'the house', Fort Belvedere, you know? It's one of the royal hide-aways. All the staff were given some for Christmas. Seems they'd over slaughtered. You're welcome to have some,' Les replied. He'd said it in such a nonchalant way, that they couldn't think there was any other reason, and it all seemed quite normal, but as the neighbours surveyed the room, looking at the bohemian fabrics, and then, when their eyes settled on the African fertility statue, a look of horror struck their faces. They'd never known anything like it.

'Are you admiring our statue? Les's brothers gave it to us as a wedding present. It's an African fertility statue.'

The neighbours stared at Gwen with a look of sheer terror as she described it to them,

'Fascinating isn't it! Incredibly sensual. You know I do feel it has real powers, don't you? The piece could be Voodoo for all I know. Be careful looking at it, they say it could take hold of your soul!'

The neighbours downed their whisky; choking it back they almost fled from the house, muttering something about 'she'd left a cake in the oven' and leaving rather flustered. Everyone fell about laughing, not able to believe what had just happened.

'Well, that's the last of them I'd say!' shrugged Les playfully. 'Sis, you didn't mind me using you as a scapegoat, do you?'

'That was close, sorry Eva,' Gwen muttered at the same time.

'No, don't worry!' Eva reassured them, 'I thought it was all hilarious! The look on their faces! Oh Gwen, you are a tease!'

'Well, I thought they knew I was just joking! I didn't realise they were that tedious.'

'Neither did we!' added Albert.

Everyone fell about again, pulling the strained faces of the neighbours. Les went around the whole evening pulling faces of distain and laughing.

'Come on everyone, let's eat this wonderful meal,' Les announced, as Gwen was laying it all on the table.

The talk again fell to how lucky they were to be there, all together, and of friends who weren't so lucky; four were away fighting, they'd not be so lucky tonight. The talk of call-up started. Gwen couldn't stand it and got up, taking the plates to the scullery. As she did, she heard a surprised cheer go up and she walked back in: Sam had arrived after all. He'd had trouble getting there because of the blackout. There'd been an accident along the road, and he'd stopped to see if he could help.

'All dead, three passengers, and a driver; looked like a whole family to me. I think the driver just couldn't see,' he reckoned. 'They had veered into a tree and off the road into the woods, the car was shredded.' Sam looked quite pale and tousled.

'Give the man a Bourbon.' Tom said, half cut by now. 'That'll sort him out.'

Gwen served him up a plate of food and put it down in front of him. He looked up at her and smiled. Aware that she had almost brushed her breasts on the back of his head whilst reaching over, she pulled sharply away and went to the kitchen. The thought of any physical contact was too much. She loved Les and didn't understand why she could feel so. She didn't want any problems and would just ignore him; nevertheless, however hard her rational head tried to keep a lid on it, her body would disobey and send wild messages. They all sat round the table, drinking, smoking and having a good time.

Gwen got up and went over to the gramophone to put a lively 'Fats' tune on. Sam also rose and approached her, saying something to the others about helping her choose some decent music. They were out of earshot of everyone else, as it was in the lounge.

'Gwen, I gather you'd rather I'd not come over, but it is Christmas, I want to be with my family. Oh heck, to be honest, I just had to see you again.' He paused, then slowly, deliberately said, 'It's good to know you're not so far away now.' He looked deep into her eyes and held her glance for a moment. A moment long enough for Gwen to know she had to get back to the table with the others.

She didn't even trust herself to speak to him, she couldn't risk him hearing the quivering in her voice. So, she just turned and walked away.

The night ended and Sam decided he would drive them all back as Tom and Albert were plastered, and they could all squeeze in. They left with everyone telling each other how lovely they were, what a great night, and how they'd help each other through these terrible times -no matter what- they were there for one another. Mr Hitler wasn't going to make them suffer. It was a lovely end to the night, and Les and Gwen stood there waving the family off. As Sam drove away, he gave a wink to Gwen. Les saw but made nothing of it.

'Do you think they'll be ok? There's hardly any light coming from those headlights, all masked in like that.'

They reached for each other, drew in close and looked up at the starry night sky, clear with not one cloud and no moon. The stars seemed to be a wondrous, hypnotic mass of glistening diamonds.

'Well, that went well didn't it! Don't you worry. Sam's a good driver, they'll be fine. Now where were we before we got so rudely interrupted by my family...?'

'Les, you are so naughty! They've only been gone two minutes.'

'Yes, but I've been wanting you for over two hours and it feels like two days,' he said in that sure, strong voice of his. She loved how his voice could make her weak at the knees. With the thought of such pleasure to come, rushing and rising in her body, she let him lead her back in, and closed the door.

As they lay there contented and curled up after having proved and reassured each other of their love, Les lay stroking her beautiful body.

'I'll remember these days forever.' he said, wistfully. 'These times are so special, even with war going on. I want to savour this moment.'

'Talking about savouring moments! Where did you get the pork?' Gwen said inquisitively.

He told her the story, and she was amused, 'Well we really nearly blew it with the neighbours!'

'They won't do any harm. You bewitched them anyway; you're a witch and you spooked them -I saw you!'

'Well, I felt we were in a bit of a hole, and you know the power of my eyes when I want!'

Didn't he just! Her eyes were dark like his, but hers were almost black, almost impossible to tell where the pupils started.

They fell into the most contented sleep they'd had in ages.

Chapter Sixteen

London,
Spring, 1933.

Wallis and Edward met many times after their dance at Fort Belvedere, through friend's house parties or up-scale events; he always managed to find a way to steer her near him.

Wallis was loving it and by the summer, safe with the knowledge that Lady Thelma Furness had gone to New York for a few months, she could really move in for the kill. Poor dear self-absorbed Thelma, not realising whom she was up against. She had almost handed the Prince over to Wallis at their farewell luncheon at The Ritz. It's known Wallis said:

"Oh Thelma, the Little Man is going to be so lonely."

At which the innocent mistress replied:

"Well, Dear, look after him while I'm away."

The Prince of Wales had already given Wallis a stunning diamond and sapphire brooch, muttering something to her about how she was the moon and stars to him. Wallis found this rather pathetic and taunted him saying these weren't real gifts as he'd just taken them from the royal vaults. If he really wanted her to understand how he felt, he'd better have something personally made,

'Stop decking me with dead relative handouts,' she snapped, 'What do you think I am, a Christmas tree you can adorn with dusty baubles?'

But he could tell; he was starting to get to know her, and he'd worked out she just adored jewellery. Her eyes sparkled in a way he'd not seen before. He wanted to know it was he who made her eyes sparkle like that; even if it was with jewellery that he accomplished it. But it was the jewellery; the reassuring splendour of wealth touching her skin; that really turned her on. Jewels made her excited in a way different to anything else: the value and beauty of the gems and the hard cold platinum, reflecting her character, gave her a sense of security that she'd been searching for, for a very long time.

Back in Mayfair, Wallis and her husband were discussing an invitation to dinner with Edward, again. Ernest had never quite got over the night they'd had guests for supper (an elaborate affair with Thelma, Henry and Grace Flood Robert all seated at the table), when suddenly the maid came into the room,

'Sorry to interrupt Ma'am, but the royal car is waiting outside. His Grace requests your presence, Ma'am, for you to accompany him immediately to Fort Belvedere.'

Ernest's heart sank, there were almost tears in his eyes. Thelma looked shocked. Wallis, in her cool, collected manner, never flinched; she didn't say a word, stood up, went for her hat and coat and walked out, leaving everyone at the table flabbergasted.

Ernest must have tired of this charade by now, and on the next occasion had to voice his growing concern, exclaiming,

'God, Darling! Do we have to go to this? I've so many worries at work. I could do with a night in for a change.'

'Well, that's you -a boring unreliable underachiever! Don't you know what it means for our social standing being invited to these dinners?'

'Well, no, not really; other than the fact I'm going to be sat next to some horsey blond 'aristo' and be bored to tears all night; trying to refrain from yawning into the soup and slipping down into my chair come the brandies.' He started to raise his voice slightly, 'Let alone hiding the sheer embarrassment of knowing you're up near 'Him'; laughing and flirting outrageously whilst there's damn nothing I can do about it. All for the sake of not upsetting royalty!' He shrugged and carried on his rant, 'You were the one against this whole 'shebam' if I remember rightly. You've certainly changed your tune.'

'How dare you!' she retorted, haughtily. 'Just because he makes you feel inadequate! And so he should! As we all know you're failing in most departments of your life. You're lucky you've got me along for the ride! Although, I do wonder when I'll be hopping off.'

'Yeh! I think you've already started with the 'hopping' bit. I'm no fool Wally. I know you've also been sleeping with Ribbentrop. How could you do it? I'm not stupid you know. I'll put a stop to all of this, somehow.'

But even while uttering the word 'somehow', he knew it was futile. There was no way he could pull Wallis back to him, she was seeking so much more than he could give her, although what that was, he'd no idea. She was never satisfied, more was always on her mind, sexually and socially. He thought at one time everything was great; they were together, he had a good job; but her horizons were blinded by wealth and fame, nothing could satiate her avaricious nature. He knew he'd have to let her go one day; but not to Joachim von Ribbentrop. He'd noticed it when the two of them were introduced: the way she arched her back, straight as she could, when she was interested in something. Wallis was finding all this 'Hitler politics' so sexy. She was sure she was right, believing in Hitler's movement, sure she was backing the winning horse: the more England went against it, the more compelled she was that she was right. She was spending a great deal of money entertaining these figures and keeping in with it all: money Ernest just didn't have.

He tried to diffuse the situation for the meanwhile,

'Look, Darling, let's not row, but we must find some time to talk properly, just you and me. I need you to understand that things aren't going well at the moment. I wish you could stop this high spending. We're going to have to tighten our reigns until I can pull this business to a stronger footing.'

'Are you telling me that I'm to lock myself away in this gilded cage? Unlike you I need people around me. Clothes and cocktails are what I do." She was fuming. "Remember, it's my wit and wisdom that's got us this far. So, tell me what are you saying exactly? That you can't afford me? My lifestyle? Or is it more like you can't keep up? You just don't have it in you, do you?'

'It's not you, Wallis, don't be so insecure! We're just going to have to let go of some staff,' he said, shaking his head in exasperation while walking to the bar to pour himself another bourbon.

'Christ! We've already downsized to this apartment, sold the car and let go of our chauffeur. Tell me exactly who do you think we can spare now?'

It seemed that he was going to have to go along with her that evening; maybe there might be another loan, or some deal he could make to secure things a bit.

This talk of money worries reminded Wallis of the insecurities of her youth. She didn't like to think back to those times, but to be unsure financially was something she'd made up her mind she wouldn't be again: Whatever.

That night at dinner Prince Edward was particularly attentive to Wallis, he wouldn't leave her alone for a second. It was noticeable to all attending that he failed to spend time with his other guests. He was fuelled with an overwhelming desire.

The Prince had commissioned an emerald and diamond bracelet to be made for Wallis, in a modern art-deco style, and couldn't wait to give it to her. It was up in his 'wing,' his private quarters, in his bedroom. He had to wait till he could whisk her away from the guests after dinner, as they leave. He was plotting all through the dinner, imagining the ecstatic look on her face. Wallis had said 'prove it,' when he'd tried to tell her how much she meant to him. 'Show me in ways I can understand... I have others that do mean it you know.' Well, this bracelet would do it - it must. He was getting desperate to know she would be his and only his.

Ernest was looking around for Wallis. It was time to go. Everyone was making their way home, but he couldn't see her anywhere. A member of staff came and discreetly told him that his presence would not be required any further, and there was a car waiting to drive him home. He shook to his very core with anger and shame,

'What is she playing at? This is getting dangerous! Does she realise what she's up to? She's married to me, for God's sake...I'm her husband!' These thoughts gave him no comfort as he had to face the driver and make his way home alone. With the images of Wallis and Edward together consuming his mind, he was in for a rough night's sleep.

Prince Edward finally had Wallis alone. It was the moment he'd been waiting for.

'I hope this is worth all the secrecy,' she said, flippantly. Nevertheless, she also had been wanting to stay; she was going to make him bed her. She knew how he felt, and she knew what she wanted.

He handed her the beautiful, leather bound Boodles bracelet case. She hadn't been expecting anything, but there it was: a box of hope, of security; and it was all hers. At these moments she showed her only signs of true tenderness towards the Prince, treating him as she should. Looking up at him with excitement, almost like an innocent girl, she opened the box.

'Well, David! This makes me think I'm not just one of your concubines!'

She stayed that night, in his bed. Caressing him and torturing him with desire as she writhed all over him: tantalising him then denying him any touch; he became so responsive he couldn't believe it.

There were witnesses and as the report says: "There was evidence of a physical act". Just what this meant is intriguing. Was it dirty sheets, a used condom, groans of pleasure or Wallis's pubic hairs - one dreads to think! But there it was: Wallis had bedded the most eligible bachelor in the world, the next in line to the throne: she -a divorced, married American, that wasn't even particularly beautiful. It must have given her such a sense of power, lying there in his bed with nothing on but the bracelet, glinting on her wrist.

Edward was besotted from that moment on: possessed, obsessed. No one had been able to make him enjoy sex like that before. His reputation of being a 'little man' and of being premature at the most crucial of moments had preceded him and affected his sexual performance. Where-as, Wallis's knowledge of Fang Chung had liberated him from this feeling of sexual inadequacy that he had carried as a heavy burden, for a long time. She knew, through the art of perverse stimulation and delayed abstinence of touch, how to enhance men's senses to increase the time before ejaculation. This, for Edward, was a revelation, and it was as if he'd found a new lease of life: his confidence increased, his drinking abated and the deeply maudlin look in his eyes disappeared - for the while anyway.

There is evidence of another bracelet, given around this time, with an inscription referring to a sexual moment in a bathtub.

There are also debates on whether an "actual sexual act" had actually occurred, due to his problems with penetration. He, himself, denying any 'intercourse' to the King: while all around him knew otherwise.

Chapter Seventeen

Sunningdale,
Early Winter, 1941.

It seems strange that even though there was a war going on Les and Gwen could be so happy. Les was right to have moved nearer to his family and friends, they all fended for each other and somehow always got by. Les was also enjoying working at the farm. He'd finished the buildings, or as Ronald proudly called them, 'barn conversions', by the summer, and was now helping with the running of the farm. He picked up some useful tips from Ronald's extensive knowledge about the earth and growing produce.

Les put these farming tips to good use back at home, as throughout the year he'd gradually made a productive vegetable patch in the garden, yielding almost the whole spring and summer needs: spinach, tomatoes, celery, leeks, courgettes, runner beans; and now with the bountiful autumn harvest: potatoes, swede, squash and onions to help through the winter. He needed to store them well.

He was tireless; either working at the farm, in the garden or on the cottage. His only worry was this foreboding feeling he got every now and then that it might be soon; that he'd have to leave Gwen on her own and be 'called up' to go to war.

It was one of the last autumnal afternoons of the year. The sky was a crystal-clear blue, with a crisp edge to the air. There was the sweet, woody smell of smoking leaves pervading through the air as they smouldered on the bonfire. He'd been preparing the garden for winter, while also finishing making a shed.

Little Pattie had been sitting outside among the perennial spinach plants, watching his every move with fascination. Then, up she sat, all of a sudden, as one of the last Red Admiral butterflies of the year sailed past her; its wings displaying their finest uniform and regalia. She giggled. Her hair lit up like golden flames in the late sunshine and she stretched her little arms trying to catch the creature: the messenger.

'This is a magical moment,' Les thought to himself. He called out to Gwen up at the house. Music wafted down, she'd been singing in the kitchen again,

'Queenie, I want you to come and see this!'

'Ok!' she said, as she ruffled her hair and took her apron off.

The light behind her took her silhouette and made her look as if she was floating as she glided along the path through the grass. He'd made a shed out of bits and bobs he found here and there. It would be good enough for storing the vegetables in the winter and for potting the tender plants in the spring.

'It's brilliant!' she said, as her eyes widened with excitement. She truly was enthralled. 'It's the best shed in the world!'

'Well,' he said, pulling her close to him, 'we've really made this our home and laid down roots now, my girl. It's our safe harbour from any storms life has to throw at us.'

They sat down on a hollowed-out tree trunk, arm in arm, lovingly admiring the higgledy-piggledy shed and watched as the wind took the sparks from the fire and twisted them, spiralling up and up. Pattie was chattering little noises and clapping her hands, watching her very own fireworks display. There was a sense of timelessness in the air. It was as if this moment stayed and was set true, forever, as the sky turned softly to twilight and for a fleeting moment illuminated shock pink upon a fishbone of wispy clouds catching the last of the sun's deep sunset colours. They kissed and went inside as the first star appeared and the harmonious moment passed, sent on up to the gods on the smoke curls, receiving their true and peaceful love.

The next morning, there it was on the mat: an envelope. Such an innocent object; so small, delicate and as light as a feather: paper. As water can cut stone, wind lift water, so can paper shape lives. It held such power of change, fear, destruction and pain.

'O H M S'

On Her Majesty's Service was typed unsuspectingly on a plain and simple small brown paper envelope. This was no ordinary brown envelope. These were the bullets and bombs of disintegration of families; dropped through the letterbox by one's friendly postman. The letter of doom; but also of duty, necessity and patriotism. The ultimate protection of one's loved one is to keep the enemy at bay - come what may.

Unfortunately, it was Gwen who found it, there on the mat. She froze as if she'd been stabbed in the back. The house suddenly seemed so dark and ominous. She stood there for a good few moments, staring at it. She'd known it was to come eventually but she'd not wanted to face it really happening. Gwen had found the death of her mother, the bombs and moving, all more traumatic than she let on. So, she secretly feared how she'd be able to cope once Les was away from home. She loved him so, he was her rock in every way, he kept her calm and content; not that it wasn't her nature, for she had a way of getting by, but she loved being with Les.

'Now all that will change, I know it,' she thought to herself. As she bent down, she felt the winds of change spiral around her, whispering taunting chants. Her shaking fingers cautiously picked up the laden envelope and took it into the kitchen, placing it on the table next to the teapot.

Gwen stood at the sink, shivering and sweating from head to toe, all at the same time: it just came over her like a cloud. Leaning forward with nausea she turned on the tap and tried to cup water in her hands to bring to her face. She was trembling so much the water was just falling between her fingers. The more she trembled the more she seemed to need to drink and re-freshen her face, as if the shock slap of water on skin would bring her round: hoping the water itself would heal her and cleanse this foreboding feeling. It did bring her to her senses, and trying to calm her breathing she decided she'd not let Les know how she really felt. She'd have to be strong. She didn't want him to worry about her; not if he had to leave her. She always got by, somehow. She knew he'd go crazy fretting about her and Pattie.

'Get to grips,' she said firmly to herself, thinking what he'll need when he gets in from work was a lovely potato and herb pie, something to feed him up.

Gwen busied herself in her familiar surroundings in the kitchen. She'd turned to creating in the kitchen, it had become her new passion and release.

By the time Les came in that night, there was not a top that hadn't been dusted, a pillow not 'puffed', and a glass not shined. The table was laid beautifully with a candle and a stunning centrepiece made of sprigs of branches she'd amassed while getting the potatoes from the shed. She'd skipped through the trees, knowing no one could see her, praying to the spirits of nature to look after him. Barefoot, she whispered and touched the tendrils and branches, promising her soul away if only they'd spare him.

The true give-away that made Les think something was wrong was when he saw Pattie, clean as a whistle with her unruly curls neatly tied down with a red ribbon and her best Sunday dress on, sitting angelically at the table. As she saw her daddy a large grin appeared,

'Look...Pretty!' she said, touching her dress.

He just had to go to the table and scoop her up out of her chair and whirl her up into the air, landing a smacker of a kiss on her adorable cheek till she squealed with delight. He placed her back down, turned towards Gwen, she walked out of the scullery and as he saw the frozen look in her eye, he caught sight of the brown 'OHMS' envelope on the dresser.

'NO!' he exclaimed, his spirit sinking to the ground in one breath.

'I don't know,' she said cautiously, stiffly. 'Open it.'

'After dinner. Let's enjoy this first.'

'Wise decision,' she said, as she put her arms up around his neck and kissed him with all her might.

That supper seemed to taste so good. All their produce and fresh herbs really came off. The rosemary bush in particular just grew and grew; healthy like a happy old witch sharing her wisdom. They cleared the meal. Les put Pattie to sleep, telling her a story. She played with his hand the whole time, till her own hand finally slid onto the covers with slumber. He walked back in the room. Gwen was sitting, waiting for the news.

'Ok then,' she sighed, 'let's get this over and done with.'

He picked up the French knife and slid it through the envelope, garrotting it with contempt. There it was. His future written in unknown hand.

'Leslie Albert Holmes

Report for duty for the
King's Royal Rifle Corps

on the
Fourth of December 1941.

'It can't be. That's in under a month,' she whispered.

That it was, and just before Christmas too.

'Queenie, I don't know what to say.'

'There are no words: it is as it is. You'll be the most almightiest of warriors, I just know it, and they need you out there. Pattie and I will be fine here, with our safe harbour and garden of plenty you've made for us. You'd better not preoccupy yourself with worrying about us,'she looked directly into his eyes, 'you must concentrate on the target, as they say.'

Gwen leaned towards him, and as he brushed a stray hair away from her eyes, he saw a determined woman. He was reassured and grateful. He loved her so much; to leave her in distress would have been impossible, something he may not have been able to do. Les had wanted to keep her safe, wrapped in cotton wool if he could; but he couldn't. He promised he'd make sure all would be well, and he'd look after her every step of the way, together in this life. But he wasn't able to keep this impossible promise. Life had gotten in the way. Destiny had different ideas.

He couldn't stand the thought of her alone, so he rallied round everyone he knew, asking them to keep an eye on her. His sister Eva tried to assure him everything would be alright. Les was so pleased when his farmer friend Ronald told him he'd make sure she had a bit of meat every now and then, as she was getting thin.

The days flew by with not enough hours in the day. He wore himself out preparing all he could for her: chopping logs, preparing the vegetable patch for the next season. He gave Pattie a pet rabbit; something to cuddle when she misses him, he explained to her. Les even made a chicken coop and Ronald gave him three chickens as a good luck leaving present.

'Something to keep the missus company,' Ronald muttered sentimentally. 'They'll remind her of your scrawny self!' jokingly under his breath. Not daring to show emotion, big as he was, he added, 'You just get back here. I need good strong workers like you Les. You go over there and give those Gerry's what for! Sort 'em out, then get home, you hear.'

Les said nothing. He stared with his dark spiritual eyes straight through to Ronald's soul, saying all his gratitude and depth of camaraderie, in one look.

The day dawned. Gwen woke first, went to the range in the kitchen and started poking and prodding the fire to wake life into the embers. She jabbed and stabbed at the fire in the grate, as if she could kill the reality of the situation, it would all go away and everything would return to as it should be. Nevertheless, she knew this life was no easy ride, she'd been forewarned, and so she stopped the torment, blew softly onto the dying embers, and there at the bottom crackled a glowing sign of life, of hope, of warmth.

'It will be alright, it will,' she told herself.

Gwen put the kettle over the range and prepared an egg for his breakfast. She popped her head round the bedroom door to have one last look at him, where he belonged. There he was: so handsome, so strong, so special to her; his dark hair all tousled with slumber. Pattie came padding across the hall and put her hands up to be lifted onto the bed. Les obliged and as she was lowered onto the bed she snuggled up into her father's arms. Gwen joined them. They lay there, the three of them, in silence, enveloped in such love resonating back and forth. A wonderful feeling, the safety of love, there in his arms. She wished she could capture it forever.

Suddenly remembering his breakfast, she jumped up and ran for it, laughing and hooting as she got to the stove, 'Just in time!' as the white frothy water rose up in the pan she delved in and fished out a perfect poached egg.

'Fit for a king, or my warrior at least,' she said triumphantly. She kissed him tenderly and handed him the breakfast tray. He ate in silence. Pattie fell back to sleep, curled up like a little cat, snuggled into the blankets. They didn't want to disturb her as Les slipped out of the bed.

Gwen went to the wardrobe and took out his uniform. It hung there: heavy, unfriendly, tough. The rough green material scraped at her skin as she ceremoniously handed Les his clothes. He stood there, getting dressed, still in silence. Handing him the shirt, they looked deep into each-others soul, trying to reassure one another. He watched as she did up his shirt buttons and then slipped his jacket on over his shoulders. As she concentrated on feeding the belt through the loopholes, he took her face in his hands and brought it up to his and stared lovingly saying,

'I love you to the ends of the earth, you know that don't you. I am always with you; every single minute, wherever I may be.'

'I know,' she said, biting back tears. She delicately finished buttoning up his uniform jacket, displaying such tenderness towards a uniform designed for such hardship.

They were both in a trance; their emotions capped as they made their way to the Sunningdale Train Station. Before he knew it, the face he lived to love was disappearing behind billowing clouds of steam, fading away. Their eyes strained to keep locked together as the train shifted into gear and sped up. The noise of all the other men and families; sobs, tears, and whistles; were silenced to them. They heard nothing or took in anything else but the painful feeling of separation.

Then, he could see her face no more, and it was time to face reality. He found a seat, and was sure he could feel her, lingering around him as he looked out from the train.

She was still with him, emotionally. After his train had pulled away, she stumbled from the platform, threw up and then passed out, there, right near the entrance, with everyone bustling around her. When she came round, somebody was cradling her head and waving a handkerchief in her face.

'Please, excuse me, I'm so sorry,' Gwen apologised.

'Don't worry yourself, Pet, just catch your breath.'

'I don't know what happened.'

'Shock does queer things to folk y' know,' the kindly woman said. She was so homely, motherly, that Gwen could have let herself be comforted by her, but her pride suddenly awoke.

'Let me get you home, Dear,' the lady offered.

'No really, I've troubled everyone too much, I must get back.'

'But you must take it easy,' she said, concerned.

'I will, but to be quite honest I could do with the walk.'

Gwen rose to her feet, smoothing down her skirt. 'Oh Ma, just let me get home,' she muttered to herself, trying to muster up some strength from somewhere.

The need to get back to her 'safe harbour' as Les had put it and rest up was overwhelming. It had all been so fraught. Nevertheless, she reminded herself she was not the only wife that morning, there on the platform, watching their heart being wrenched out of their bodies.

Chapter Eighteen

London,
Winter, 1933.

Wallis was, by now, deeply embroiled in her affair with Prince Edward, relishing everything that came with being the Prince's mistress. Edward was noticeably needing her more and more. He would phone incessantly, throughout the day and night, or turn up at her doorstep in the early hours, desperate to see her. Staff would have to be woken, and drinks made. They would talk and talk, realising they had a lot in common, especially in politics. Wallis shared his views on the 'peace movement,' being pro-Nazi, and had been interested in the Fascist movement ever since her lover Count Cianni had introduced her to his views. They both thought Hitler was impressive and became devout Hitler sympathisers.

Exclusive evenings were being held entertaining Hitler's Nazi opinions and the highest of society were engaged in the movement. Nevertheless, all this excitement just wasn't enough for Wallis; still needing more she'd embarked upon a passionate liaison with Baron Joachim von Ribbentrop, Hitler's advisor and foreign liaison in London. She found his self-confidence and domineering masculinity a relief after HRH's emasculated sexuality. Von Ribbentrop was fascinated with Wallis; known to have sent her 17 roses every day for a year. He was continually turning up at Bryanston Court, spending much too much time 'in-residence' for the gossip mongers not to start rumours, so they had to meet secretly. It was hard to find a place safe enough, away from the watchful eye of the press, as she was starting to be followed everywhere.

'I must see you, Vallis.' Ribbentrop said in his clipped German accent, cornering her one evening.

'I know, I was dreaming about you last night, your wonderful firm strength. I need to know what a real man feels like again. Remind me...' whispering into his ear as the cocktails flowed and canapés swirled round the room. It was another pro-Nazi evening held at Lady Emerald Cunard's; always one of Wallis's favourite soirees.

'Edward's looking at you Darlink,' Ribbentrop warned.

'Oh, Edward's always looking at me,' she snapped, rolling her eyes, 'I can't even breathe without him admiring how I breathe. But it's you I'm thinking of... carry on talking. He's too weak willed to say anything right now, and more importantly, I need to see YOU, soon,' she murmured sensuously.

'Vell, we've got to vork zis one out, haven't ve!' he said.

'I've got it, I know. Oh, it's just perfect- flawless. Anna, my dressmaker, have you heard of her? She's the daughter of Admiral Wolkoff. Well, she's an avid supporter of the cause, and maybe we could meet at hers. She's incredibly discreet.'

Wolkoff had to be, as she was a Nazi agent sending information back and forth.

'Yes, I know her, zere vill be no trouble zere.'

'I have some vital secret information for you,' she said excitedly.

'I've got somezing vital and secret for you too!' he announced, with a sexy spark in his eye. 'Ven shall ve meet?'

'Tuesday,' she said, flushed, even for Wallis.

Wallis seemed insatiable at this point in her life, what with her lovers, her husband, the Prince, and her spying antics (passing information on to the Nazi's whenever she could). She was finding it all incredibly exciting being fuelled on adrenalin.

Wallis taunted Edward with the knowledge that she was seeing others as well as him, and this was driving Edward to absolute distraction with jealousy.

'Well David, you yourself are not totally faithful to me. So what do you expect of me! I see the way you look at Fruity. It's abhorrently obvious you have a longstanding crush on him.'

'Please Wally Darling. He's my best friend, my equerry. You can't deny me his company.'

'Well, your father and I finally agree on something, and that's Fruity Metcalf.'

'May I remind you that you're not exactly in Father's favour either. Please let's not squabble. I want you all to myself, is it so much to ask? I've got an idea. How about we go on a little holiday? I know you like France. Let's go, and I can have you near me day and night.'

She thought of how she would miss Ribbentrop but would also like to get away for a bit. She'd finished with the decor at Fort Belvedere, having torn through the place like a tornado, changing most of what Thelma had done. It was her way of making her mark and letting everyone know she was 'in position.'

She'd also fired staff left right and centre -as she did- but this time even the Prince's butler 'Finch' was ousted. He had refused to follow the rules of this brash American. Finch had been with Prince Edward since childhood as his valet. He was supportive and parental in his role, offering him needed comfort and held a calming influence. She of course was jealous of the closeness and influence he held over Edward, and so he had to go.

Edward knew how she loved France, so he arranged to stay at the Castel Meretmont, outside Biarritz. It was high summer 1934 and the Prince was feeling brave. To be travelling abroad with Wallis, without Ernest, was blatantly risky: the press interest was high wherever the Golden Prince went so Aunt Bessie was tagged along to the entourage to show willing as Wallis's chaperone.

'Come along Bessie. Leave that! The staff will sort your cabin for you, that's what they're for.'

'Oh, yes I know dear, but I do like to do some things for myself you know!'

'Well, I want us to go up on deck and wave goodbye to good old 'Blighty'!' Wallis said, with scorn in her voice.

'Blow away the cobwebs, you mean!' Aunt Bessie chortled, as they made their way to the aft deck. There, looking back, were the last sightings of England before the sea enveloped the horizon; the last green strip of land disappearing among the blue.

'Good riddance is all I can say!' she said, as she pulled her jacket tight to her thin frame, the winds strengthening as they made their way out to sea.

They made their way on to Paris, where they were to meet up and continue the journey with the Prince. He'd flown in, whereas Wallis adamantly would not, detesting flying.

Edward looked at her and was so glad to be finally getting 'his' Wallis away from all the rigmarole that always surrounded their clandestine times together in Britain. Here felt freer to be himself. Europe always relaxed his mood a notch and as the train pulled out of the station and they headed south to the sun and rugged coastline of the Aquitaine, the rhythm of the train easing his mind.

They settled in at the Castel, relaxing in the sun then mixed and dined with the best marquis' in town. Edward even saved a young boy's life. The child had become caught in the strong sea currents that lie along this treacherous coast. The surf always up and roaring, like a large wall of charging tigers the waves roared in, relentless.

'The sea won't rest here, will it!' Wallis exclaimed, worn out and upstaged by the energy of the sea.

'It's invigorating Darling!' Edward said, finding it exciting.

'It's deadly,' she said flatly. 'You must be kidding if I'll ever swim in that torrent.' She turned her back on him and walked to the bar. 'I do like the gentler sea of the Med, don't you?' she drooled.

'Well, let's clear out and go visit my brother. He's in Cannes right now.'

'Well, that sounds just fine,' she said, lounging into a sofa. 'The press won't leave us alone, now that you've become some sort of swimming hero!' she commented sourly, as she pointed at the newspaper headlines, and then picked up and started browsing through a fashion magazine. He shook his head,

'All I want is for us to be left alone, but what was I to do? Stand by and watch and do nothing? I couldn't let the boy drown, could I?'

'Yes! No! Oh, I don't know, but you could have drowned yourself!' Wagging and pointing her finger at him. 'And as for the rain - its forecast real heavy for days, you know,' her eyes hung low.

'That's settled then. We'll fly to Cannes tomorrow,' unable to see his Wallis down.

'Teddy honey, I don't fly. You know that.'

'Ok well, let's...' thinking of the best way. The train was difficult, having to connect back as far as Paris to get over on to the Orient Express. 'I've got it, we'll sail down, it'll be wonderful. I'll get someone onto it straight away.'

There was only the 'Rosauria' in the area, available for charter, equipped with full crew. She was a worked, battered, ocean going steamer that Lord Moyne had recently bought and turned into his floating scientific exploration vessel.

'Of course you can take her, Your Highness. It would be my honour,' was Lord Moyne's reply to the request to 'borrow her'. Really, he was very wary to be handing over his pride and joy; he'd rather not have been asked. 'But I do warn you of the weather. It's going to blow a hoolie out there in the Biscay.' Warning them of the bay's characteristic temperament.

'That's fine as we're just skirting round it really.'

'Uhhuh!' groaned the lord. He knew how the spiralling energy whipped up all around the bay. The sea could really rock.

So, there they were, setting out to sea, having ignored all weather warnings. They sailed into the bay and right into a tempestuous storm. With their decks awash, thunder and lightning cracked in the skies over them. The night was a-flash as they sailed out to the ride of their lives.

Wallis was petrified and finally, four days later, they were able to put into safe harbour at Corunna, Spain.

'This is absolutely crazy. I can't take this anymore, David. It's not just the sea, but look, what is this monkey doing? It's going wild all the time and it's driving me insane!' she exclaimed. 'Just look at it, are we meant to put up with this? In our private quarters?'

Lord Moyne's monkey, as if on key, screeched right at them, then darted round the room, wiggling its bottom, mad with abandon. They looked at each other and just had to laugh, with Edward announcing,

'Performing this evening, 'The Monkey Dance'; the one that broke the camel's back!'

'David, but seriously!'

Staying in the area, they had time to visit the famous Santiago de Compostela, blessing the sacred tomb, then travelling through the grapevine fields as they made their way back to the boat to continue the journey round the Rock of Gibraltar. It was harsh; the weather conditions were rough, and it kept the adrenalin up. They gratefully pulled into the shelter of Majorca's northern side and breathed a sigh of relief as the weather was wonderful and sunny: the bad weather had stayed out at sea. They had sailed through the eye of a storm, come out alive, and now were safe, together. The couple had become closer through this ordeal, but their own storms were yet to brew.

Wallis had only warmed slightly to the Prince through all this, whereas Edward was falling deeper and deeper, head over heels in love with Wallis. He abandoned every plan he'd made; all other engagements were cancelled as the holiday continued, letting down his brother, and others. He just couldn't tear himself away from Wallis's side even for a minute. She hypnotized and captivated his every thought. He so wanted her here, alone, just the two of them, together, away from the hounding press and monarchy. The perpetual protocol of royal lineage was abandoned: along with his shirt.

They spent some glorious romantic days tripping around the enchanted private coves, sunning themselves in secluded rock pools and gathering shells as they walked the seashore.

From there, they went on to Cannes, cavorting around, and went ashore, staying at the Hotel Miramar despite all the attention of the press. He wanted to take her dancing to the Palm Beach Club. They famously Rumba'd all night long, way on till four o'clock in the morning. He was a great dancer, and they whirled round and round into a perfect Tango.

The next night, on board a friend's yacht, they dared each other to go for a swim. The warmth in the air lifted the smell of the Mediterranean to a warm salty invite.

'It's crystal clear! Oh, go on, in you go!' They undressed, hooting and giggling then dived off the boat, splashing each other and disturbing the moonlit ripples.

Edward's love and admiration for Wallis had become so set in his mind. He wanted to prove it, make her know he was serious, and so, the next night, in a love-crazed moment at one o'clock in the morning, he phoned down to the reception desk, ordering,

'Get me the manager of Cartier, urgently!'

The Cartier staff had to be woken and assembled in the middle of the night, to serve Edward's eccentric whim. He walked into the elegant room oozing luxury. Edward was beside himself with excitement at the thought of surprising Wallis and giving her something to make her eyes sparkle.

For the Prince, the gems bought a symbol of solidity, showing how their relationship had grown serious, and the gems merely cemented their relationship. Whereas, for Wallis, they meant much more; the magic of the stones was incredibly exciting for her, flaunting them proved her to be the envy of all women, whilst the powerful colours and radiance took her breath away in the knowledge of their worth.

Which gem? What colour for his Violet Queen? Cartier displayed the jewellery, with stones of the finest cuts and colours. Rubies from Mogok that looked like blood on fire, Kashmiri sapphires the colour of the moonlit sky or Colombian emeralds, as green as if nature itself had been frozen in time.

The magic of his love for Wallis and the bewitching glint of the stones mingled with his soul and he decided to keep her with him forever. In reality she had actually been pretty vile to him, in private and in public, often in front of the guests on board, putting him down and belittling him as usual.

'Oh, but, you know, I can't decide!' he explained like a kiddie in a sweetie shop to the Cartier manager. He looked at the jewellery laid out in front of him, glistening in the night light. Pointing with his cigar he said, 'I'll have that, that, those... and those.' Thus, solving his problem of having to choose. He bought some beautiful pieces late that night. Excitedly, he rushed back to the hotel and woke everybody, ordering them back on board the Rosauria.

'You are quite insufferable sometimes!' Wallis threw at him, but he just looked on with admiration as she picked him to pieces. 'Aunt Bessie really needs her beauty sleep and so do I!' said triumphantly, then asked, 'What on earth have you made us come back aboard in the middle of the night for?'

'I want to wake up with you on Lake Como, tomorrow. We have so much to see, Darling, things I want to show you... I want you to know how much you mean to me.'

Wallis softened towards him,

'Ok then. So, what's the plans now Capt'n?' she joked.

'You and I get back to our bed, here, rocked aboard Rosauria. We set our course for the romanticism of Italy and wake, tomorrow morning, with our beds floating on the misty Lake Como.'

He opened her hand and placed a small leather-bound Cartier gold encrypted case.

'One now, one later, and one when we get there.'

'David, for me? What a decadent prince you are! Adorable!' she said in a French/ American accent, dragging the middle 'a' in her heavy drawl. She snapped open the lid, eager to see; as she did, he moved in and kissed her.

As he kissed her passionately, especially for him, she realised she just couldn't reciprocate the same depth of feeling. It really had been all about the chase, the thrill. Having grown close she liked to be in his company, but there was just no fire in it for her anymore.

He thought he'd be able to sway her with time, forever for him, and the jewels helped. However, he'd noticed she was already starting to admire the physique and manly ways of Guy Marcus Trundle, one of their guests aboard.

Wallis stood holding the gift, 'I just love your gestures,' she purred, as she looked at Edward then back at the box. Expecting a decadent gift, she wasn't too impressed when faced with just a charm for her bracelet, a mere trinket for her wrist - all be it emerald and diamond. The charm bracelet she wore was to become like a romantic love letter between them; always secret code encrypted messages in remembrance of particular nights of their love, and of course a cross and a teddy, all jangling from her wrist: as if to remind Wallis of her situation.

That night the boat pushed out to calm waters, following the moonlit path across the ocean. The stars, candlelight and diamonds dazzled them for a moment, and everything was almost perfect.

Chapter Nineteen

Wormwood Scrubs,
Feb 28th 1947.
The night of the storm,

Another thunderclap shook the very foundations of the prison. Les shivered at the intensity of the boom; it seemed to shake his very soul. He'd never been shaken before, not even with the life-threatening situations at war; but now, looking back, he realised how the political storms of Europe started to change everything. Gwen was forced to survive by herself. He'd not known the full extent of what had gone on without him, but he'd known it had been rough: catalytic to her mental stability. Feeling so helpless, he prayed. He didn't know what else to do. He prayed for his family to be protected somehow; but the gods weren't listening to his pleas that night, destiny had other plans.

Asking for forgiveness, but again visions of newspaper articles flashed in his mind, as if the higher judges were taunting him with his crime. At home he'd followed the papers for weeks, as the CID searched high and low for any clue.

The Western Morning News had led with: "Yard Combs Underworld. CID believe a gang of international jewel thieves may have followed the Duke and Duchess from France, awaiting a suitable opportunity."

The Bristol Mirror headlined: "Windsor Jewel Robbery. £25,000 worth vanished... The stolen jewels were covered by insurance. Jewellery possessed by the Duchess is estimated to be worth £250,000. It is believed that the thief might have entered the grounds by the main gate and walked into the house by the main doorway."

Then, Les remembered the Evening Telegraph's words: "Continent Wide Drag-net For Jewel Thieves. Hundreds of detectives were today checking the movements of all known French and Continental criminals... Mr R. M. Howe, Assistant Commissioner in charge of the C.I.D, at Scotland Yard, has taken personal control of the manhunt, the greatest in the history of crime."

Les curled up in a ball, feeling incredibly vulnerable, guilt weighing heavily for his actions: he'd not wanted to spark such a spiralling turn of events. He'd not expected it to unfold into such a charade. It became too big for him to admit to; to come forward would be like putting his head on the block. Les had never really intended on doing it, things just spiralled out of control. He'd been made so mad by the 'ex-King and his mistress' waltzing back over to Britain and demanding rights to the nation they had relished deceiving, spying against and plotting for its demise at every turn. Les remembered being warned about the Duke whilst in France and whispers Eva had heard about Wallis's affairs, all echoing round his mind, tormenting him, that stormy night. But who was he to judge? he asked himself; what on earth had he been thinking of? Did he not realise the severity of his actions? And not least, the full extent of the consequences? He'd got carried away for the first time in his life. He'd lost his cool and acted irrationally. Maybe Post-war Traumatic Stress Disorder had hit home, hard.

He couldn't get warm as he shivered uncontrollably. Being just skin and bone the freezing night penetrated through, his bones shaking and his teeth chattered as he played it over and over, tormenting himself. His mind went back to when he was first sent to the front, when he started as a 'batman'- at which he was to excel.

Chapter Twenty

France,
Winter, 1941,

Les took a deep breath and surveyed the train. It was packed with men and all their kit. There had been a massive surge in call-ups, everyone was in high spirits: the bravado hiding the fear. Rotten-dirty-Gerry jokes were being told among the stories of bravery, only to be played out on the battlefields. All were united: not just by uniforms, but the compelling wish to put a stop to this Adolph Hitler and his Nazi massacre of Europe.

'Do you want a smoke?' the young guy next to him asked, pushing a packet of 'Piccadilly' cigarettes in Les's face.

'Cheers, why not!'

'You know, I've got to get at least two blasted Gerry's to make up for my uncle and cousin: blown to smithereens they were. These Germans just have such good kit. It's an unfair advantage I reckon.' The young lad suddenly looked afraid. He turned back to Les saying, 'The thing is I don't even know if I can shoot, you see, I've never used a gun. What if I'm no good?' Doubt and worry creeping into the young guy's voice.

'You know what? This war is not just about how well you can shoot - but I'll bet you'll be a 'sure shooter'. I can see it in your eyes, you have strength of purpose. Just remember, squeeze the trigger gently but firmly, and most importantly, don't hesitate for a moment, then you'll be fine.'

‘I’m in the sixth battalion, what are you?’ the guy said, lighter than before.

‘I’m in the Kings Royal Rifle Corps.’

‘Oh, you must be good with a rifle then.’

‘Not bad.’ Les said, as he remembered shooting his targets straight through. He was a sharpshooter, fast and accurate, deadly.

As they milled out onto the inner Waterloo station, all placed in their own platoons and battalions, the KRRC gathered Les along with others, and took them to the headquarters.

Les was lined up and briefed. Bunk beds here, food over there, training starting at ‘five hundred hours’ tomorrow morning. Be ready or be in trouble. He got the gist of it.

Over the weeks it was noticeable how he excelled at the training: his aim impeccable, his attitude on the ball and his natural born instinct to protect or kill was obvious.

Captain Carper noticed Les’s skills and decided he’d take him on as his personal ‘batman.’

‘I need someone like that around me...’ he explained to his senior officer, ‘if you’re saying I’m to be sent out ahead of others, on specialist missions. I know he will be useful. He seems to be able to succeed in any tricky situation we throw at him.’

‘Well, you’d better bring him up to speed as to his duties, ASAP, as it’s just come through that you’ll be leaving on a covert operation, next week. You’ll know more when you need to. You have some leave to take?’

‘Yes, Sir,’ he said, with the excitement of the unknown glinting in his eyes.

Sternly his superior ordered, ‘Take it.’

‘Yes, Sir!’

‘I think it’s time I promoted you and made you ‘major’. Right ho, Major Carper. Good luck!’ said as he dismissed him with a wave of his hand; his head down, already busy with something else.

Major Carper saluted his senior officer and clicked his heels against his highly polished boots, turned and quick marched out of the office. Carper was a shrewd, intelligent man. Like a hawk, he could see to the core of things, straight through normally fathoming problems, he also had an uncanny way of predicting his opponent’s next move. He was invaluable for reconnaissance information, not having let them down yet.

Les didn't know it, but this had been a lucky move for him, and they would work well together. Ok, he wouldn't be an officer, but he was to share some of the perks and be able to put his view across in major decisions.

Les, now as a batman, had to make sure his officer had what he needed with him: clothes, maps, ect... thus enabling the Major to concentrate on the flow of the operations. Les was also expected to protect his officer and their surroundings, so was a bodyguard, butler and sharpshooter, all rolled into one.

This job was made for him. He was to keep alert, keep his brain in gear, always on the look-out for a sniper or worse, but also had the 'keys to the stores.' The first thing he did was change those unforgiving, torturous boots of his. They were a bad fit and his feet wouldn't relent in complaining -not that he ever did.

There they were, packed in, sitting thigh to thigh in the bomber plane. It was freezing cold up there in the thin air that night, just before New Year 1941. The sky was jet black but alive with stars; no moon, perfect for parachuting in. They had a lot of kit to be dropped, and it was all ready to roll. The deep drone of the engine almost reassured them, hypnotising them into a tectonic trance. They were facing the unknown, but it was the most peaceful moment Les had since before he'd boarded that train in Sunningdale. He loved the feeling of flying, up through the astrals, anything seemed possible.

He prepped himself, checking his wits were razor sharp. He'd really bonded with his superior, Major Carper, and wanted it all to be a successful mission, if he could help it, whatever the real aims were. Les was never told more than he had to know.

All he did know was that they were to get in, get something or somebody, destroy what they could and get the hell out.

Gwen's face flashed through his thoughts, she was laughing and kissing him, he felt this was a good omen as he tightened the harness straps of his parachute and took a deep breath. He was ready.

His timing was perfect, as whisky was passed round and the door to the plane was rolled back to reveal the French countryside below. The ground was closer than he thought it would be, and the air rushed in making the guys take a sudden breath of freezing cold air.

'Alright my men, 'jump to it' as they say! Keep bearing to the left, don't end up north of the river and for Christ's sake avoid any lights! There shouldn't be anyone, but we never know.'

'Go, Go, Go!'

The first few were pushed out before they even knew what was happening to them. Suddenly, they were unfolding like paper flowers and then floating like jellyfish in the night sky. The sudden silence after the loud sound of the aircraft was mystical.

Again, Les had that feeling of being suspended in time, the world had stopped for a minute: he'd literally jumped off. Looking down it all seemed so trivial, so unreal; the tiny fields coming closer and a dark silver river oozing its course along the country. But this was no time for philosophical thoughts as he prepared his body for the impact and the ground rushed towards him. He aimed his shoot, releasing as he went, guiding himself down into what looked like a soft grassy verge of a field. He crumpled on impact with the ground, allowing himself to be flexible, but still his breath was knocked right out of his body. His ankle took a bump, landing on a side of a stone, but he was fine: he'd made it down. He packed the parachute as quickly as possible knowing what a danger it was, being so highly reflective, let alone the rustling sound the silk gave on the grass as it was packed away.

Looking around he heard a soft bird whistle. It was his officer, Major Carper, and so Les gathered his shoot and made his way towards the sound. He still wasn't sure of his surroundings, not having had time to check it out; so he stole through the night, from bush to bush, with his rifle poised and cocked in front of him. The gun had already become an extension of his vision: ready to react.

He could make out other shadows looming in the same direction and felt safe that they were the rest of the group. There were five of them in all: himself; Jack on radio; Mike, 2nd Lieutenant; Captain David Reger, intelligence, who spoke French like a native; and of course, Major Carper, now promoted.

'Let's keep in this coppice, it seems to bend round the valley, and aim for the west side over there,' Carper said, pointing through the branches. 'There should be a farm to the south of that field - they're known to be friendly. We can re-assess once there. We need to get there within the hour.'

'Let's get to it then,' said Captain Reger, or 'Reggie' as he was known.

It was hard work and slow going, stealing through the pitch-black denseness of the old coppice with branches strewn on the ground of bracken and bramble bushes scraping at their uniform. They made their way over all these obstacles without making more noise than a snuffling wild boar. Before they knew it, they were there. They could smell the smoke from the farm guiding them through the night-time jungle.

As the skyline opened, they could then see the smoke reflect and rise up into the night-sky, leading them to the low barn buildings in front of them. They heard a door open and German voices carried through the air. They froze, Major Carper gave the signal to get down and hide. Luckily the German officers couldn't see them hidden in the dark denseness of the woods, but the Germans were on full view to them, displaying high ranking uniforms.

'I'll just give them their Christmas presents shall I, Sir?' Mike was already cocking his revolver.

'No one move!' Major Carper said, so sternly, no one even dared breathe.

The German officers piled into their car and drove out of the farm onto the dusty track, sending up a cloud of dust whirling behind.

'What on earth were they doing there?' Reggie asked Carper.

'It does seem intriguing, such high officials out at a farm at this time of night. I was reassured this place was safe. If we'd attacked those Gerry's, the whole area would be ripped apart. Let's suss out the situation before we draw any attention to ourselves.'

After a while somebody from the farm came near the edge of the coppice, whistling. Major Carper signalled back with his duck whistle then they ventured to the farm.

They squeezed through the low doorway; the thick heavy carved door pushed open to reveal a large kitchen, a range at one end and a long heavy wooden table running the length of the room. The table must seat all of twenty people in its prime but now was covered with cheeses. The men just couldn't believe it. The French 'madame' of the farm, solid but beautiful, threw some garlic in a frying pan and the aroma sizzled up and attacked the soldier's senses. They'd done well so far but didn't want to relax just yet; they still had a lot of travelling to do before dawn.

'Nous ne voulons pas vous déranger, Madame. Mais....' We don't want to bother you, Madam, but... explained Reger.

'Non, Messieurs, vous êtes ici pour nous aider, et pour ça, je veux que vous mangez quelque-chose avant que vous partez,' she replied in French, then translated to the others by Reger,

'She says that as we're here to help them she wants us to eat something before we leave.'

She turned and gave them such a warm and encouraging smile. Muttering something in French to the others in the room about, 'When would these lads have their next cooked meal?'

'Allez, asseyez vous,' one of the French guys said as they pulled out their own chairs.

'Ok then, sit everyone.'

'Laissez moi vous rassurer...' Let me reassure you all... The French farmer explained that the Germans would not be back. It had been a random visit, wanting to test the farm's oldest cheeses because the Germans wanted some for their New Year celebrations. It made the farmer sick with hatred to have to deal with them, but they had to do it to keep the cover of the resistance.

'We shall be taking you as far as we can at dawn, but we must be back here for morning.'

The five of them looked quite dumbfounded as a succulent, fried garlic and herb field mushroom, almost as big as each plate, and a glass of wine, was put down in front of each of them. This was not how they'd imagined this evening to go. Lovely as it was, there was something unnerving about it all to Les.

As they ate, the French told them of such hardships they were under, explaining how the Germans took everything and had killed their neighbours. They weren't quite sure why they'd been spared, jokingly stating it was because the Nazi's liked their cheese so much they kept them alive merely to make it. Les liked being in that kitchen even less.

'Sir I'd just like to know. How exactly are they transporting us?' he asked, his mind still focused.

'On the cheese cart of course! We are delivering cheese to the chateau early this morning -c'est parfait!' the farmer said, finishing his glass of wine.

Les could see the fatigue in the eyes of the elderly farmer, mingled with the edge of adrenalin at playing the enemy at their own game. Times must have been tough.

'Je vais dormir un peu. A tout a l'heure,' and with that, left the room.

Slumber took them too, and soon they were roused by the sound of people busying around, loading out in the yard.

'This is our move,' said Carper.

'About time too,' Les said, relieved, 'I've felt like a sitting duck all night.'

As they were shown to the cart, Les felt even more unsure about things. They were to be covered over with straw, then the cheeses to be packed nestling on top with a tarpaulin thrown over it all.

'I need to make sure I have access to throwing back the tarpaulin,' Les stated.

'If necessary. Ok, you go to the back, first.'

They were 'loaded' on and all was packed up. The journey was about 5 miles and the horses plodded along. The farmer and his son were sitting chatting away about the cold weather and if their cows needed to come in to shelter if it got worse. Les let his body be rocked and swayed with the undulating rhythm of the cart in motion.

After about an hour, the cart slowed and the voices of the French turned to hushed panicky whispers. It was a makeshift checkpoint for all transport along the road. They were known to be delivering at the chateau so it shouldn't be a problem. The Germans wanted them to take off the tarpaulin, the French saying there's really no need, as it's just cheese. Les thought the French voices were floundering a bit in their tone.

'Here goes!' Les thought, as he saw a highly polished boot through a crack in the wooden base of the cart. The German was standing right alongside.

It seemed the soldiers wanted to have one of the cheeses. Les could make out only two German voices. He knew where one was, right by him to his left and the other was still in front of the cart, ordering the farmer to take back the tarpaulin.

As the farmer climbed down to comply with the German's wishes, Les knew he had to act and the only way to do this was with the element of surprise. He nudged Mike as if to let him know he was ready for action as the farmer started to untie the tarp. Les had always been holding the edge of the tarpaulin in his hand, so sprung up onto his feet like an apparition. The Germans looked startled. Les was right, there were only two of them, luckily, and they looked of lowly rank; on the scrounge most likely. He had to do it quickly. He shot the one to the left, and as he turned, Mike gave full barrels to the one in front. The Nazi gave his last dance as his body reacted to the force of the shots, then dropped to the ground: they hadn't known what was coming to them.

'Easy now, Mike, you don't need to let off all your ammo next time, ok,' Les said calmingly.

Mike, the 'ammo man' jumped down off the cart. He was white as a sheet and green around the gills. He lent forward and threw up. It was the first time he'd shot to kill.

'Quick, get these guys into the woods, over there, and get this cart back on the road,' Major Carper ordered, deciding, 'I think we'll go by foot from now on.'

The old farmer made some quip,

'Thank God he'd not vomited all over the cheese!'

They all laughed, heartily; that type of laugh where there are no boundaries of right and wrong, just the surreal humour of life and death. It was decided there and then that the farmer would carry on immediately as planned. This way, with no lapse in time, the farmer would be exempt from suspicion: old and slight as he was, but so wise and brave. He said he had nothing to lose as he cracked the whip and gave them a resolute look of determination as he rode on.

His grandson, Francois, young as he was, was also wise to the area. He always used to be out hunting before the war. He was in his early twenties with dark hair and the bluest of eyes; as if sparkling on truth and the need for freedom and fairness in his belly. He knew how to find the ancient pathway through the dense forest that surrounded the chateau. The old 'pas du bois' bought you in around the back, through a maze of caves that he knew the Nazi's had not yet discovered. The cave system had been used in ancient and medieval times: secret cool stores, perfect in the hot summers when the rivers were low. He led them swiftly and surely through what looked to the eye impenetrable; but by somehow twisting and manoeuvring through they made it to the far side, and there were the caves with the mountains as their backs. The group waited there, safe whilst sorting themselves out for the night.

Major Carper briefed them on the mission of the evening. His strategy was always to tell as little as needed and explain just before-hand. Thus, the aim still fresh in the soldier's mind, with no time for worry.

They were to enter the chateau, find the room on the north back wing and stop the communications that were being transmitted any way possible, also to pick up anything of interest. By the floor plan Francois drew in the earth, it seemed the cave would bring them in on the side that they needed to be, so things started to look feasible; it had seemed bleak until this breakthrough.

It was decided to leave as much of the kit there, hidden in the first cave. They would take only what was necessary, so avoiding being weighed down. They knew they were to bring things back: if they could make it back.

They each took some space and set to, preparing themselves physically and mentally, visualising and going over the maps and orders of events. Mike sorted the ammunition they would take, a couple of grenades were the best defence they had.

The sky stilled as twilight struck; silence fell for a fleeting second, the birds quietened, even the leaves stopped rustling. Les was drawn to a stream leading out of the cave. He bent down to wash his face, to cleanse and strengthen his soul. The leaves then started to rustle and an owl flew right over and seemed to squawk right at him, as if a shrill warning: have your wits about you. He dried his face then put his fingers deep into the mud, scooping out enough to apply to his face, looking just like an Indian applying war paint. Camouflage was vital: the most important of weapons.

They travelled through the caves and waited for the right moment to strike. This was the hard part, but also another of the most useful of weapons: timing. The timing had to be perfect: not too early, nor before midnight, but just before the end of the midnight hour. Everyone would be really inebriated after all that good French champagne, totally in the swing of the evening, enjoying the band and more brandies. There weren't too many Germans in residence, it was just a communications outpost, but it had to be stopped. Francois had known about the band playing through a female friend of his. Her sister was singing there and was getting information for the resistance as she worked her way through the officers in town. It was New Year's Eve after all. Les surveyed the rear of the castle, soaking it all in; the lights twinkling, the smell of a good party wafting in the air with the fine mix of wine, pine logs and cigars. The walls of this stunning and majestic of medieval buildings had hosted and withstood its own battles during the revolution and before; and now, sacrificing itself to the future.

Les suddenly thought of New Year, last year, all curled up with Gwen; her beautiful skin touching his as they lay together in the moonlight that flooded the bed, kissing and making wishes for the year ahead. It was the most arousing and tender of images. He sent her all his energy, beaming her love if he could as he looked at the star twinkling above. 'That star will be there whatever happens to me tonight,' he thought soberly.

Les tightened his pack for the last time, good and tight, and they approached the rear window. The night's work was more or less over for the Germans, even the guards were having their moment of frivolity. The frantic hours in the communications room had died down, there was just someone left sorting out some paperwork.

As Carper peered through the lens, they were close enough to hear the band throwing out a lively jazz beat. Then a soldier came into the room, half-cut by the look of it, and slapping the other on the back dragged him out to the party.

'This is it! Remember, keep it simple, in and out, OK!' whispered Carper.

'Ok.'

They approached the building. Les cut the glass out of the window and they entered the room. Major Carper searched every file and folder he could, and Captain Reger quickly photographed the maps on the wall. There was a safe in the corner,

'Damn, it must be in there,' cursed Reger.

'You want that opened?' Les asked, seeing the frustration in Reger's eyes.

'I don't think we can blow it, Les.'

'No Sir, but I've opened one before on a job in the building trade. I could see if I can now?'

Les put his ear to the cold steel box and froze, not even breathing as he felt the subtlest of vibrations quivering his skin. He clicked here and there, this way, then back that way. Suddenly there was a noise as the young officer walked back along the passage, to the communications room. The captain and major had just enough time as they flew, like birds into their nest, out through the window. Les made it to the window, but not with enough time to dive through, so he hid behind the thick tapestry curtain. The door handle turned and the officer walked straight to his desk, picked up his glasses, turned back round whilst putting them on and walked back out.

Les had felt the very life of that young man. He could smell his spirit: intelligent, shy and nervous; dominated by these powerful Nazi's; but he had obviously wanted to have a closer look at the sexy French singer. Les knew he wouldn't be back for a few minutes as Claudette was to do a sort of striptease at 'o' one hundred hours.

Wrapping himself back around the safe, he caressed it until the door went a satisfying 'clunk' and the protective sheet of steel swung open. Carper had disbelief in his eyes as he climbed back into the room.

'You are incredible, Les!' he said, looking at Les with new appreciation. 'That's just what we need.' Major Carper leant in and took some contraption out of the safe; some sort of typewriter it seemed.

'Go!'

They ran out, and as they left, threw a couple of hand grenades into the room, just enough to destroy the communications machines. They reckoned that what with the thick stone walls of the chateau and the loud booms of the band there might be a chance the muffled sounds wouldn't be heard, letting them get a clear escape.

They were back over the far side; back at the first cave before they knew it, assembling their kit and congratulating themselves on their incredible achievement. They wolfed some shortbread and took a swig of whisky. They had to get as far away as possible, as quickly as they could. Francois had waited and was going to take them to the river. From there, it was roughly a hundred miles downstream to a British outpost where a Battalion was hauled up, holding on to what was known as the Free Zone, separated by the Demarcation Line.

They walked all night, following the side of the fields giving them protection until dawn when Francois led them to a glade, and there in front of them was the river tantalisingly rippling the way forward. The cold mist was rising up like magic vapours, making it difficult to clearly see the way ahead. Francois, at this point had to turn back if he was to get back to his village. The rest of them were told to follow along this river to where they could eventually cross; as they were still in the Occupied Zone until then and had to be careful. There were Germans everywhere.

Chapter Twenty-One

London,
Autumn, 1934.

Prince Edward and Wallis were back from the Mediterranean. Wallis had been grateful to get back to her own life, back to her husband, Ernest, even if she was still swept along with the Prince's social events. She had tired of having Edward around her continually, finding him a little claustrophobic.

'Ernest, it is good to be back, it was all so lovely, but I did miss you. You would have loved Lake Como. Maybe we could go there sometime.'

'I don't know that I could do it in the style you're becoming accustomed to, Honey.' His face looked haggard, and his eyes were tired.

'We'd find a way to have fun, though, wouldn't we?' she said, sympathetically.

She'd realised while she was away how she liked the reassuring, down to earth companionship of Ernest. She was quite happy being married to this man and didn't necessarily wish for this to change. But that's not to say she wasn't caught up in her affair, loving the power and prestige she held, being the Prince's mistress, and she wasn't likely to give that up either.

In a letter to her aunt around this time it's known she wrote how she was loving basking in the public attention she was receiving: "laughing a lot inside" about it all, but grateful for her private life with Ernest when she wished to 'retreat' from the public eye. Wallis seemed to want to 'have her cake and eat it'.

The marriage of his brother Prince George was important to Prince Edward, and he wanted his Wallis to be there with him, placing her on the guest list. There then ensued the first battle of wits, as King George would not have her anywhere near the event and promptly took her name off the guest list.

'David!' Wallis fumed, 'No-one will take me seriously if I'm not to attend these types of events with you.'

Prince Edward was literally livid with his family and defied his father, arriving with Wallis on his arm; nothing could be said or done on the night. The newly married Princess was dressed beautifully, in white satin, and the other ladies had also worn subdued colours; the Queen herself in silver brocade, so enhancing the wedding feel of the night. Wallis turned up wearing a dress in violet coloured lamé with a bright green sash, glittering in all the jewels the Prince had given her and a diamond tiara, hired from Cartier for the event. Everyone was horrified. Prince Edward blatantly introduced Wallis to the King and Queen then went on to dance all night with her alone, as if she was the only lady in the room. This did Wallis's reputation with the royals no good at all.

Christmas came and went. Edward spoilt Wallis with a present of a beautiful diamond pin with two square cut emeralds set either side.

If the events at the wedding hadn't done her enough damage in the Royal's eyes, she was then to make a faux pas that she would live to regret. She'd unfoundedly decided that Princess Elizabeth was annoyingly sweet and way too 'perfect' with her boarding school manners, and that the Duchess of Kent rather dull and uninspiring, so Wallis started to sarcastically mimic them for fun. One fateful day, Elizabeth was to walk into the room at Fort Belvedere, just as Wallis was in full swing, nastily imitating Elizabeth's mother, the Duchess of Kent, and Elizabeth herself. It was to cause a rift that Princess Elizabeth, rightly, would never back down from, having seen Wallis' true opinions.

'I seem to have blown it, David.'

'Don't worry about them, they'll come round in time, you'll see,' he said, in his innocence. 'They love me terribly and once they understand how much you mean to me... Let's not forget how you make me deliriously happy,' he said, as he swept her onto her feet and swirled her round the room, 'then they'll love you as much as I do.'

'You are so naive, David. Naive!' she said, abruptly breaking from his grip and sitting down. 'It all seems rather difficult at the moment. I just don't know where I stand, and Ernest is struggling financially. I can't afford to ...'

'Darling Wally! You should have said something.'

Edward slid onto his knees, sitting on the floor by her feet, holding her hand in his and looking up at her, with her perfect hair and clipped suit,

'I will make sure Ernest has some financial help, and you, my darling, need your own allowance. So, you don't need to worry your beautiful head about such matters,' he said, while kissing her hand. 'That's that, then. Can I?' asking for her permission to have a cigarette. 'I've also been thinking, we'll get away for a bit. It was such bliss, you and I away from it all, wasn't it?'

He stood up and went over to a beautiful mahogany drinks cabinet. The silver gleaming and the highly polished glasses almost singing. The cabinet laid with everything freshly cut and prepared: olives, lemons, fresh tomato juice, soda; but his hand went straight to the whisky and poured himself a large measure into a stunning seventeenth century cut-glass tumbler -even though it was early in the day.

'I have a chance to go to Austria and then on to Hungary.'

'Really? When?'

'Soon. I know you'd just love Vienna. You'll come, won't you? I won't go without you.' Edward pressed.

'Well...'

'We'll get you some clothes for the occasions. It'll be exciting. This time of year is so beautiful, what with the mountains and the snow. We will have the use of the Simplon Express Train. I'll take you to Kitzbuhel. We can go skiing!' he said, excitedly planning ahead, 'Oh how I love skiing!'

'Hold on, David. Why exactly are you thinking of this?'

'Well, I'm able to be of use to the political game of chess that seems to be sweeping through Europe. I want to see it for myself.'

'Now that's more like it! That's fascinating!' she said excitedly, her eyes gleaming. 'You're thinking about the situation with Austria aren't you? Whether Mussolini takes her, or if Germany would take her under her wing, as Hitler has been promising.'

'We'll see,' he pondered.

This was the beginning of Prince Edward delving into politics. The government would regret having encouraged him to strengthen the British influence in Europe. Royals were not meant to dabble in politics: their image being a separate entity entirely and 'the people' needed them to be loyal to the country, not to a particular political party. It could dangerously influence their popularity, not necessarily for the better.

As for Prince Edward, he was fully aware how his popularity with the masses (not only in England but also in Europe) could influence their decisions. He understood the power he had, but then, so did Hitler.

They travelled through the Tyrolean Mountains. Edward skied every day, whereas Wallis preferred to stay warm and play poker with the 'boys'. They danced at the ball and partied for days. When they made it to Vienna Edward gave a speech in perfect German to the awaiting crowds. There had been riots for days and there was a feeling of danger in the air as the Austrians didn't quite know which side Edward was on.

They then travelled on to Budapest; the capital was the epitome of elegance and excitement at this time. Wallis adored the baroque decadence of the Danube Palace Hotel, the lavish casinos and the shops, where she purchased some ornate antique Hungarian jewellery for herself. The journey had been a success and Prince Edward had been able to influence both Austria and Hungary to lean towards the Fascist Mussolini for help, in doing so restricting Hitler's power.

On their return, King George realised what an influence this 'Simpson woman' was to his son and swept into action worrying this relationship could ruin the position of the throne for Edward. He couldn't understand any of his son's liaisons, but this one was going too far. It had to be stopped. He looked upon Wallis as a divorced, married woman of ill repute, obviously after the Prince's money, with no sexual morality, of base manners and no aristocratic breeding whatsoever. He needed to find something on her, which he was sure there was, to use to sway his son away from her, or to use against her to make her leave Edward alone.

Lord Trenchard was contacted, as he was an old faithful friend of the King, and also now the Commissioner of the London Metropolitan Police. In his time, he had designed and created the Royal Air Force. He, being incredibly successful, must have found this lowly task of 'digging for dirt' on Wallis's sordid sexual liaisons rather beneath him. Lord Trenchard, being patriotic, dutifully complied with the King's wishes. Scotland Yard's Superintendent Canning was placed in charge, and the investigation began.

Meanwhile, Wallis had indeed fallen for the blond Arian specimen, Guy Marcus Trundle. He was an American, working for Ford motorcars. He had heavy Nazi tendencies, was brash and cocky, and she was infatuated. Wallis just had to have him; but he'd been avoiding her.

'You don't understand, I want you,' she said, cornering him one day.

'Well, I'm not so sure you 'need' me at all. You've plenty of men in your life at the moment as far as I can see, and,' as he looked her up and down, 'to be quite honest, Honey -you're just not my type.' Vaguely unimpressed.

'Don't you like a risk though? Don't you think it would be exciting? To be fucking me right under the Prince's nose?' Said as she blatantly placed her hand on his crotch. 'We could meet secretly and pull the wool over everyone's eyes!'

'I suppose it would be a thrill to know that I was secretly 'serving' the Prince's mistress!' Looking down amusingly at her strategically placed hand.

'I'd make it worth your while,' Wallis panted.

'So, what would that make me? A gigolo?'

'Yes, if you like! Paid by the royal courts!'

'A royal gigolo!' He threw his head back and laughed out loud.

'It's quite simple: I satisfy the Prince, and you will satisfy me.'

He looked at her with amusement in his eyes, 'You're really serious!'

'Meet me at my new dressmakers, Elsie Schiaparelli's. She'll be discreet.'

'How can I refuse!' he said, slapping her pertly on the bottom.

'No!' she turned angrily, 'You are NOT to leave any marks on me,' she snapped. 'No bruising and no biting. David just can't find out! You understand?'

'Loud and clear, pussycat!' He winked at her and walked off.

Chapter Twenty-Two

France,
Winter, 1941.

After walking for three nights and most of the days, Les and his fellow soldiers, now exhausted, crossed through some fields to cut off a bend in the river they'd still not been able to cross. In the far corner of the field was a mazet, a small hut farmers used to sleep in when doing the harvest, as this place was in the middle of nowhere.

The men saw the hut and approached with caution, it looked deserted and was perfect for their needs. They had to set up camp for a while, transmit their findings and information from the chateau, and take a much-needed rest. They were shattered and starving, rations had been the barest minimum. They needed something hot to eat, to help them get their strength up, but also somewhere sheltered to sleep. The weather had taken a turn for the worse and the snow clouds were drifting overhead as the temperature plummeted and their fingers stuck to the metal on the guns. The ground had become rock solid, unyielding and slippery, making their progress very slow. They knew they had to take cover somehow, somewhere, tonight.

On entering they found the hut abandoned. The farmers hadn't used it that year, probably fighting at the front. It was just perfect: some hay-bails, a tin cup, a saucepan, and a stool. Jack set to, immediately setting his things down and started to unload what he needed from his rucksack. He transmitted messages back and forth for six solid hours. Captain Reger gave him instructions about the coded typewriter to relay to England. England replied that they were to keep their present position. Ammunition would be dropped to them in the next 24hrs.

They had no food and the fire smoked incessantly. The wood they could find had been frozen and damp. It was time Les went to forage. He needed to understand the area around the hut and see about food.

It was a few hours before dawn when he set off. He covered a five-mile circle and found another hut; this one had a stove, so he dismantled it and carried what he could this time and would come back for the rest. He'd also found some turnips and potatoes still in the earth.

As he neared the hut, travelling back through the woods, he saw a deer, there, delicate, all on its own -what was he to do? They desperately needed protein, but would anyone hear his gun if he was to shoot?

Les took his jacket off, slowly and with no sudden moves wrapped it round the gun and shot the deer; the slaughtered lamb. He sorted the carcass, there and then, as he had done with Ronald the farmer and his pig. He also piled up a load of wood, near the back of the hut, under the shelter of a tree.

'Venison for breakfast!'he said, bursting back into the hut. Les beamed with triumphant contentment as he held up a whole leg. The men's eyes stared up at him with disbelief.

'Les, you really are a walking miracle.'

At home, things hadn't been all that easy for Gwen either.

'No, you don't understand, I don't want your help, Sam,' she exclaimed one wet afternoon. She'd been putting on a brave face, but Les being away was harder than she'd feared.

Sam had called by to check on her and found her in the kitchen; flour everywhere, baking scofa cakes she'd said; but she seemed unsettled, almost hyper.

'Ok, don't accept my help! But you can offer me a cup of tea, can't you?'

'I'm sorry, Sam, of course,'

'How have you been? Any news of Les?'

'I'm fine, and Les better be,' she said, brushing a flour covered hand over her brow, 'I don't know what to do. I've not heard a word since before New Year.'

'I thought of you at New Year. Here, alone.'

As he said this, his concern burned through his words and through to her soul.

'Really Sam, Pattie and I are getting by just fine - other than the fact I can't sleep for fretting.' She turned away, not wishing to show how his kind concern was enough to break her. 'Stop looking at me like that. I'm not on inspection, am I?'

He walked round the house like a tiger stalking his area, as if claiming it for his own. He couldn't get her out of his mind, wherever he went. As he poked his head into the bedroom, he saw a bucket on the floor collecting drips falling from the ceiling.

'I knew you needed me!' he exclaimed jubilantly.

'I didn't want to put you out,' she said evasively.

'I'll come at the weekend and see about that for you.'

'Ok,' she sighed, resigning herself to the veritable inevitability of them being alone in the house together. The work needed doing and the days had been so cold and lonely. It was a relief to have some company, even if it was Sam. From then on, it casually became a regular thing that he'd call by, play with Pattie and have a cup of tea with Gwen. They were respectful and became relaxed in each other's company, the flow of conversation and laughter entwining them.

'I'll get that,' he said, one day, as he went to take the whistling kettle off the range. As he did, he innocently laid his hands on her hip from behind and as she moved to the side he could sense the smell of her perfume from her neck. With this close physical contact the passion stirred between them; like a wind blowing the leaves into a whirling circle, the flame for each other rose again.

'Please don't complicate things,' Gwen said distantly, still aching for Les to return.

Les was freezing cold, his shoes were like icy weights round his sore feet. He'd been out hunting but had found nothing. It had been a week since they'd found the hut. The snow had come and settled. It was packed hard, frosting the top crust of the earth making it almost impenetrable for him to dig to find any food. Most of the fields were frozen with ancient, craggy grape vine stumps rising stubbornly through the snow; they unfortunately offered no nourishment at all, and he just couldn't bring himself to use them as firewood. He returned empty handed, except for some welcome firewood from his stack. They had found the ammunition box that was dropped: plenty bullets and grenades, but no food as yet.

That was how they were when the Panzer tank rolled into the field. Suddenly the men were in flow. They'd prepared for this. Radio had told them to hold onto the hut -whatever. It seemed it was strategically placed, and if the allied troops could reach it, they would have pushed the line forwards 50 or so miles.

A German, cockily confident behind the shield of the tank, was standing up pointing at the hut. Les aimed and shot him down, there and then.

That was it: the Germans knew they were there. The tank fired and missed. It seemed it was on its own. Carper aimed a grenade, and it damaged the tank, but the tank still spat bullets, another grenade seemed to really rock the tank and stop it in its tracks. It wasn't going anywhere anymore, even if the Nazi's were still alive within.

This was the start of an exhausting battle, it lasted days. It seemed Germans were in the far side of the woods and were attacking them from afar. Luckily the range was just short of the hut, saving it by the grace of God. As there were only five of them it was a continual strain. They were past exhaustion, in a war trance, eyes glued to the surrounding area: kill or be killed their mantra. It all seemed so surreal. This beautiful snowscape had now become so deadly.

Mike turned to load up the fire, it was hanging on by a thread. The dusty embers were still showing brief moments of glowing life, but if they didn't sort it now, there'd be no warmth that night. It had been -9 the night before.

'Cover me,' Mike said, as in his impatient way he opened the little door round the back and crawled on his knees to the wood stock. It was only a few metres away. He started to load up the sack with the last of the logs; next time they would have to get to the trees for some firewood.

Out of nowhere appeared a German soldier. The German stood blatantly in front of Mike: his greeny-grey uniform, shining black patent-leather belt and shoes all immaculate. It looked unreal as to how this soldier could be out in these conditions and yet so pristine. The metal star near his neck glistened and caught Les's eye as the Nazi shot right at Mike. Les fired, aiming for the star -the jugular- and again for luck. This one had been way too close. What were the Germans doing getting so close?

Mike was dragged back into the hut. He was in a bad way, groaning with blood pouring from his left side.

'Get the wood... Did you get the wood?' was all he said, as his body started to shake heavily. Jack moved the radio, and they laid Mike on some straw. Major Carper came over to Mike.

'Mike, hold on. Yes, we have the wood. You were very brave. How is your pain?'

Mike's eyes were wild, like a startled fox. 'Ok Sir, really.'

But the Major knew different, he saw Mike's lips trembling and eyes screaming with pain. Jack was trying to wrap a body tourniquet around him. As Major Carper reached for his rucksack, for the supplies of morphine, Jack asked,

'Should we have a look?'

They injected him with the painkiller, then assessed the situation. Les was keeping cover, he was so mad he wouldn't let anything more happen to them that night if he could help it. He blamed himself: he just hadn't had enough time to reposition himself before Mike had been shot. The Nazi's face kept popping up in his subconscious -just like it had in real life.

The wound was deadly. Mike's left lung had been ripped through, and it was only a matter of time. They'd slowed the bleeding, but the gurgling moans, deep and distorted, were haunting the air that night. He struggled to speak around dawn,

'Les, tell me about your girl, she looks so pretty.'

Les came to his side.

'I have a girl you know,' Mike murmured, 'she doesn't know I'm going to marry her, but she's mine alright. Alice is her name.' He struggled to speak, gurgling and breathing heavily. 'I've loved her since I was a young boy...' He started to cough, blood poured from his mouth. 'What...what's happening...' His eyes looked shocked, wide open, then calmed. His breath slowed right down and his lips started to turn blue. Les took his hand, and Mike gave it the softest of squeezes, then his body relaxed as he faded away.

'Oh Lord. Protect us all,' Jack sighed, as they looked at one another. Silence fell, the sun rose, and they knew this was all so transient.

'What are we to do with his body?' Jack finally asked.

'We can't exactly dig this earth, hard as it is?'

'I know this sounds gruesome, but we're going to prop him up at the little window, over there, to look as if he's still a player,' Major Carper explained.

'He'd want that: to be a soldier, in life as in death,' Les replied, sombrely. Things were getting to him. The killings he could deal with, but this death, someone so close to him, hurt deep. He had to bury the hurt just as deep, inside.

The radio crackled and Jack jumped straight on it. The bleeping, tapping, dots and dashes, carried on for a while. Then Jack looked up,

'Some good news at last! It seems the Yanks are on their way to help us! We just need to hold on till they get here - should be by nightfall.'

'We don't have enough ammo to last till then. Let's hope they do actually find us.' Carper said, showing the only glimpse of pessimism Les had ever seen in the major's eyes. Carper was always so strategically positive, but they were so exhausted, it was affecting their mentality.

The Germans tried to approach again, though thanks to Les's sure shooting, there were no bullets wasted, and no Germans were able to get any closer.

It was a sight for sore eyes when, to the rear of the hut, a tank and about 12 men approached.

'It's them, it's got to be!' cried Jack.

The Americans arrived and entered the hut, all full of bravado and stories of their escapades.

'Don't worry lads, we're here to relieve you! I guess you'd better get some well-earned kip first. Don't wanna say nothin'- but you guys look awful!'

They then looked at Mike.

'We'd better get rid of him too, now that we're here.'

One of these guys pulled out a bottle of French brandy, handed it round, and then offered Les a Winston cigarette. Les slid down the wall, onto a pile of straw, and took a long slow drag on the fag; it was his first cigarette in days. He watched the smoke unfurl and finally started to relax into a needed slumber.

He woke at three in the morning. Two of the Americans had been shot. They'd been taking Mike's body out of the hut, and at the same time the Germans had started approaching. Les could see them in the field, disbelief in his eyes.

He rushed to the window, getting back down in his position, just waiting for something to move and he'd kill it. There was nothing but anger and adrenalin in his belly.

Chapter Twenty-Three

London,
Winter, 1935.

Lord Trenchard resigned: possibly because he didn't want to deal with relaying the contents of the 'China Dossier' to the King. It was becoming incredibly potent, shocking even. Its very existence was to be questioned, nevertheless, the proof was there.

King George was presented with the dossier by the soon to be Prime Minister, Stanley Baldwin. Summoned into the King's room, and after the usual formalities King George asked Baldwin to get down to the nitty-gritty:

'So, what exactly is the situation on this Wallis woman?'

'Your Excellency, I just don't know where to begin...'

'Well?'

'I suppose I'd better start at the beginning.'

The King nodded, wishing him to get on with it.

'Your Excellency, it seems there is rather a lot of 'dirt' on her, some I'd rather not express in front of Your Majesty.'

'Oh, do carry on, please. You're not usually one to be shy! Remember, this is my son involved here, and I wish to know all the facts.' He smiled reassuringly.

Baldwin took a deep breath, 'It seems to start in the United States. Her first husband, Win Spencer, was a naval officer posted to San Diego. He is an alcoholic bisexual, and their marriage was floundering. This is where she first started fraternising with the Fascist Count Cianni,' he stammered, looking at King George. 'After that, there seemed to be a string of affairs, often with men of Fascist leanings. She was rumoured to be helping them to 'spread the word' as such.' He took a nervous breath and continued, 'Her husband was posted out to China. We're not sure but the US Navy have implied she had worked for them, carrying documents and suchlike, but then had become unreliable, possibly leaking information; they weren't sure but wanted her out of the way. Her time in China...' he paused and sighed, 'Well, Your Royal Highness, it really is unbelievable, but she became involved with the 'sing–sing'.'

'Explain,' King George said, rather clipped. He knew all there was to know about China, having been fascinated with the country for years, but wished for Baldwin to explain everything.

Baldwin, blushing slightly, carried on, 'They are floating brothels, where it seemed she spent some time, maybe even working in them. They train their ladies in the 'art' of 'Fang Chung'.' Clearing his throat, he continued, 'This is an ancient art of fornication, but it seems to lean on the side of the perverse if you ask me.' He turned even redder, and cleared his throat, 'It doesn't stop there I'm afraid. She was known to have slept with wealthy, important men... for money.'

'You mean to say she prostituted her services?'

'That's not all. They believe she also helped launder opium drug money on the casino tables for the people she was in with. They think she possibly helped in the supply of drugs too. Again- no proof.'

'I just don't believe this,' King George said, his face pale with shock in his eyes.

'At the moment, she seems to be mixing with Fascist and Nazi supporters. She's been seen leaving an establishment with Baron von Ribbentrop, arm in arm, very cosy together. And right now, she is in a known Nazi dressmakers, Elsie Schiaparelli, where she secretly carries out her affair with an American, a Nazi sympathiser, Guy Marcus Trundle. They meet regularly, thinking they've fooled everyone meeting there, but I'm afraid they can't fool us. We have photographic proof it is where they carry out acts of fornication.' He took a long breath,

'Our main worry, Your Grace, is how much of a liability she could be. Whether she would ever hand over information that she may get to hear of, being in such close proximity to your son, and of course, the worry that the obviously highly important and sensitive content of information that comes his way,' he paused, at a loss, 'may be leaked.' At which he shook his head with disgust.

The King, mortified, replied, 'This is of the utmost importance. Yes, we must make sure that will never happen. If anything, limit what my son is to be told in the future, as he seems to be besotted with this woman. I feel he tells her absolutely everything. I will be speaking to him but whether that will do any good, I don't know.' The King's eyes dropped with remorse. 'Good work, please carry on. We need to keep a watchful eye on this Wallis-woman. She could be very dangerous for us, for my son's right to the throne, and even more importantly, for this country.'

'Yes, Your Majesty, I understand completely.' He rose, bowed, turned, and went to the door.

'Baldwin,'

'Yes, Your Excellency?'

'Prince Edward must never know of this, you do understand. We don't wish to look like meddling parents; it would only make things worse. Never, you hear, never, must he find out we are following his 'Mrs Simpson'.'

'Of course, Your Royal Excellency. Goodbye.'

And the door was closed behind him.

Queen Mary was to be informed in private; the information was to shock her to her very core. Later, together, the Royals discussed what they could possibly do. King George decided,

'We have to do all we can to make sure that woman does not become the queen of England.'

'But that is impossible, that will never happen, Darling,' the Queen replied, 'she's a married divorcee!'

'Nothing is impossible,' he said gravely. 'I do not wish her to get her hands on any of our heirloom jewellery either. She is not to have any of Queen Victoria's diamonds, or Alexandra's emeralds. I know he's already taken from the vaults. I also feel strongly he mustn't be told she's cheating on him. He'd just fall apart, I'm sure of it.' The King paused, shaking and weak with emotion,

"That woman in my own house!" he exclaimed, exhausted and disgusted. This was all taking a toll on his health.

And so, together with the Duchess of York and the Duchess of Kent, the King and Queen discussed what could be done to prevent any of this happening.

Wallis and Edward were to go out that evening, but beforehand Edward wanted to give her something. He had another special gift for her: a beautiful necklace of the most splendid emeralds. He had her spellbound as he lifted the stunning necklace and placed it round her bony neck. The emeralds, torn from the vein in the earth, came from the Muzo mine in Colombia, centuries before, when these stones were revered, believed to hold the powers of the gods and when the influence of nature still stood strong in people's lives. The emeralds had been taken: robbed from the Royal Aztecs throats at their moment of death. The powers of these impressive emeralds were not able to shield these innocently trusting warriors from the double-crossing lies of Pizarro. The stones had been shaped by the hands of wise craftsmen, worn by the powerful rulers, only to be shipped back to Europe, given as strategic trade to the monarchy, then sit in dark vaults. The curse, if there was one (as the ancient priests so thought), was now wrapped around Wallis's jugular. So, in a way, the power did remain, as her life was to be affected from this moment on, as addiction to wealth and high status, notoriety, and the extreme 'richesse' of life greedily enveloped her. However, she was also to take the life of the Prince; take his destiny too. Wallis wore the emeralds that night, blatantly, for all to see, flaunting them around town.

She was seen at the Covent Garden Opera House. In the interval it's known she belittled Edward, saying:

"Hurry off now David. You'll be late for the London County Council Ball. And take that cigar out of your breast pocket. It doesn't look very pretty!"

The King and Prince met to discuss Wallis. Edward famously denied any physical intimacy. The King tried to remind his son of his impending destiny, to no avail.

Lord Wigram wrote of this event in his diary: "The Prince's staff were horrified at the audacity of the statements of HRH the Prince of Wales. Apart from actually seeing His Royal Highness and Mrs Simpson in bed together, they had positive proof that His Royal Highness actually lived with her."

In June, the Prince gave a speech at the Queens Hall. He went from one political blunder to the next, beginning to openly express his blinded political bias, and in so doing, wreak havoc with the British position of diplomacy necessary at that time. The King became even more exasperated with his son voicing his opinions as Edward appeared incredibly naive and showed himself to be confused as to where he stood exactly: agreeing with both Hitler's anti-Semitic and Mussolini's fascist ideals.

'David, will you stop pacing around. It's exhausting me. We're meant to be catching some sun!'

Wallis was stretched out; her androgynous body cleverly positioned in a blue swimsuit; sunglasses on and a Hermes scarf wrapped around her hair.

She'd found his tireless energy and childish need to be with her at every moment, or discussing with her every thought he had, rather exhausting. Letters written to Aunt Bessie had expressed that she definitely was not in love with him.

They were, yet again, back in Europe, on another 'political holiday'. He'd realised that he didn't have to carry on pursuing the dangerous game of playing Mussolini against Hitler. It had, deviously, been put to him by Pierre Laval to try and influence them to join together, so weakening the Franco-Soviet power.

Edward had driven great strength from Wallis's presence, now even taking her to these high-brow political meetings so she could be a part of his decision making. She loved being treated so highly, as if she was a princess on tour, or a politician of importance. The lifestyle was becoming irresistible, but for His Royal Highness.

'I've decided to take your friend, Gregoire, up on his offer, and position him as my lawyer.' Wallis announced. 'I'd not realised he represents Elsie and Ribbentrop. I'm going to tell Ernest to use him for his company's interest with those shipping lines in Europe. I mean... Gregoire is perfect, what with all his contacts.'

'You liked him then, I knew you would!' Edward replied while still pacing around.

'Yes, he's fascinating. I think the scar on his face just adds to his character; it makes him seem quite formidable!'

This was one of the many damning decisions they were to make. Albert Frederic Armand Gregoire was one of the most dangerous of Nazi spies. For them to have such close contact with him would do nothing for their reputation as Nazi sympathisers. From this point on, the Secret Intelligence Service had to step up their surveillance on Wallis.

Chapter Twenty-Four

Sunningdale,
Spring, 1942.

It had been over four months since that moonless star-filled freezing night when Les had been dropped in by parachute, onto French soil, starting their mission. He'd spent some harrowing months there, protecting the line, fighting endlessly. The cold harsh winter not relenting as the Germans ceaselessly kept the pressure on them. He had seen people standing right next to him, talking one minute, blown up the next. The brutality had changed him: the senseless slaughter of good men. Lad's screaming, praying in their last moments for their mother to take the pain away. Every time he closed his eyes he was like a wild cat on the prowl, ready to shoot anything that moved.

Meanwhile, here he was. Somehow, he'd made it out alive and was walking up the all familiar road with the cottage in view. Home on leave. His battalion was being reassigned, and he was to sort out all the 'kit and caboodle' as they said. So, it meant he had a good few weeks in England. It all seemed surreal; how could he be here? Back in Sunningdale with no real signs of war; where-as out there, in France and throughout Europe, they were fighting for their lives. The stench of the trenches and the memory of the hut all seemed like a bad dream, a nightmare.

As he walked in, Gwen ran straight to him and kissed him through her tears.

'Oh, dear Lord, you are the sweetest sight for sore eyes,' she said, kissing him again and again. As she found his lips, the tender warmth and inviting caress of her tongue made him sweep her up and carry her there and then into the bedroom.

'Queenie, it's only the thought of you that's kept me going,' he said, low and sure.

He looked at her, her tousled hair, her soft skin beckoning for his touch and her eyes full with love.

'I've hated it with you away,' she moaned. 'I can't bear it; I start imagining all sorts of terrible things,' crying and kissing him.

'Don't worry, I'm here now,' he said passionately, as his uniform fell to the ground and her dress was thrown up in the air.

Les made love that night as if his life had been saved and he was reborn. As he held her at dawn, cradling her in his arms, knowing this to be one of the loveliest moments of his life, he knew he would do anything to protect his Gwen, even if it meant fighting to his death to fend off the Germans.

The next week he went over to Eva's. She was so glad to see him.

'Les! You had us guessing for a while. Tell us, is it as bad as we think over there?'

'Worse. Really Sis, let's not talk about it, if you don't mind. I'd rather know what's been going on here.'

'Well....' she started, noting his avoidance. She did like a good yarn.

They chatted about this and that, how her work was going, up at the 'Big House' as they called Fort Belvedere. She told him everything, how the house just wasn't the same since Prince Edward left. She told him all the gossip between the servants, how his 'Royal Prince and his mistress' (as she always called Wallis), were, as if, barred from his own kingdom.

'Imagine that!' She explained how they were sure the couple had leaked vital information, spying for the Germans.

'Eva, tell me you're making this up. I'm out there, risking my life at every second, for King and Country, and our own royal couple are spying against us. Like snakes behind our backs, that's just outrageous!' Shocked, he shook his head in disgust, sickened at the thought, unable to comprehend the full extent to what she'd relayed.

As they talked, Eva looked deep into her brother's eyes. There was something so very different about him. That open approachable look had disappeared and in its place were these dark fatigued eyes, haunted by what they'd seen and experienced, trying desperately not to bring it out into reality, trying to keep the distant harrowing visions inside. She could feel his pain, see the torture, but knew as they spoke, he wouldn't talk about it; as if saying, 'just leave it there, in my eyes, if I don't vocalise it, it's not real.'

So, she just chatted on about any old thing, trying to soothe him with her voice. She changed the subject to insignificant daily occurrences, hoping to calm him down and make him feel safe again.

'Things have been ok here, and Sam's been so helpful. He's been keeping an eye on Gwen. He pops round now and then, making sure all's well.' She hadn't realised what she'd said, or what consequences it could have between the brothers. Les's eyes suddenly started back to life, like a horse bolting through a gate,

'What was that?' he shot at her.

'Just that we've been keeping an eye on Gwen, as you'd hoped.'

'No, what exactly did you say, Eva?' Les's urgent demand forced upon her.

'Well, that Sam was the one to go over. I often couldn't get away because of the little ones and all, and there were a few odd jobs to be done over there. Sam was only thinking of how he could help you. I know he was.'

'Don't talk nonsense. We all know what he's thinking when it comes to women.'

'Les, please don't be like that. Sam was going over there with nothing but good intentions,' Eva pleaded.

'Exactly my point! And why, if it's been so innocent, has Gwen not mentioned anything to me about it?' said Les, brewing up with emotion.

'Probably because it was 'innocent' as you put it, and totally inconsequential, so....'

'Eva,' he sighed, lowering his head, 'sometimes you are just too naïve.' His eyes froze back over, glazed, gone somewhere else. It was as if he was back in survival mode.

'I'd better get back,' he said, as he reached for his hat and stood up, 'You will always tell me the truth, good or bad, won't you. I have laid my trust in you, Sis,' piercing his dark eyes into hers.

'You know you can. I promise you nothing untoward was going on. You've really misinterpreted me.' She looked sad as he bent to kiss her cheek. Les looked around, surveying the room, soaking everything into his memory, then left and closed the door behind him.

He had to come to terms with his jealousy. It was kind of his brother to keep an eye over his wife; but he also knew and felt the fire between the two of them: there was no denying that. He worried it would only be a matter of time before something 'untoward' happened, if left alone together so often.

He returned home to find Gwen singing to herself, happily doing the washing.

'How wonderful! You can help me hang the washing on the line, like you used to.'

Les picked up the basket, while looking at her joyous innocence shining in her eyes, and rep-remanded himself for ever having thought that she would be unfaithful. The pure love emanating from her eyes towards him was intoxicating and there was no doubt this was how she felt. Even-so, he also knew how naive she was, easily manipulated by shows of affection. His tension eased from his body as they shared a kiss over the washing line, and he believed, as he always did, that life would have a way of working things out.

As her lips withdrew from his, she looked at him with a naughty spark in her eye, the kind of glimmer that changes lives.

'How are you feeling right now?' she asked.

'Good. Why?' he said, questioning her.

'I've got something to tell you, maybe you should sit down!' she announced, starting to laugh that enchanting laugh of hers.

'Go on, you're intriguing me now,' he urged.

She looked deep into his eyes, took his hand and placed it on her tiny belly, giving him that 'knowing' look.

'Oh my, are you sure?'

'Yes, I am. I just know!'

'So soon? How!'

'I just do! I'm sure it was that first night, when you'd arrived back, remember?' she said, slightly blushing at the memory of their intimacy.

'How could I ever forget!' he said, now laughing. He kissed her and swirled her up in the air, 'Oh, you are so magical, and so full of surprises!'

'So, you're glad?'

'Well, I know the circumstances are awful, but that's life, and so is THAT!' he said kissing her belly. 'Together we create magic, my dearest.' Then his face dropped, realising he'd soon be sent back to the front. 'Don't you worry, I can't have you on your own. I know...' he said, his mind racing, 'we'll see if your dad wouldn't mind coming and staying with you. How about that?'

'Les!' she said, covering his whole face in little kisses. 'That sounds fantastic, he'd love that. He's lonely, and ever-so sad up there alone with Ma gone, and I find it so hard without you.' A tear of truth welled in her eyes, not wanting to tell him to what extent she missed his presence.

'I know, Queenie.'

So, that was the plan. Les felt so much more comfortable knowing she'd have her father: no more need for Sam to come round. That'd put a stop to that -full stop. He loved his brother very much but also knew his brother very well.

That sorted, they had a wonderful time, with Gwen glowing and blossoming under their love, curled up tight, talking promises into the night. They dreamed on, planning their lives and what they'd be able to do once the war finished. She flourished when pregnant, emanating some sort of inner contentment. It was as if the human role she played was playing its best performance yet, and it spilled out to everyone in her presence.

He knew he didn't have long left on leave, but just enough time to settle her father, George, in. They, luckily, got on like a house on fire, and had a few days of jovial family banter, all together: Gwen, Pattie, himself and 'Father-in-law', as he always called him, never forgetting his position in the family, and glad to have an elder male around having lost his own father in World War 1.

The day came, and the uniform had to be donned again. Gwen couldn't deal with it, her heart froze; the pain too great she evaded the whole event and carried on as if nothing was going on, as if he was just popping over to see his big sis, Eva. So it was, that, one minute he was there, the next, he was gone.

She dealt with it, in her own way, by focusing on the good things, pouring her love into Pattie: spoiling her with such affection, kisses and cuddles, tickles and giggles. She kept within their contented bubble, not allowing the sharp edges of reality to pierce their idyllic fantasy world. On arrival, her father took great pride in the gentleness of the family scene his daughter had created and was so glad to be near her, helping her in any way he could, only too aware she was momentarily slipping into other worlds for escape.

Time passed and the weeks rolled by. The weather had turned nasty and rain fell relentlessly for days on end. The roof, unfortunately, opened up its leak again, and the continual sound of the drip landing into the bucket became almost like an unexploded bomb, a clock ticking. Instead of marking the passing of time, it was a constant reminder of the situation; of the reality that Les wasn't there to mend it, that he was away at war fighting for his life, that they'd not heard from him since he'd left. Her mind could 'black-out' and ignore everything, except when such an innocent, simple thing like a drip wore down her stability. She had started to drift off out of the room mid-sentence, leave the kettle on the boil totally oblivious to the piercing whistle, not get washed or dressed as she normally paid such attention to. Her father would find her floating around the garden in her nightie talking to the trees; and all the while Pattie, playing with her mummy's hand, content and oblivious to the ticking bomb of her mother's sanity starting to gently slip away.

Her father noticed these signs, of course. He was concerned from the first moment she'd become over animated about the news on the radio a week before; since then he'd heard her secret fearful tears all night, 'Thank the Lord I'm here,' he thought.

'Honeybee,' as he'd always called his girl, 'I'm going to get up there and fix that leak for you, I think it's driving you loopy!' he said, with a wink.

The moment George had said it, the reality of the situation and how it was affecting her, brought her back to earth. She looked straight at him and laughed, full and strong.

'You know, Dad, you're absolutely right! I've never even noticed, but now you come to mention it: it's driving me round the bend. I can't stand it!'

They laughed together, and then she said, 'Can we get up there NOW! This minute! And fix the damn thing?'

'Wait a minute!' he said, so relieved to see her return to herself, just like that. It could come and go, as he knew with her ma and grandma: so quick; but so harrowing.

'You're not going anywhere near a ladder in your condition -and that's a fact!' he said sternly.

'Ok, but I can help,' she said stubbornly.

'Yes, you can -by staying at the bottom of the ladder and holding it for me!'

'But I'm still so agile, Dad. And your legs are weak!'

'Don't you fret about me, my girl. Let's just get this job done while the rain's stopped.'

So, they decided he'd better climb up there first and see what he'd need, assess the situation, as such.

So, like a trooper, up he went. It wasn't easy, and the leak, of course, was in a difficult place to reach, but he made it there. He was shouting down to Gwen, telling her the status of the leak, when the clouds suddenly rolled in, so black and ominous. Everything went dark and a wind came up from nowhere. Fear got into his belly: he hated heights. George had always had a touch of vertigo, but never so strong as now. Afraid, he froze; the wind seemed to take him, and his balance was lost. As he tried to stabilise himself, the slippery wet tiles gave no grip, and he started to slide. There was nothing for him to hold on to and he gathered momentum.

'It's no good,' he thought, 'this is it! Oh God, not right now, Gwen needs me.'

He fell through the air and landed twisted on the lawn below. If he'd landed on the path, only inches to the left, he would have surely died from impact, but the grass cushioned his blow just enough to save his life. Excruciating pain came over him, almost exquisite, and he blacked out. He came round with Gwen running and screaming around him, a hysterical look in her eyes. He tried to move then realised that he could not.

'Dad! Dad! No! Dad please! I need you. Stay with me!'

'Get me a blanket and go get help,' he whispered.

'I can't leave you!' she said, panic-stricken.

'You must, Honeybee. Go now...'

Gwen ran down the road, and into the Police Station, normally a 15-minute walk but she must have been there in 5 minutes flat.

'Please help! It's my father. He's fallen.'

The ambulance came and he was taken to hospital. He had a broken leg but worst of all, a broken back. The spine had snapped: and so had his spirit. He was in agony and felt more hopeless and helpless than he ever had in his life. The last thing he'd wanted was to be a burden on Gwen. He'd wanted to help her; not hinder her. He couldn't comprehend that just being there for her helped her in ways unfathomable, keeping her calm and reassured.

George spent a good while in hospital. She couldn't easily get over to visit him and this stress started to seep into her psyche again. She would find herself getting all dressed up and beautifying herself, but not able to actually go anywhere. She would dance around the room, dancing round and round, losing hours and hours, imagining Les was dancing with her. Pattie would play over on the heath, all day sometimes, playing Cowboys and Indians, or just catching insects, or playing with friends.

By the time George, was able to come back to the house Gwen's state of mind was really quite vulnerable. The schizophrenia was ebbing and flowing, like a sea searching its shore. He felt so hopeless. George saw it straight away but couldn't do anything. All he could do was talk to her, through his incessant pain. He would talk with her, in whatever world she was in that day; he would join her there and keep her company, only hoping this helped her keep her feet on the ground. She was looking so beautiful; stunning in-fact, and he hadn't really taken it in, until the German Prisoner of War that had been assigned to help them (as George needed to be lifted, and carried to the bathroom to be washed, ect), arrived at the door and just stood there – dumbfounded - at this angelic apparition that had opened the door. She stood, humming a tune, pushing her hair away from her face, smiling and welcoming him in.

Gwen innocently inquired after the uniform, telling him how assertive he looked. She reached forth and touched the metal insignia on his collar and, as if feeling a glimpse of his cold soul, she suddenly withdrew her hand.

The look of lust that fell over that German's face put a shiver down George's back; even though his back was numb with pain. He could foresee this might lead to problems. Over the next week he tried to get to know this man who had to enter their house. This German, 'Victor', was a cold fish, there was no soul to speak of. Victor was callous and calculated. He'd obviously been vicious in the war and hadn't regretted a minute of it. He despised the English and resented the fact he had to help an English family. He brutally threw George around while washing him, whenever Gwen wasn't in the room. Victor always had an edge of danger when he moved George, as if he knew what power he had, with one slip, how much pain he could cause. But the worst pain for George was watching this man sweet-talk Gwen. Victor was like a viper approaching his prey. He would adapt, as if a chameleon, to show her what she most wished to see. He became a soft-spoken gentleman, but still assertive and masculine. He praised her looks; flattering her, subtly flirting, making her feel special. He brought her gifts: stockings, butter, and sweets for Pattie. He knew how she loved to laugh, and they passed their time having tea and him telling jokes, together in the kitchen. It was as if his hatred for the English was accumulating into a warped, twisted, resentful desire for Gwen.

George tried to make Victor understand that he must leave Gwen alone. He explained that she was delicate, mentally. As soon as he'd said that he realised that it was a grave mistake. He saw the German's calculated thoughts twist this information to his own benefit. George realised he'd just made the situation worse than before and didn't know what to do. He spoke with Gwen, trying to make her understand what this German was really like, but she couldn't see this side of Victor's character. Her mind couldn't comprehend such manipulative, calculated behaviour. She saw no harm in their tea times together, certainly not any unwarranted behaviour; explaining how kind he was to help them, and how they just couldn't manage without his help and that they must be considerate towards him. Her point being that they mustn't forget that it may be Les one day, in Germany, who may be a prisoner of war, and she only hoped that a German family would treat him with as much compassion.

One fine day, the viper, Victor, arrived bearing gifts, but unusually, this time, gifts for George. It was a bottle of beer, George's favourite ale, and was much appreciated. Victor poured it into a tall glass and handed it to Gwen's father after he'd been washed and changed; they'd even changed his sheets that day. Victor seemed jovial, and it led George to question his judgement, 'maybe I'd been too harsh to judge the man, it may just be the war that's made him as he is. Lord knows it's enough for any man to keep rational, that may be his reason for his cold nature, effects of war, and all that...'

Nevertheless, as he thought this, he saw the glint in Victor's eyes as George then started to fall into a slumber. 'There was something in his eyes though, I just know it,' George thought as he fell asleep. The sleeping drug Victor had slipped into George's beer had taken effect. Gwen was doing the laundry, Victor approached her saying he'd help her hang the sheets on the line. He followed her outside, his eyes watching her every move, almost feeling her breath as it rose and fell. The sunlight was shining, flickering through her cotton dress. She was oblivious to the fact that the dress became almost see-through, revealing her perfectly shaped body. He could smell her scent, slightly floral, that she always wore. She turned around and smiled, so innocently, offering him one end of the sheet.

Within a split second he'd taken the sheet and wrapped it around her. She was laughing at first, giggling, saying, 'No, silly! No...' But then, she screamed. It was the shriek of the sudden realisation of the deep fear of 'invasion'. The disbelief of what was happening to her echoed in her scream. He ignored her. Wrapping the sheet around her mouth, gagging her; then around her eyes, blindfolding her; around her head, shoulders, her whole upper body; mummifying her alive. She could do nothing, wrapped tightly in her own matrimonial sheet as he dragged her to the garden shed. The place that was erected so lovingly; a symbol of her and Les's contentment as a married couple; was to be used as the place of extreme violation of her body and soul.

He threw her down, ripping at her dress. He just couldn't wait for her now. He'd had enough of these days with her tantalising him, he thought, she deserved this, she wanted it really, this English whore. She kicked and kicked; but he got hold of her, turning her over and onto her stomach. She could kick no longer. He parted her legs and so roughly, with all his hatred of England, and his confusion of his desire for her that had turned into pure anger, he raped her. Forcing his way, penetrating deeper, and deeper, his desire was not satiated, every touch of her skin turned him even wilder, hitting her harder, he wanted to feel his power over her, see her submit to him, feel her respect his being.

This was, of course, all lost on her. Gwen, in the depths of absolute fear had disappeared: shocked to somewhere else in her mind. He, resenting her as he climaxed, reached forward and pulled at her beautiful hair. Clumps falling to the ground as he, arching her body back on itself like a dead animal, thrusting his might deep within her, groaning with distorted animalistic pleasure, bashed her face into the floor.

When he was finished, he stood over her, telling her how if she ever said anything, he would have her put away in a mental asylum; locked up forever, claiming extreme insanity; that she'd attacked him, that she was a wanton woman: he knew it, she knew it, and she'd got what she deserved.

'Think yourself lucky you've had me; and don't think I won't be back for more...' he said, staring at her possessively as he buckled up his leather belt. His eyes piercingly evil, proudly surveyed the scene. She was scratched, bloody and bruised. Muddy bloody tears ran down her delicate face, and her hair was tangled beyond knots.

Gwen tried to hide into the sheet, trying to cover up her feminine parts as the blood and sperm seeped from her. She cradled her belly, talking to her baby inside, telling him to hang on in there, how lovely he was going to be, how he was needed to keep Pattie company and how Mummy was going to be just fine.

Victor turned his back on her and walked out. The clipped march of the patent leather boots on the gravel path echoed in her mind. She could still hear the sound of his heels on the ground: 'No soul,' she was thinking, 'Heels, but no soul.' Huddled, shivering in shock in the shed, whispering to herself for hours till way after dusk,

'Heels, but no soul.'

Chapter Twenty-Five

Fort Belvedere, Windsor,
January 1936.

Wallis and Prince Edward returned to England, to the English winter and to the failing health of his father, King George. Edward seemed to need Wallis even more. Time spent with his father was strained as King George found no peace in his son's actions.

Edward would phone Wallis incessantly, for hours on end, and as the time of his father's death approached all Edward wanted was to be at Wallis's side. The pressure, the thought that now was his time to step up and become the monarch of this country was something he hadn't exactly been relishing and was now resenting. He was known to have said:

"...my brother Bertie would make a much better king than I."

The role as king was now also tainted with the taste of loneliness. He couldn't bear the possibility of not having Wallis at his side and naively thought with all his popularity among the people of his country, something would be achieved.

It was a cold January day, Prince Edward walked into his drawing room, shaking off his tweed jacket and giving a shiver as he threw the jacket over the sofa. Wallis was sitting by the fire, ablaze with logs.

He'd been out hunting in the grounds of the Windsor Great Park that surrounded his beloved Fort Belvedere, trying to shake off this feeling of impending doom. The sky darkened and grey clouds had rolled in bringing freezing fog. He'd had to get back before he became chilled to the bone.

'I don't understand what you were doing out there, the weather conditions are terrible,' she snapped at him, almost caring in her way.

'I needed to get some air I suppose.' He approached her, bending down cupping her face in his hands, to give her a kiss.

'Get away from me, your hands are freezing.'

'Darling, just one kiss! Please?' he begged, as he planted a kiss on her turned cheek. 'Read this,' he said, offering her an envelope.

'What is it?' she asked inquisitively, whilst unfolding the elegant envelope of the royal stationery.

'Oh dear!' she exclaimed while continued reading the note. It was from Queen Mary, in her own handwriting:

"I think you ought to know that Papa is not very well."

The King had developed bronchitis and was getting weaker by the day. Wallis and Edward sat together, holding hands, staring into the fire, knowing things were going to change dramatically. She comforted him and made sure that he was to go to Sandringham.

Off he went, till there in front of him was his formidable father, reduced to a frail shivering invalid, wrapped in a Tibetan robe: like an ancient monk on the edge of life. Edward stayed a while at his father's side and then sped off into London to speak to Baldwin. He wanted to discuss his request not to become king, explaining how he'd never had the courage to talk about it with his father. He wondered if now, as the time approached, there was anything he could do to get out of his hereditary role of responsibility.

Edward immediately left Downing Street and headed into town; having arranged to meet Wallis at a nightclub. They drank and danced, whiling away the small hours while his father battled for his life. Those concerned (the royal household and the Prime Minister in particular), were outraged at the audacity of his playboy behaviour while his father fought for his life and lost.

The King, put to peace by euthanasia, three quarters grain of morphia and a whole grain of cocaine, slipped from this world. His famous last words, hours before had been:

"How is the Empire?"

Lord Wigram replied:

"All is well, sir, with the Empire."

Edward, once told of the passing of his father, was beside himself; confused and ragged by guilt and fear he stayed at Sandringham. He hounded the telephone: unapproachable and ignoring his fellow sibling's feelings, he just wanted to disappear into the solace of Wallis's voice. He phoned her again, and again. She could hardly refuse him at a time like this; however, was finding it all such a strain and started to wish she was not caught up in it all.

On 22nd of January London was in mourning. The procession and all the pomp and ceremony that go with such an event had got under way. Edward's ascension to that of king had commenced. Wallis was eagerly watching it all from the windows of York House. She felt a hand slip into hers. She turned, surprised to see Edward by her side.

'What on earth are you doing here, David?'

'I needed to see you.'

'You should be out there, with the rest of them,' she said, pointing out the window to the precession.

It was a shocking move that he'd made: leaving his mother's side on such an occasion and breaking protocol at such an important time as his own ascension to the throne. The whole country was looking to him to lead forward and rise-up triumphant, as it were. The signs were there from the beginning, for all to see, that things were awry with the future king.

Later that night, after the reading of the will, he fled back to Wallis. Waking the household, he came storming in. He'd had rather a lot to drink, and his temper was raging.

'David, will you calm down!'

'Calm down, you say?' raising his voice. 'This is calm for how I should be.'

Wallis rang down for the maid to make some drinks.

'Well! You're going to have to calm down if you want to be in my company.'

'It's all so terrible,' he said, crumpling to the floor by her side.

'You will have to tell me what this is all about, David, if you expect me to understand this erratic behaviour at such late hours of the night.'

'I don't understand it, help me Wally,' he said, breaking his rage and turning maudlin. 'My father is so cruel, even to the end. He's locked me into this life of servitude to the country. He's left me nothing. Nothing!'

'I don't believe you! You're the king now,' she snapped back.

'Yes, that as maybe; but Papa didn't leave me any money, Wallis! How am I to look after us?'

'What do you mean? You will become one of the wealthiest men in the world, won't you?' Wallis's voice broke her normal cool tone.

'He left my brothers and sisters an inheritance. I wasn't even mentioned.'

'You what?' Panic rising in her voice, 'You weren't mentioned?'

'No, that's what I'm trying to tell you. Clause after clause; the reading of this damn will seemed to go on for ages; but never was my name mentioned!'

'You can't mean that, David.'

'Yes, I do!' His voice was becoming even more elated, 'I kept on saying, 'Where do I come in? Where do I come in?''

'And?' she said desperately.

'That stupid man, the royal solicitor, Sir Halsey Bircham, -you saw him the other day, remember? Well, he just treated me as if I was an annoying interrupting so and so!' He took a breath, 'the audacity of him! He dared to tell me that: "I had not been included in the will!" Wigram then went on to say that I was meant to have 'amassed' a substantial sum from the Duchy of Cornwall!'

'Well?'

'As you know it's only about a million in investments: nothing secure. How could he have not included me in his will?' Edward was becoming hysterical. He downed another brandy and lit another cigar from his last smouldering stub. Turning back to her he added, 'There's so much we want to do, so much I want to give you, and it all needs cash, Darling. Cash! This is all so unfair!'

'Well let's think a minute. What exactly is the situation, what do you have?'

'I don't know! Lord Wigram ran through it all after the reading, stating I was to have all the substantial benefits I gain as my position as king. However, it's not personal assets as such.'

'Maybe so, but it's yours to do as you wish, isn't it? You must have inherited some property?'

'A 'life interest' in Sandringham and Balmoral. Then, Wigram insulted me by telling me the details: Duchy of Cornwall £364,000 a year, and £425,000 to be received from the Duchy of Lancaster,'

'What about the civil list? That alone must bring you in a decent amount of money?'

'Over 2 million, but...'

'Well then, David!'

'I know. There's also the gold at Buckingham Palace. I hadn't realised it's worth over 10 million.'

'And all the artwork and jewellery - that must be worth a fortune!' Wallis said, touching her bracelet.

'I know, but it's not really ours to dispose of how we like, is it?'

'I don't see why not!' she snapped back.

'Hmmm. It's not that simple. I'm going in there tomorrow to make sure I get every penny I'm owed, as Duchy of Cornwall.'

'I thought we were meeting with Charles (Duke of Saxe-Coberg-Gotha, Edward's cousin, and a member of the Nazi SS) tomorrow?'

'We are, Darling, don't worry about that. Oh, and did I tell you I saw von Hoesch today. I made a point of telling him that we'd love to visit Germany, and how we really wanted to see Hitler's 'Olympics' this summer.'

'Good, there you go then,' leaning in affectionately, 'something good came out of today after all.'

Wallis titillatingly stroked the back of his neck, sending a shiver down his spine. 'You did praise Ribbentrop to him, didn't you? He's done such a good job on that shipping deal.'

'Of course,' he said, then changing the subject, 'Come here, I want you to hold me tight tonight.'

The solicitor and other members of staff were so outraged by the new King's behaviour that they immediately resigned from their positions: not wanting to have to deal with this insensitive king, some gave delayed dates but resigned all the same.

The first thing the King did with his new-found position was to order a replica of the royal Buick for Wallis's sole use, he was later to also settle £300,000 on her, this sum was almost a third of his life savings, and realising, suddenly panicked, withdrew his offer and reduced it to £100,000.

'We've so much to do!' Wallis drawled.

She was being lead through the corridors of Buckingham Palace. It was weeks later, and they were deciding what to do with 'this old mausoleum', as Wallis called the palace.

'Firstly, we'll get rid of most of the staff. Their appearance is not right, some of them look like they've been here forever. We've gotta clean out the deadwood and start afresh. I think the whole place needs an overhaul, don't you?' She explained in that way that made Edward comply with her. She was taking the country's heritage and throwing it away on a whim.

'I've decided Lady Mendel will do the refurbishments.'

'Do you think that's wise?' Edward asked, taking into consideration his past with Lady Mendel. He didn't wish to 'rub her nose in it', as such. Wallis was loving every minute of her newfound position loaded with increased power and prestige; she just couldn't pass up the chance to throw her weight around, and place people in their pecking order.

'I think she would really bring the ol' mausoleum up to date. Out with the old silk tapestries and velvets,' Wallis announced while sweeping her hand round the room. 'All these ancient hangings everywhere are so passé,' she paused for effect, 'and in with the chrome, green paint, and angular patterns. Let's make this palace fashionable, up to the minute. Reflecting our good taste. That'll be our stamp on this mausoleum! Wha'd'ya'think?'

Wallis may have been able to control the redecorating, and the sacking of the staff that treated her with distain, but as to the ladies-in-waiting: she had no control. They were against her, and even went out of their way to avoid her; it was known one even dropped her handbag deliberately rather than having to shake Wallis's hand. Wallis had made many enemies during this shake-up.

The ladies-in-waiting, of a higher stature than Wallis, were disgusted that a married divorcee should be using their dear David so blatantly, and they were damned if they were going to treat her with anything other than contempt.

As for Wallis's marriage, that was a subject in discussion. Ernest had tired of his slightly sado-masochistic relationship he held with Wallis, as the 'cuckolded husband', and had unintentionally fallen in love with Wallis's recently widowed friend, Mary Raffray.

Ernest arranged to meet Edward. Ernest wanted to explain he'd really had enough of this whole situation. Wallis was going to have to choose between them. He wanted to know what would the King do about her decision. Would he marry her? Edward, it is known replied:

"Do you think I would be crowned without Wallis at my side?"

It was then agreed and arranged that Ernest would end the marriage on the condition that Edward promised to be faithful to Wallis and look after her whatever: come what may.

Wallis however, unaware of this meeting, had expressed in her letters she was fearful that Edward would want to marry her. This was something she didn't want. She was infatuated with Ribbentrop and Trundle. The King was important to her as her ticket to being treated with high esteem in society. With this 'golden ticket' she was able to walk above her station.

Oddly enough she was madly insane with jealousy when she found out about her friend Mary and her husband Ernest. It seemed she was to be exempt from judgement of herself; but full of it for others.

Chapter Twenty-Six

Sunningdale,
Summer, 1942.

Gwen stayed there, on the floor of the shed, like a wounded animal curled up in the dark in a state of shock; until finally, she came round enough to gather the strength in her legs, pull herself up and make her way back along the path. As she stole into the house, her father, who'd been comatose for hours, came out of his groggy, drugged sleep to the sound of the clunk of the latch on the back door. At first, he thought he was imagining things; seeing an apparition, a ghost of a frail figure in a white sheet wafting along the corridor. It wasn't until he heard the bath running that he realised it must have been Gwen. He called out, but received no reply, as she still could not speak; lost in her world, unable to face the real world. As she sank into the bath, the hot water swirling up around her, steam rising, seeping into her very being she started to come back, bit by bit, breathing life back into her bones. She took hold of the soap; with its reassuring smell evoking cleanliness and floral scents she pretended she was covering herself in flowers and washing away any memory of the incident. Delicately humming and treasuring herself as if she were glass, she washed away the mud, blood and tears, only to reveal the already forming bruises. She decided these bruises were blossoms, petals of flowers covering her skin, as she poured the water over herself. She was a long time, lost in the world of steam and imagery. By the time she emerged; powdered and creamed, having covered herself in her scent; she was sure there was no trace left of the smell or any last residue of body fluids of that man on her. She hoped this would help eradicate the horrific rape from her mind, having washed it away, imagining the evil leaving her body and draining down the plug hole.

What else could she do?

She couldn't say anything, she couldn't do anything. She knew Victor meant what he said. As desperate for the arms of Les to comfort her as she was, she decided she couldn't tell him: he'd be so mad he'd do something he'd regret, let alone the fear he'd never look at her the same. She didn't want him to think of his wife as a violated victim. So, she tried to lock the memory deep within her subconscious and throw away the key, but in doing so her mind became only more troubled under the strain.

Her father asked her about the bruising on her face,

'I slipped outside on the path, Father.'

She looked at him lovingly; but he noticed her eyes were glazed, as if living another life. When the German didn't show the next day, or the day after, he only hoped that his fears were not founded and that the snake of a man hadn't hurt his Gwen. The bitter taste of truth hung in his mouth, and he had to question Gwen, only to get some babble about roses and how early the blossoms are this year.

The feeling of inadequacy engulfed George. He couldn't bear it. He had to let it rest, glaze over the situation; but it hurt him deeply, believing he was at fault. His feeling of guilt led to physical pain, and he was more uncomfortable than ever: his moans became deep and mournful.

A different German, Pieter, came to the house to help. Not a kinder, gentler soul could have replaced the viper. Pieter was really a schoolteacher and herbalist; but had been dragged into the war, threatened by the Nazi's. He hated the whole idea of the war, especially the anti-Semitic sentiments, believing in nature and the beauty of the human race.

Pieter arrived saying he was to replace Victor, explaining that Victor had been disciplined and moved to another base after having started a fight, leading to major disruption. As he explained, Gwen's father looked at him, searching for answers in his eyes as if to see if he knew anything about the other day. Pieter openly gave his eyes, with understanding of what George was searching for. Maybe Pieter had heard Victor bragging, or rumours, but George was only too glad that Pieter was here in exchange.

Gwen was so confused and afraid, she couldn't bring herself to look at Pieter; not in that uniform; the memories were too vivid, the flashbacks too real so ran to her sanctuary - the kitchen.

'Excuse my daughter. She's had a hard time recently.'

'Haven't we all,' Pieter said gently.

They talked late into the afternoon. George was glad for the company, even if it was a German. They discussed his fall from the roof, the medication he was given, and the healing process. Pieter had a number of herbs he was going to find and bring to ease the muscle swelling, hoping to ease the pain. He explained how he believed in Pranic Healing, offering to perform it if George wished. Laughing, George was a true sceptic to that sort of thing, he replied,

'One step at a time, eh! I'll give the herbs a try though!'

Eva had heard the news that they'd changed the German helper, after going days without.

'I don't like the sound of that,' Sam said while she was telling him.

'It'll be ok, I'm sure.'

'Well, I'm going round to check, just for my own piece of mind.'

'Maybe that's best then,' as she rolled her eyes. She had so much to do herself. She couldn't really spare the time.

When Sam did make it to Gwen's she was incredibly evasive, drifting out of the room when he entered. Her father also seemed unsettled. There was something in the air, but he just couldn't put his finger on it. Gwen didn't have any light in her eyes, she was as if in a cloud, muttering things about Les as if he was still at home. Sam couldn't bear to see this; something was wrong he knew it. When he came to go, he reached out for a hug goodbye, and for once, she allowed him to approach her. Hugging her he said,

'I'm here for you, Gwen. You know that. Don't you?'

Gwen looked at him with burning secret tears of fear in her eyes and gripped his jacket so tightly with her fingers, hanging on for a brief moment, then let him go. She didn't dare tell him so turned away and headed back to the sanctuary of her kitchen. It was at this point Sam decided he would personally keep an eye over her. Les may be away; but he wasn't. Tough if his brother didn't like it, someone needed to look after her. He could feel her fragility and his heart just yearned to protect this delicate rose from the harsh winds of reality.

Chapter Twenty-Seven

Windsor,
Spring, 1936.

It was now late March and spring had sprung. The now King Edward, absolutely blinded to the reality of Wallis's actions, and so sure of his feelings for her, was excitedly optimistic of their future. He thought he could see a way forward for them to be together, so, gave her his most extravagant gift yet to celebrate.

'Open it, open it!' he said, his eyes shining with delight.

He'd placed a Van Clef and Arpels bracelet box on the bed. Opening it up, she saw just a beautiful ruby and diamond bracelet, but this was no regular ruby and diamond bracelet: the stones were immaculate. Every ruby was of the highest quality from the Burmese mountains; where one finds the earth's frozen veins of purest corundum, the perfect 'pigeon blood' colour of the finest hue; having been extracted from the earth by the miners tattered hand, taking months to colour-match the stones. And then the diamonds, cut to perfection, sending the light bouncing back and forth with clear brilliance. The gems, together, made the piece a triumph of magnificence.

'David! How splendid!' She reached in and took the fiery cold bracelet out of the box.

'Turn it over...look!' he said eagerly.

'What's that?' she said, as she read the inscription. 'Hold Tight' was engraved on the back. Wallis burst out laughing: a harsh sexy laugh,

'You are disgusting, Darling! But I know how you like it, don't I!' she said, winking at him.

The inscription wasn't necessarily implying a term of endearment, but more likely, as many of the inscriptions, was crudely relating to their sexual exploits. This particular message hinting to the 'Casanova Clip'; a technique that she was said to perform to perfection. She would tightly have a grip around the base of his penis with her hands, then, as he entered her, she would contract her vaginal muscles to titillate the penis head, stimulating and increasing weak penis performance.

'Shall we try it out?' Wallis winked, knowingly lifting her skirt as the King could hardly contain himself with want for her.

These gifts didn't change her attitude to him. She still treated him with reproach, now even in public, nor did she abate from her secret liaisons, nor it seems did she waste her chance at taking advantage of her position relating to top secret documents left lying around and passing the information on to Berlin.

Baldwin, in his biography had stated:

"About Mrs Simpson, greater suspicions existed. She was believed to have close contact with German monarchist circles."

It was also acknowledged in FBI files, a particular report International Espionage Behind Edward's Abdication, stated:

"Certain would-be State Secrets were passed on to Edward, and when it was found that Ribbentrop actually received the same information, immediately Baldwin was forced to accept that the leakage had been located."

The leak was Wallis.

Sir Robert Vansittart, the piercingly astute and daring man behind the British Intelligence, took a strong dislike to Wallis, becoming her arch enemy. He was convinced that she was a Nazi collaborator. He had proof from a Russian secret agent that Mrs Simpson was frequently at the German Embassy.

Whether the King himself was allowing this flow of information was never proved; but for him not to have had any idea of her movements must have been difficult.

On May 4th, Wallis wrote, for her, a rather emotional letter to Aunt Bessie, complaining as usual of the continual strain tearing her apart. She was finding it painfully difficult to "placate and amuse two men at the same time" and to fit into their separate lives (let alone her clandestine affairs!). She was continually tired, nervous and irritable. The emotional, mental and physical stress was taking its toll. She'd also come to realise how she'd outgrown Ernest. Wallis had become accustomed to her lifestyle as the King's mistress, and she knew she'd miss all the perks of her position if the King were to fall for someone else.

The King had no such thoughts in his mind.

'Wallis, we are going to sort this situation out once and for all.'

'Stop being so over dramatic! Everything is fine as it is. Don't push it.'

'But that's it you see. It can't go on like this,' he said taking her hand and looking at her so lovingly. 'You are my Violet Queen, and I wish the whole world to know. I want you to be treated with the respect you so deserve as my love.'

'Oh David! Let sleeping dogs lie,' she said, half-heartedly; secretly enticed by holding such a position, exciting her beyond belief.

'No, you see, I can't. The Government will insist that I make a decision, not that I care, but there's also the censorship of the press -that can't hold out forever. America and Europe are already printing what they like about us. I don't want your reputation to be slandered. The press can be so cruel. I love you; I wish the whole world to know; and I want to marry you.'

'David!' she sighed, exasperated.

'Well, Ernest and Mary are coming over and we're going to arrange how we can get you out of this mess. Then you will be free to be my wife.'

It was arranged that night, as the four of them plotted their futures, that Ernest would be seen with 'a woman' in his bed at a reputable establishment. The 'illicit affair' would be witnessed by the hotel staff when entering with the breakfast tray, thus enabling Wallis's reputation to be kept intact. Wallis, for the entire evening, was so cold and demeaning to Mary, not having forgiven Mary for falling for her husband. Wallis didn't even take into consideration what Mary was doing for Wallis, putting her own reputation on the line for the sake of Wallis's future. Mary was said to never speak to Wallis again.

With everything in position, the couple went off on another of his political holidays. He chartered the Nahlin, a luxury yacht belonging to the eccentric millionairess Lady Yule, and planned to cruise the Mediterranean. It was to be dubbed the "good ship Swastika" by guests aboard, due to the goings on. Once again Wallis's attitude to the King, her criticising him every chance she had, had been noted by the guests unable to escape her screeching voice echoing on board belittling their friend, and were finding it all rather tiresome to witness.

"Wallis was not wearing well" was known to have been said.

The couple's behaviour became extreme: blatantly sleeping together in the private car of the Imperial train, they arrived in Sofia, Bulgaria. The King, not wanting to leave Wallis, refused to get out of bed, even though there were hundreds of schoolchildren with flowers to greet them and brass bands playing to herald the occasion. Wallis's influence was affecting his judgement.

Chapter Twenty-Eight

Sunningdale,
Summer, 1943.

Months passed, George's wounds healed, and Pieter was becoming as if part of the family. He was always so calm and gentle, especially around Gwen, and finally she started to trust him. He was admittedly a godsend during the birth; it had all happened so quickly, and he knew just what to do.

'You really should have been a doctor, or at least medical,' they said, as they thanked him. Little 'Dickie' was born, a ray of sunshine bursting through the clouds of troubled times. Gwen was secretly so relieved the baby hadn't been damaged during the assault.

They couldn't deny things were getting harder. The war was taking its toll; so many had died, so much had been destroyed. The farming was affected, rations were in full force, anything of any 'nicety' was now scarce. Gwen's nerves meant she never really ate much, as long as she had her cigarettes, so the little ones had her share most of the time. She busied herself nervously knitting socks for the front. George was stabilised and more comfortable but still totally invalided. He would never walk again.

It was the nights that were the problem. Gwen had been dealing with so much, keeping it all to herself: the death of her mother, her new baby, her father's accident, the rape, the worry the baby was harmed, and of course, Les at war. Les being away seemed the worst, seemed the way it was to stay; it had now been years he'd been away. She missed his companionship so much, his maleness, their bond, the way he always made her feel secure. She understood he had to be away, but the worry was taking its toll as she yearned for affection, for that feeling of security when wrapped in his arms, especially after the rape.

Then one afternoon she walked in on Pieter and George discussing the war. News had come from the front, and it wasn't good.

'I don't want to hear, please don't tell me,' she begged, and fled from the room, but the damage had been done. That night she came round in cold sweat screaming, 'No, no no!' having had the most vivid hallucination; seeing Les being tortured by Victor. Her body trembling, her heart pounding it was too real not to be true, or a premonition, and fell to the floor in distress, rocking back and forth, calling Les's name.

She longed for Les's arms around her, longed for him to tell her he was ok and they'd be together again, that everything would be alright as she harboured in his affection; but the dark offered nothing but silence and the cold reality of dawn; of being alone with nothing but her demons and the voice of Victor threatening to return. This hit her hard and something snapped.

Gwen became terribly afraid of the nights from then on and hardly slept a wink for fear she'd see Victor again. She thought she'd pushed it all away, only for it to resurface stronger than ever in her subconscious; his evil deadly eyes and the sound of his boots crunching the ground torturing her mind.

Desperate for the feeling of security to keep her stable, of the comfort in the arms of her man to hide her fears, but Les was far away as she fell down the abyss of escapism in any form.

Sam came round as he'd decided, and each time Gwen let her guard down a little further. After a few more months it had got to the point he just couldn't wait to see her whenever he had leave. Well aware she missed Les terribly, but also aware she was becoming more vulnerable, he worried for her and wanted to make her happy in any way possible. Sam thought he felt her eyes were starting to light up when he came through the door. He hoped his presence made her feel better, that deep down, she knew what magic they could have together. He felt her lingering in his shadow, basking in his gaze.

Gwen admittedly did feel better when Sam was around, he was such good company. Somehow, he helped her forget the demons, forget about Victor, about if Les was dead or alive and for a split-second, she could enjoy the moment. She was craving the reassurance of physical contact; she also knew she didn't have it in her to fight the energy between them much longer.

It was at the end of the summer, Sam had been round all day. Pieter and Sam had helped deal with her father, the three men had a good chat, laughing and discussing the politics of the day. Pieter had finally gone back to his base. George was asleep and Gwen was sitting out in the warm sun. She was catching the last healing rays of the day. The colours were starting to deepen and go richer as the sun dropped into a sunset and the roses were abundant, and their scent intoxicating. Sam stood staring at her as the sun lit her hair as if on fire. His love for her was so intense he didn't know what to do. He didn't want to upset her, but he felt he had to be truthful. He had to talk to her. He couldn't keep his feelings within anymore.

She looked up at him, as if feeling his heavy burden, and stood up, turning to approach him as he started to speak,

'Gwen, I just don't know what to do...'

'I know, Sam.'

'But if only you did, my angel.'

'Sam, if only *you* knew...' she said distantly, the pain of fear apparent in her eyes.

'What, Gwen? You know you can confide in me.'

'I...' She couldn't hold it in any longer, but didn't know where to start, 'I'm afraid, Sam, so afraid they're going to come and get me...'

'No one will get you, I'm here now, I promise.'

With all the want in the world he pulled her to him, this time she gave in and came responding to his needs as their lips met. She needed to feel loved, to feel safe, to feel something other than fear. After all these years of trying to deny the pull that their souls subconsciously had on each other they were bound by their lips: in pure passion, attraction, possession and appreciation. They looked into each other's eyes as the feelings they held unfolded like the petals of a water lily, then backed off as she laughed, the first time in ages,

'Oh bugger! Now we're done for!'

'Don't fret, my angel. Please, don't feel bad, guilty...you know...'

'A gift of the Gods to counteract our loneliness?'

'Exactly so,' and he kissed her again until, blushing, she broke the embrace.

Pieter came the next week. He noticed how much lighter in spirit Gwen seemed, she was unusually full of smiles and giggles, a little hyper but happy all the same. She had even made him a cake from the extra supplies he'd been bringing her over time. The little ones were well, but he was worried about her father. George's eyes were bright, but his skin had turned pallid, he had enlarged sores on the verge of infecting, and his pain had also increased again, but he wouldn't hear a word about going back into hospital.

Pieter looked at Gwen and wished that all this wasn't put on such a delicate soul. He'd worked out that she was borderline schizophrenic, and that worried him, as he'd hate for her to be 'treated'; knowing what damage the forms of treatment the hospitals used could do to one's body and mind.

He also knew he himself had fallen for her, as he knew everybody fell for her. He couldn't help his feelings, they were protective, but also incredibly profound. He loved her, no doubt about it. Nevertheless, Pieter decided he would keep it to himself and help her in any way he could.

Aware there was a magic between her and Sam, he didn't linger on thinking about it. He knew how incredibly lonely she was and how little Les had been able to be in England in the last few years: if he was alive at all. They'd not heard a word again for months, not since before the birth of Dickie. So, he really didn't begrudge her if she found a little solace, almost wished it for her.

Within a few more months, her father's health really started to deteriorate, and as he did, Pieter grew closer to Gwen. They would sit and nurse him together, talking in-depth through this hard time. She opened up, finally telling him of her torment, of the continual black cloud hanging over her: the nightmare of losing her mind for good.

'Pieter, it's oppressive. I'm so afraid sometimes. It's there you see, always.'

'Don't let fear get to you, as that is all it is.'

'I know, but my mind plays tricks on me, it's so real. It plays with my conscience, tells me Les is being tortured because of me, even dead, tells me I'll end up like my grandmother, naked and abused, strung out in those horrible institutions. I have the most horrific nightmares...flashbacks...and,' she paused, pushing hair from her eyes and biting her lip, 'I know it's around me. It seems worse this time, the demons...' Then shook her head as if to shake away the torment. 'I don't want to lose it again.' Her hands noticeably trembling as she lit another cigarette.

'You won't, you're doing well, you're still with us! Gwen, it's understandable you're a bit anxious at the moment, you're dealing with so much, everyone is. Let me tell you everyone is having nightmares, I know I am. You must do what you can to feel better, happy come what may, as they say.' He smiled reassuringly at her. 'But do you mind asking, are you aware when you have a full-blown episode or do you go off in another dimension as such?'

'Yes, I suppose I am, well, not once they are happening, but maybe at the very beginning. I start to feel more cut off from the world, more separate in a way I could never explain. Not all of it was bad though. I was more aware of the spiritual, the essence between life and objects. I see and hear everything, maybe things that aren't necessarily there for everyone to see or hear, but they are there, I'm sure. Recently it's been intense. It's just I have to keep it to myself, as you can imagine.'

'Yes, I can understand,' he said, but not quite knowing the depth of her torment. 'My grandmater had a 'gift' we called it. She was wonderful. I learnt so much from her and Grandfater. They lived, well... we all lived, deep in the woods, the Black Forest. They lived by nature; the seasons dictated our life and we followed the moon for planting and hunting. I learnt all my knowledge of the healing herbs from her. Many a night she'd sit by the fire, sorting out her drying herbs or preparing tinctures or poultices for people. She was so wise, so...' He lowered his head and whispered from a pained place in his heart, 'she was taken by the Nazi's. They both were. She'd hidden some friends of ours who were Jewish. We'd known them all our lives.' He spoke so slowly as if trying to comprehend and justify the past. 'I've never seen her or Grandpater since.' He sighed, breathing out his sadness, 'I was forced to go to war to survive; but I can feel her - even now. She made me believe there is more to life than meets the eye. She made me promise to 'listen to the plants' and follow the lunar cycles. Grandmater said she used to 'hear messages' from the forest, and I have to say, I believe her.'

'How fascinating!' Gwen was engrossed in what he was saying, reassured hearing there were others that believed in the spirits she saw.

'It sounds silly I know.'

'No, not at all. Thank you so much for telling me this, Pieter.'

Silence fell as Gwen absorbed this information. It had gone dark outside. The fire embers were dying down and a peaceful stillness fell over the house.

Her father slept comfortably that night. She felt a strong kinship towards Pieter which made up for the awful past experience with the German, Victor. She felt as if Pieter had been sent to help her understand it all, not only events but also understand herself. She was so grateful for his help and asked him if he'd teach her about the herbs.

'Of course I will Gwen. It'll be my pleasure.'

'Excellent! It seems so fascinating.'

He kissed her goodnight, as he often did, and as he did she felt his sadness: the weight of the oppression of the situation that he had to endure; that they all had to endure. Somehow, she knew she'd found a real friend, even though he was the 'enemy', she'd found a true 'ally'. She knew he was someone she could count on, even in the most difficult of times or situations. She felt Pieter would be there for her - whatever.

Time rolled by, Christmas came and went, and winter faded out. Finally, Les came back on leave. He was over the moon and Gwen nervously ecstatic. They could be a family, together again. She'd hoped and prayed for these times, for him to be home, but when it actually occurred it was so unsettling, so painfully brief, disturbing her dreadfully. She knew just as soon as she got used to him being around, he'd have to be off again, possibly never to be seen again. She was hearing of many women who were losing their husbands.

Gwen knew this was out of his control, nevertheless, she needed to feel safe, aware she was becoming more vulnerable. She couldn't trouble him with all her worries as she could see he was so affected by the hardships of the war he was almost a stranger himself; her insecurities seemed trivial.

Les's heart broke. He'd been shocked at the change in her, so thin, her eyes drifting into sadness, her incessant smoking with slight tremble of the wrist as she held the cigarette. He was aware of all this but could do nothing. Nothing but hold her in his arms for the nights he was there. But this only made it worse for Gwen. She realised how much he wasn't there, how he couldn't help her through the daily problems, how she didn't dare tell him of her demons, how very different the dark nights were when he was lying next to her, how there were never nightmares, never demons when they were together. Let alone so afraid Victor would return, or that she would become unfaithful just to feel safe again.

And then there was the sad fact Dickie didn't even recognise the face of his own father; not responding when Les picked him up.

Les knew Sam had been coming round to cheer her up, and in the end went to talk to him, he had to thank him for looking after Gwen when he couldn't. Brother to brother, they promised to look after this angel, together, if it came to it. Les was gutted he'd had to do this, aware of what trouble it could bring but had no choice, the thought of his precious rose all alone was worse than he could bear. He could see how difficult it was getting with the rationing and her father deteriorating and was only too grateful for Pieter's help, unaware of the true extent to her situation. How ironic, he thought, there he was, plotting and planning to kill every darn one of the damn Nazi's, when this kindly German soul was the most instrumental man in his household: healing his sick family.

'That's life, God-damn-it! Just roll with it.'

He left, heavy hearted, back to the front, knowing he was losing a grip on his own home, his family; more-over, it was no-one's fault, merely consequences of war.

Somehow, they all scrimped by and with Pieter and Sam around she felt safer and more stable emotionally than she'd been for a long while. The children loved the male presence in the home, giggling and clambering all over them and her father felt more at peace about her than he had in ages. Sam and Gwen inevitably grew closer, with his line of work meaning he was based in England as his injury stopped him from doing anything far afield.

So, Gwen's days became centred round Sam's visit or her chats with Pieter, but she couldn't deny that when Sam was around she felt free, more herself, not afraid. No voices.

Nevertheless, at night she still battled: supressing the visions and voices, the trembling with fear for Les, with her conscience, with intoxicating moments of consuming guilt for enjoying Sam's company. Afraid of her emotions for Sam when she loved Les so much. Les was her love, her life; she hadn't wanted any of this to happen. To calm her confusion, she decided she wasn't to question the gifts of life, just go with them, as Pieter had said.

Her father took a turn for the worse. The doctor had been called, and explained there was nothing else he could do. Pieter was sent for at the base, requested to come and help.

They stayed up all night, the two of them, her and her German friend, lighting candles, praying, wiping his fevered brow and soothing his sores. Nevertheless, they knew with every breath George drew, they were counting down to his last few. Pieter kept her so calm she was able to hold on to her emotions and see it for its reality.

It was true, her father was so uncomfortable. She hated to hear his moans of excruciating pain, knowing she could do nothing. So, now, as the moment was drawing near, she just wanted to love him and make it easier for him in any way possible. She held his hand and prayed, and sang, softly; sang anything, letting her melodious voice waft over him, calming his spirit. Pieter was also slowly chanting, she didn't know what, but together it made a magical, hypnotic environment.

Her father opened his eyes, looking directly at Gwen; his eyes full of love and wonder he murmured through weak breath,

'We love you, Honeybee; you are not alone. Remember that. Your mother and I just love you so ...'

Then the light in his eyes faded, the spark that one measures life dimmed and he was gone.

Pieter held her close as she sobbed. Gwen, through her tears, was saying how she needed to be held. How everyday her father would always hold her when she was little, whenever she was 'ill' he would hold her; how she only really felt ok, in her mind, when she was being held.

Pieter held her, rocking back and forth, chanting his prayers, until dawn. Gwen had a grip by then. Her tears had all run dry, and she kissed Pieter on the forehead.

'I will never forget your kindness, or your strength of spirit in helping me, Pieter.'

He was so touched, he tried to hide it; but she saw the tear, the sole, lone tear of joy and sadness, roll down his cheek.

'None of that. We have no choice but to continue.'

And with that she got up, went to the bedroom, dressed into her faithful navy dress, powdered her sore red eyes and placed a hat, jauntily on her head as she did,

'I have to find the Vicar. I'm going to have to go out there and face the world somehow; it's only thanks to you, I can.' A cool barrier against the grief had momentarily descended.

Gwen did deal with it all well, even if it was all a front, she kept it together. At the funeral she was surprisingly a tower of strength, standing there, stunning in black with a long black feather in her hat that waved about in the wind, reminding everyone of their free spirit as they laid her father to rest.

The wake was a modest affair: Eva, her husband Albert, all the kids, the doctor and a few others. She'd decided Pieter best not attend, what with the German uniform and all. She didn't want him to be afflicted by any animosity after all his kindness. She knew people would only gossip. They didn't have the mentality to comprehend how boundaries were able to be so blurred.

Chapter Twenty-Nine

London,
Autumn, 1936.

Back in the royal world things were moving swiftly for Wallis and Edward. He had moved her from Bryanston Court into an elegant Crown-owned Regency house, 16 Cumberland Terrace, which, of-course, she immediately started redecorating.

It was under heavy surveillance, not just the Secret Service, but also a swarm of reporters from around the globe. The British press was still under autonomy, not able to release anything about their affair. The problem being that this censorship was becoming harder to control as Europe and the United States were not under such illusions: there were no restraints concerning what they could print.

So, the American press hounded her, she was starting to get a taste of how extreme the public lust for snippets of their private lives would tear apart their intimate moments. Associated Press had stated that, to date, the King had lavished over £200,000 (roughly 11 million in today's moneys) worth of jewels on Wallis and that £10,000 of the finest silver fox furs had been imported by a British company from Julius Greene of New York as gifts for the royal mistress. The attention of the American Press concerning her imminent divorce drove her to go and stay at a cottage at Felixstowe to get out of the limelight for a while.

Wallis was incredibly nervous about the impending divorce proceedings, knowing how much of a farce the whole thing was. It was blatantly obvious to anyone in their circles that she was the one having done the extra marital bed hopping. It only needed one slip up and the whole plan would fall like a pack of cards, leaving her humiliated and destitute.

Her nightmares were unfounded. Mary played her part perfectly, having written the exhibiting love-letter. The waiters, the innocent two pawns in this vital game of chess were blindly manoeuvred to state that they, as witnesses, had been the waiters at the Hotel de Paris in Bray, and had delivered breakfast in bed to the accused and alleged lady in question -'buttercup'. All went to plan.

Wallis appeared at court. Immaculately turned out in a royal blue skirt and jacket; pale, with subtle trembles of fatigue; she still seemed to look stoic. The only clue to the beat of her heart and the lie she was pulling off was the tension release of her flicking her tongue around her mouth: her snakelike qualities coming out under duress. The judge disliked her, and subconsciously knew something was afoot, but due to the high profile and public interest in the case, and all the information laid on a plate, it was a simple open and shut case. He had no reason not to say:

"I suppose I must come to the conclusion that there was adultery in this case. Very well, Decree Nisi."

It was all over in nineteen minutes.

Wallis and Edward couldn't risk being formally seen together and had to wait 6 more months before he could publicly make her his once her Decree Absolute was granted.

After the ordeal of the court was over, he secretly met her at Cumberland Terrace for dinner. He wanted her to know £100.000 from the funds of the Duchy of Cornwall Estate was at the jewellers, Van Clef and Arpels, for her to spend as she so wished. He'd also brought over many royal possessions: decadent furnishings, elaborate mirrors, bed linen, royal china and lashings of silverware. He was excitedly setting up their love-nest, but he just couldn't wait to perform the final 'pièce de résistance'.

'David, I really am so shattered by it all. I must have an early night,' she said irritably, not in the mood. The last few days had taken their toll.

'I know, Darling, but I just had to see you...'

With that he placed a ring box on the silk damask tablecloth. Such a small thing, a simple 2-inch squared Cartier encrypted box, but such explosive potential. By opening this box and accepting the ring within, change would swirl like a wind and blow out across the world, affecting not only their lives but many others.

Wallis had expressed a strong desire for a Mogul Emerald but wasn't sure he'd been able to get hold of one. She lifted the lid of the box, and there, glowing in all its power and glory was the most prestigious of stones: a massive rectangular cut emerald, emanating such strength of purpose nothing could take away from its magnificence.

Mogul Emeralds were famed and sought after by the wealthiest and most powerful leaders and families throughout the centuries. They were very old emeralds, dating back many centuries, and who knows, possibly mined many centuries before that. The stones had made their way to India. The smugglers claimed the stones were of Indian origin, from the fabled 'Old Mine' of India, but most have been (in recent years) proven to have come from Colombia, making their way, ensconced, through treacherous trade routes and falling finally into the hands of these reputed Mogul leaders.

The people of India, at that time, used the emerald not just for jewellery but more as a talisman. They believed the stones had the powers of the elements, 'the forces above and below' and could give the beholder spiritual and alchemical enlightenment whilst guarding one's soul. The emerald would enable a leader to be wiser and more powerful, win wars, see lies and deceit around him, and know his enemy. The stone, as an ayurvedic curative of many diseases, was believed to hold incredible healing powers. It was ground and ingested, or worn, and one's health was protected. Also, it was said to be used as an antidote to poison. Some even believed it predicted the weather.

The craftsmen often inscribed sacred religious prayers as scripts into the stone, similar to the historic 'Emerald Tablet'.

One most famous Mogul Emerald was owned by Emperor Jahangir's son the Shah Jahan. He reigned from 1628 to 1656 and owning a massive emerald of 78 carats on which was inscribed: "He who possesses this charm will enjoy the special protection of God." It was his most revered possession.

Wallis had heard of these fabled emeralds and had wanted one like crazy. There were rumours there was one of the finest available and she had to have it: what Wallis wants; Wallis gets.

Edward contacted the famously talented jeweller, Jacques Cartier in Paris and asked him to see if he could get hold of a Mogul emerald for Wallis's engagement ring.

After Cartier had scanned a worldwide search, his spies were led to Baghdad. There was one available, but the syndicate required a hefty price. Once all parties agreed to the 'conditions', Cartier set the stone with all his skill into a breathtaking ring, and it was couriered post-haste to the King in London.

The gossip goes that the King then declared that the price was way too high, and that he would only pay half of the requested sum. This deeply upset Cartier, humiliated after all his time and effort, let alone the fact the price had been pre-arranged in a gentleman's agreement: Edward had already known how much the syndicate was asking before Cartier went ahead with the setting. Therefore, Cartier withdrew the emerald, and was driven to make the drastic decision between himself and the syndicate to cut this fabled massive magical emerald in half, ending up as what is today, the engagement stone, now known to be 19.77 carats. By doing so, Wallis's greed could be met, and Edward's wallet would be able to reach.

It was a tragic start for a couple on the verge of a tragedy. The 'magic' of the stone was ruined, and maybe, from this moment on, the luck of this popular couple took a turn for the worse.

So, there it was on the table that night - the fabled Mogul emerald- shining, emanating the light of life in front of Wallis with the most weighted question hanging over it.

Wallis's eyes stared into the stone, hypnotised by its powers, and she accepted, as we know. Well, she could hardly refuse that stone. If it hadn't been such a magnificent gem, taking her breath away, she may have been able to keep her sense of reason and decline his offer of marriage. Nevertheless, she accepted, and in so doing, hadn't taken the full consequences of her actions properly into account. Wallis had not really intended to marry Edward, she would have liked to carry on as they were, but this was now not possible.

The King, however, was pushing for marriage. He'd already had heated talks in which Baldwin expressed his request that Wallis "abandon the proceedings". All was not as rosy as the King wished it to be.

Chapter Thirty

Sunningdale,
Summer, 1943.

After the death of her father, Gwen fought her fragility, fought her worry for Les and the sleepless nights fretting he'd never make it back; her fear became an abyss she fought falling into, as her mind played tricks on her in the dark dawn shadows, sure she'd heard the sound of Victor's heels coming up the gravel drive to get her.

Spending time with Sam helped banish these fears, without realising needing him more than ever to keep her together. They'd shared nothing but that one kiss, but now becoming so afraid her fears would slip her into another psychotic break she really needed to feel the arms of the man that she had come to rely on.

Sam was aware she needed him. He'd battled hard with his emotions, but he loved her more than anything. He'd wake in bed sweating with desire for her in a feverish trance. He'd see her in his mind, even when he was doing the simplest of jobs. He also battled with his conscience, the fact that she's his brother's wife and how this could destroy the whole family. Les was the strongest spirit of all of them; he worried Les might even kill him if he found out but whatever he tried to think, or whatever angle he took, nothing could dissuade him from wanting to love Gwen.

He arrived late one evening to find her staring into the fire,

'Good evening, Gwendolen,' He liked to call her by her full name, knowing Les never used it; but as he approached, he noticed her hand nervously twitching as she held her cigarette.

'Oh Sam,' she said, her eyes wide with worry. 'I'm so glad you're here.'

'Why you look like you've seen a ghost. What's wrong?' Concern in his voice.

'It's so scary alone here at night,' she admitted, looking up at him, trembling.

So, when he saw her eyes, asking him to banish the nightmares she felt so deep, imploring him to reassure her, to hold her and not let go, he couldn't resist his overwhelming desire to hold her, to look after her, to love her and put her in his arms. He knelt and held her tight, then feeling her need for more he stood.

'Come with me, my angel.' He took her hand and slowly led her into the bedroom. 'Let me love you.'

Then silently, he undressed her, kissing every inch of her skin, blessing her beauty with his lips. Gwen responded, desperate for the reassurance of skin to skin, her fingers slowly undressing him, tantalising his body as she took off his shirt, making him yearn to take her and make every inch of her his. She started to shudder with desire, begging him to kiss her, to take her, murmuring how she needed him, needed his maleness, and that was it -he couldn't hold back.

Sam had to have all those years of restraint wiped away, taken on the wave of true love, or lust or desire or whatever this was he was consumed with. They kissed as he laid her down on the bed. Lifting her legs around his neck, caressing, massaging and kissing them, following them down to the tops of her stockings, buried his face into her French cami-knickers, kissing her and then parted the knickers to one side as he kissed her there, sending shocks of exquisite sensations searing through her body. She reached to find him, feel him, to free the throbbing manhood locked in his trousers. He allowed his body to take over and he just had to be inside her. The feeling of extreme bliss soured through their veins as he entered her. They made love till dawn, deeply, madly, bonding them in bodily paradise. Finally, they fell asleep.

Now that she was on her own at home it was easy for them to spend nights together. With Sam lying by her side she had no nightmares, the demons were silenced and her trembling hand stilled. They couldn't bear to be without one another, consoling each other during such terrible times. As the planes droned overhead, it reminded them of the dangers of war, aware it could be merely a transient affair they clung together in the fleeting moments they shared.

When they were together the feeling of security and stability Sam gave outweighed Gwen's tormented thoughts of guilt. She loved Les deeply forever, but she knew her worry was killing her mental stability; she needed this more than ever, escaping mental torment by diving into the emotions she loved, escaping deep into where she felt most comfortable - that of sensuality. To make Sam happy made her feel good again.

They never talked about tomorrow, or yesterday, knowing that right now was probably the only thing that could be as real as their love.

He'd bought her -no questions asked- a beautiful silk underwear set; French knickers and a camisole top, in cream, with tiny burnt orange flowers on it. She loved it, and lay there, sprawled out on the bed, wearing nothing but her present. She looked stunning. He thought how 'she is entwined with my soul,' as he admired her auburn hair tousled all over the pillow, her skin glowing in that after sex aura and her lips sexily blowing him kisses. Gwen was looking right into his eyes, tantalising him to make love to her again, beckoning him with her beautiful legs, taking her hand down, counting the flowers till they were going towards her own forest. Her breath erotically low she said,

'Get over here.'

As Sam made his way over to her, they heard the gravel path crunch as someone approached the house.

'Oh my God!'

Gwen's face went white as a sheet afraid it was Victor come back for more. Sam stood still for a split second, not sure he'd heard right; but there was no doubt, footsteps were approaching. He knew his brother's light rhythmical footsteps only too well, and there was no mistaking the sound of military boots, that harsh regimental sound one couldn't help but make when walking.

'Les's back,' he uttered in disbelief. Gwen, reaching for her dress muttered,

'But he's not due back for months.'

'Well, he's here now!' Sam said as he scrabbled around, gathering his clothes as quickly as he could and flew out of the bedroom window only for Les to see him, or rather his butt, disappear from the house.

Sam was gone, through the bushes at the back of the house, sprinting for his life as he streaked across the golf course.

Les, like a tiger, had started to chase him through the bush and decided he'd seen enough. He knew it was Sam. He also knew his blood was boiling so high he was capable of anything at that moment. His training came into play, he stood there, frozen for a split second as he decided the best way forward. Les knew if he got hold of his brother right now he wouldn't stop until there was no life left, and even though he felt Sam deserved it, he didn't want the blood of his brother on his hands.

Trembling with anger he didn't know what to do: he couldn't face Gwen, just wouldn't be able to look at her, then he thought of his superior, Major Carper. This man had been such a good influence on him and Les really admired the strategic mind of the major. He decided to go to him. The major would help him to sort this out properly, man to man, not fist to fist; but God only knows how he wanted to lay one on Sam right now.

Les went back to base, walked in a fury, entered the establishment and Major Carper took one look at him and knew something serious had happened. They'd been through so much, out there in the field together. He also knew how much Gwen meant to Les, and this had to be handled carefully. They decided to summon Sam to a meeting here at the base, in a controlled environment, with acting superior officers also present in the room. This would give Les a chance to get some answers from Sam without the brothers going too wild. They gave Les a cup of tea as he sat in wait for his brother. Les had wanted a brandy to calm his nerves, but the major didn't think that was a good idea, given the circumstances.

In the operations room, there at the barracks, on his familiar ground, with his people at his back, Les waited, deadly calm. He took out a cigarette, lit it, and with every drag it was as if he was sucking the life out of Sam, planning how he'd put it to him. Something in Les had snapped, this was more than he could bare. Gwen had been the only thing that kept him going while out there, at the front. The fact his own brother had betrayed him, when Les had counted on him to help Gwen and the children, broke the few remaining tattered strings of faith in the human race that Les had left. He was never the same again: his heart hardened.

Finally, Sam and his superior officer had made it over. Sam entered the room, the fluid way he moved not giving away a thing, but his eyes too bright, too quick, to be innocent,

'Hey Les, what are you doing here? What's all this about?'

'Don't you feign surprise with me,' Les said, slowly forcing every word out.

'Easy tiger!'

'Don't address me or even look at me! I'm going to have you.'

Sam, shifting in his seat, said, 'You're not threatening me, are you?'

Les looked right into his brother's eyes and replied, 'I know what you've done. I just want everyone else to know what an untrustworthy, conniving, worthless adulterer you are.'

Les's superior cut in, 'We have called you here, as Corporal Holmes accuses you of the act of adultery towards his wife.'

'Give me a break here Lieutenant Stanton! This man, my brother, is making this up! I mean how could he even know anything, he's never here to know.'

This infuriated Les even more, 'Exactly! That's how you've been able to wangle your way in with my wife.'

Sam's face clammed up, he took a good look round the room, realising the whole situation was starkly serious, he had the feeling this interrogation could get nasty, the officers looked intimidating. The fact was, he could lie till he was blue in the face, but not to Les. His brother had always been able to tell when Sam was trying to pull the wool over someone's eyes.

'We are here for you to confess to your acts of adultery against Les's wife.'

'Les this is stupid, is this all really necessary?'

Les just stared, deadly cold, directly at Sam, piercing his conscience.

Sam felt any friendship left, due to the fact they shared the same blood in their veins, had disappeared. It was as if he was sitting in front of a total stranger. War had made Les hard. How could Sam explain to such a man how he'd loved Gwen from the moment he met her at their flat in Birmingham; how he'd hated to leave her alone every evening with this war going on and raids overhead; how he felt he had to look after her while Les was away; and how he knew deep down, she'd been raped by the German. He knew Les wouldn't understand any of this.

The same way that Les knew he'd also broken his own heart leaving his sweet vulnerable wife each time; having to go to war; how just the thought of her had been the only thing that kept him going and had given him the strength to crawl out of the trenches alive; how the solace of her arms was the only place in the world he ever wanted to be; and how he would go to war, do anything, to protect her.

They stared at each other, as if transmitting all this: their fears, their sorrow, their love for the same woman.

‘Can’t you just be bloody truthful for once? I want you to admit what you’ve done. Admit it!’ Les beat his fist down onto the table with all his rage rick’o’shaying throughout the room.

‘Ok Les,’ Sam whispered in a sigh, his energy spent.

There was nothing but the truth left, and no corner to run to but admit to what he lived for. He didn’t care what they did to him: court-marshal or punishment. His brother deserved to hear the truth. He deserved to be treated with respect.

‘It’s true.’ Sam hung his head and continued, ‘I’m sorry Les, I’d apologise, be full of remorse but I’m deeply in love with Gwen. I have wracked my conscience many a time for an answer. I truly am a brute to come between you both… It’s all my fault. You mustn’t blame her in any way. I’ll take my punishment but just don’t blame her. Don’t stop loving her, she needs love you know.’

‘You think I don’t know what my wife needs. Shut your mouth, Adulterer!’

‘Corporal Holmes, calm down. That’s an order!’ Sam’s Lieutenant was serious.

The brothers both looked up at the same time, and realising he was talking to Les, they looked at each other and a truce fell over them. They loved one another, they’d always been close as children, and this situation was awful, but a form of peace had been found.

‘Promise me,’ Les stammered, ‘Promise me, you’ll NEVER see her again.’

‘Anything you want, Les,’ Sam said slowly, his heart splintering into pieces as he uttered the words.

Les was no fool; he’d known the risks when he’d asked Sam to look after her. He’d been aware the power of the love between Sam and Gwen was stronger than he could ever have with her. He couldn’t give Gwen the same passion she desired and had found in Sam’s eyes, but he’d hoped theirs was more lasting, more real, more secure. Les’s feeling of inadequacy was to last forever. That was the saddest thing to come out of all this, as Les had been so caring, so loving, so complete; but now was torn apart and emotionally frozen.

He decided he wouldn’t take his leave; he’d stay in the barracks. He was too ashamed to see her, knowing she’d loved those stolen moments with his brother. He also felt guilty; guilty that he’d not been able to do what he promised and look after her through all life’s troubles, knowing she needed someone to be there for her, whatever. He needed to get his sense of pride back, so stayed there, at the bar, staring into a bottle till there was nothing left. Then slept. He slept for two days and not once went to see Gwen even though his division was to leave on their most dangerous mission yet.

Chapter Thirty-One

London,
Autumn, 1936.

The government was furious that Wallis should still be continuing her blatant affair with Guy Trundle: "It's one thing to cuckold a prince, it was quite another to cuckold a king."

They expressed to her privately that she would never be able to be queen, hoping this would dissuade her, explaining how she would never own the title 'Her Royal Highness'. Wallis could have the title of duchess, but she would never be on the official Civil List, so would never earn an income from her position. If they were to have children, they would never be able to rise to the throne or inherit the wealth of the monarchy.

Wallis felt threatened by all of this and was becoming increasingly paranoid that there was a plot to assassinate her, to save the monarchy from ruin.

'David, this is all getting too much for me. Can't we find a way to stop all this? I've come to the conclusion it's not worth all this heartache. You must think of your position and your country first.'

Edward looked distraught, and took another sip of brandy as Wallis continued,

'I hate being hounded like this. I think I'll leave the country. It's for the best. You must see that. Everyone is against us being together. Then, if possible, I can come back once this has all blown over and you are crowned king.'

Edward became mad with rage,

'I'm not bending on this one, Darling! You must understand, I love you. If this government won't approve our marriage, then there's nothing other to do than leave this torturous throne. I want you, Darling, YOU!'

Wallis couldn't believe what she'd heard him say, realising her pleas were futile. She never thought it would have come to something so utterly drastic as this. She knew the cabinet were aware of her other affairs, secretly understanding their resentment towards her. Tears of guilt and frustration ran down as she tried once more.

'No, you can't do that! You can't give all this up, just for me, you can't!' she said, changing tack; realising full well it was her manipulation that had led him to this decision. 'You must let me go, even just for a while. This is your country. They love you.'

'And I love you. I'm not hearing any more about it. I will consult Sir Hoare and summon the Prime Minister. I'll threaten them with abdication and,' he paused, taking another massive gulp of brandy and a long drag on his cigar, 'this will all come out in our favour -just you see if it doesn't.'

At which Wallis turned and sobbed even harder, knowing Edward was facing a losing battle for a woman that didn't truly love him.

'They won't want me to leave the throne, don't worry.' Nevertheless, his words had no strength to them and fell flat.

It was later made perfectly clear to Wallis that there was now no middle ground. The cabinet had decided there was absolutely no possibility of a morganatic marriage in which she could stay in the country, explaining how they held her responsible if the King gave up his throne. She was to leave him alone, for good, or he would have to abdicate.

Wallis was also receiving threatening letters, being followed, and then a plane of glass had been broken next door to her home, panicking, she asked for her security to be increased. This all was making Wallis a nervous wreck. She couldn't sleep for her guilty conscience and if it wasn't for her Aunt Bessie by her side she may well have collapsed.

Edward met Wallis at Fort Belvedere. They went for a walk down near the river at Virginia Water. The freezing fog was swirling around, making everything eerie and suspicious. They were on edge as it was, and she clung to his arm.

'David, I long for the balmy days on the Riviera when everything was simple.'

'Well, I think it's best that you do get away, for a while. I've some bad news.'

'Not worse? Things can't get any worse, can they?'

'Well...'

Edward stopped walking and put his arms around her, bringing her close, pulling up the collar of her coat, in an almost protective manner. How the roles were being reversed.

'The thing is, Darling, it's becoming totally out of my power to protect you...' he sighed, looking deep into her eyes and whispered longingly, 'us.' His breath lingered and the sound of the word 'us' swirled around, lost in the fog. 'The cabinet will not cover for us anymore, and the damn English press are about to have a field day. We've been lucky it's lasted this long without any leaks, considering European and American press have been onto us for a while.' He kissed her forehead. 'Oh Wallis, I can't bear the thought not being with you, but I hate to think how the press may rip you apart. They will hound you like a wild fox. I need to know you are safe.'

'Oh my God! How long have we got?'

'Not long I'm afraid. It's best you make tracks as soon as possible.'

'I'll go to Herman and Katherine's.'

'I want to make sure you're safe, you must take my bodyguard with you.'

'This is serious, isn't it? I might even be assassinated en route. Is that what you're saying?' Wallis's fear-stricken eyes looked upon His Royal Highness.

'Don't exaggerate, Darling. You're exhausted. Just remember this will all work out for the best: we will be together. I'll come to you as soon as I can,'

The fog swirled around them. They braced themselves and headed back to the house. Wallis immediately started packing a suitcase and summoned for the rest of her things to be sent on to Cannes. That night, fearing for her life, she wrote a will and increased her jewellery insurance.

It all happened so quickly, they only just caught one last glimpse of each other the next day, Saturday 3rd of December. She was packed and ready to leave, leaving with only the briefest of goodbyes. Wallis kissed him, but they had to get going,

'Wait, I almost forgot!' producing a bracelet from his pocket, 'Give me your wrist,' he said sadly.

She extended her hand, he looked at her, seeing the anguish in her eyes and placed the lovely ladybird bracelet on her wrist,

'It's inscribed: "Fly Away Home..." Wallis, wait for me, however long, because I can never, and will never, give you up.' He paused with emotion in his voice, 'I will be flying back to you as soon as I can. Wherever you are is now my home.'

Wallis was ushered out of the house, herself and Perry -the trusted friend and personal bodyguard to the King- and into the awaiting car. The Buick swung out of the drive, heading for the coast on this cold and foggy night. Waiting there on the quay for the boat to take her across the channel Wallis felt like a victim of circumstance, an evicted political prisoner. She conveniently forgot how she'd schemed against the country, doing anything she could to help the Germans with her clandestine spying escapades.

The harrowing escape had only just begun. They were racing against the press all the time. At one point in France the press caught up with her, leading to a dramatic escape being smuggled out of a hotel kitchen window; foot in sink and out she climbed. All rather unglamorous! Her usual lust for adrenalin fuelled escapades had drained out of her and been replaced with a sense of fear.

Taking a great risk, desperate to speak to Edward, she famously placed a call to "Mr James" (Edward), begging him not to abdicate for her:

"On no account is Mr James to step down. I implore you, get some advice. Talk to your friends. Do nothing rash. I will go to South America or somewhere..."

The line crackled and rang off, but it was to no avail. The power and influence she once held over him had disappeared momentarily in his fevered righteousness. If only she'd followed her instincts.

In all the kafuffle it's known she accidentally left her notebook in the telephone booth, this could have been catastrophic as it held all her Nazi contacts. The press would not have stopped till she was brought down. Panicking, trembling, she was in pieces: the guilt of her role in the cause of events was starting to catch up with her. She arrived at Villa Lou Viei a paranoid, terrified, nervous wreck.

It was days later that Edward was finally able to speak with the Prime Minister, Stanley Baldwin. It was a sad affair and both men seemed to be rather distraught throughout the whole meeting. Poignantly, at one point, claimed by Sir Edward Peacock's version of events, Baldwin tried to express that Wallis wasn't the: "type of woman to be queen."

At which Edward retorted:

"So, I can have her as my mistress, but not as my wife. That's fine hypocrisy!"

At which point Baldwin snapped. He'd had enough of this whole charade and let loose, making a comment in direct reference to the China Dossier:

"If a king wants to sleep with a whore that's his private business. But the Empire is concerned if he now makes her queen!"

On this, Edward, absolutely fuming, decided there really was nothing left to do but abdicate. His naivety over the whole situation and his obstinacy in the way he dealt with any form of a solution had driven him blindly to believe he would be best to threaten to resign from his position as monarch. His family had closed their doors, disgraced by his actions. He cried at his mother's knees; but she could offer him no solace. He, on the verge of suicide, could see nothing in his life but the love of his Wallis. He had so much but gave it all up for so little. He knew if he carried on the country may even rally into a civil war, split by controversy, tainting his reign forever. Let alone the realisation that if Wallis became his wife, his queen, her unpopularity within certain political and religious circles could destroy her.

Wallis, now ensconced behind the safe walls of the villa, fraught with worry and freezing in the cold damp winter waited with bated breath. She even famously wrote a statement to the press, stating how she would give him up: "to withdraw forthwith from a situation which has been rendered both unhappy and untenable."

Also, saying to Goddard in his urgent visit to the villa, that she: "would do anything to keep the monarch on the throne."

This did not reassure the needed parties enough, knowing how this would only endear her further to Edward.

This was all futile as Edward had decided what he was to do, and it was already in motion. His relief at the decision of abdication had given him hope for a future beyond all this. The legal and financial arrangements of the abdication nearly made him change his mind. He'd not realised, and was shocked, at the thought of giving up the income from the Duchy of Cornwall; something he was relying on. It was also put to him he would have to hand over the estates of Balmoral and Sandringham to his brother. He wouldn't comply. He decided to make his brother rent them from him for £25,000 a year. His demand so outraged all associated, that Baldwin locked him into a deal stipulating that in order to accept these financial agreements, Edward was never to return to England unless invited by the government.

There it was, in black and white: so ending his 325 day reign of England. The only thing left was for him to make one of the most memorable speeches of the century. The whole country stopped for a moment, listening to his heart-wrenching words. His popularity soared, winning his people's hearts at his emotional confession of his desire for love.

Wallis, at the villa, was listening over the radio, along with the rest of the world.

'I can't stand it,' she said, rising to her feet and starting to pace the room. She was furious. 'What has he done! Oh no, no, NO!' she exploded, shaking her head in despair. Then, at the moment Edward talked about living in his: "happy home with his wife and children" she screamed, throwing her glass of whisky smashing into the fire,

'What happy home? I'm never playing happy families!' she shrieked. Ranting, muttering curses, smashing things as she went, she stomped up to her room where she spent one of the worst nights of her life. Her dreams of always getting her way had been shattered. This scenario of being the hated and resented 'tainted woman' that was to be blamed forever for causing a king to abdicate, was never how she'd seen thing's evolving. Although she could still have escaped from it all and gone to Argentina.

In her American fairy-tale of 'ever afters' she'd wanted to stay married to her friend and confidante Ernest, have her exciting escapades, and still be the mistress to the king, enjoying all the perks of power and prestige, with none of the tiresome responsibilities. In the darkest moments of the haunting night, she saw her future; locked to him, both relying on handouts -which she so resented- aimlessly floating around Europe with no fixed purpose. She wrote poignantly: "...the dregs of my cup of failure and defeat...". She'd lost the battle to have it her way, lost it to a stronger empire than herself.

That night back at Fort Belvedere, the now abdicated King was also having a terrible time. With everything that had happened in the last few weeks he was shattered. He gathered some of his belongings, and with his beloved dog Slipper, he ventured forth, leaving behind what he knew and loved as his home.

This last wrench was one of the most painful. He'd loved his Fort Belvedere, his sanctuary away from it all, his gilded cage, his safe haven. All the energy and enthusiasm he'd put into the Fort, getting it exactly how he liked it, was now irrelevant. He looked back and remembered the good times spent with friends, the parties, the status he'd held, and realised it was to be no more.

As Edward clambered into the back of the car it dawned on him; the sheer extent of the sacrifice he'd just made was loud and clear; the reality a bleeding wound of regrets. Only the thought of Wallis drove him on that night, reminding himself it was all for love: not realising unrequited love was all he was really left with.

Chapter Thirty-Two

Arnhem,
Autumn, 1944.

Les went back to war angry and dangerous. He was a brilliant soldier and now had that element of bravery that only one who didn't care if he lived or died could have. His risks were lethal; nevertheless, they luckily paid off. The mission was to get into position; his taking over two months, crossing through France, Belgium and into Holland; then liaise with other battalions. Once together, take out significant bridges and hold Arnhem as theirs. This strategic manoeuvre was quoted to: "to save the war."

It had been Field Marshall Bernard Montgomery's vision to have a single thrust north. He believed if he could secure key bridges and towns of the lower branches of the Rhine he could significantly weaken the German force, cutting them off and bringing them to their knees, thus enabling to gain position and power greatly needed to turn the war around.

The war had become such a desperate situation it led to such a desperate measure as 'Operation Market Garden'. The plan was for 35,000 men to be dropped behind enemy lines, or positioned on the ground, and make their way, from 9 to 300 miles; during which they were to take ownership of the bridges, and the main objective, Arnhem itself.

The whole operation relied upon communication and coordinates, which would all be transmitted by radio, and all supplies then to be dropped in by air, where and when they were needed.

The Wessex Division, XXX corps, Kings own Scottish Borders, Polish Parachute Brigade, all Paratroopers, Kings Royal Rifle Corps Divisions, British 2nd Army and many more were included in the operation.

It sounded a fantastic idea, if all went to plan. There were those that tried to warn General Montgomery that the plan was flawed. It had too many loopholes; even reconnaissance had photographs showing German tanks in the area; however, advice was ignored, and orders were to go ahead.

Les, being part of the Kings Royal Rifle Corps had the hard slog of making it through France once they'd been dropped. Somehow, making their way up through the Netherlands, inch by inch, they fought their way into position. They were to link up with the 1st battalion, in the 4th Armoured Brigade that were then to link with 1st Parachute Division.

Every day was survival tactics; every day they ended starving and exhausted. Les's foraging skills had become a finite mastery: this and his wits helped to keep his major and crew alive.

It seemed like they'd been walking forever. It was the 17th of September 1944 and the first wave of paratroopers were being dropped in. It was meant to be simple as the gentle Dutch villagers were not to be a problem.

The first major problem they encountered was that the area was heavily occupied with the enemy. Not just any Germans, but the Panzer Division, known by reputation to be one of the deadliest. The Panzers were hauled up in the surrounding countryside, taking a 'well-earned rest' before embarking on their next mission with their new Tiger Tanks. The 9th SS Division were also with them, with their 'zooped-up' Sturminaubize 42 tanks: these machines were way beyond anything the Allies had rolling along the only road towards them. Not only that, but the German 20mm Flak guns were on the lookout for any aircraft flying overhead.

As soon as the allies tried to communicate to ascertain each other's whereabouts by giving their co-ordinates, the second major problem unveiled itself. Due to the terrain, the radio waves couldn't transmit through the dense forest spanning over the flat lands of the area.

There was no communication between the troops or with England. At best it was intermittent and unreliable, if at all.

The third disaster was a natural one, one that hadn't been predictable: the weather. A blanket of thick fog rolled in on the 18th of September and suspended all flying. This put a halt to any supply aircraft getting through to drop vital ammunition, equipment, or basic reinforcements.

Not able to alert HQ in England, nor able to communicate between each Division, the plan unravelled quickly: for the worse. Many were killed in the first few days. Progress was impossible. The German tanks were a wall of steel. No one was able to get anywhere; let alone to where they were meant to be.

By day 4, they had been brought to their knees: shot down, blown up and pushed back. A desperate message was sent out over the radio, hoping for it to reach England. It fell onto German intersecting ears instead:

"Out of ammunition. God save the King!"

Somehow Les's small crew had made it through. They were at the bridge they were meant to blow, before heading on only a few miles to their destination, except for the crucial fact that they were on the wrong side of the bridge. The problem was the Germans had hold of the bridge, with their tanks positioned all along it, and both ends secured.

Major Carper decided to haul up, half a mile away, out of sight in a barn, and lay low. What could they do? They kept trying the radio, but to no avail, and there was no sign of the 4th Armoured Brigade. There were Germans all over the place. Les's nightly foraging wasn't cutting it, and they couldn't risk lighting a fire to cook the only thing he could find, which were potatoes. They couldn't understand why they neither heard nor saw any sign of the supply aircraft. They knew they were near a drop, but the rendezvous position was the other side -the now German occupied side. They couldn't get through to HQ to warn them and arrange different drop co-ordinates. It had been days now and things were getting drastic.

'Oh heck, if only we could blow that bridge, that'd slow them Gerry's down.'

'Wouldn't it just!'

Finally, after days, the drone of the supply aircraft was in the air.

'Oh, no! This is the worst! Don't tell me we're going to have to watch our supplies fall over there. They're going to love this - receiving our goods!'

'I can't stand this!' said another.

This was happening all over, as still no communication was able to get through to alert HQ. Major Carper had to get his troop back on track.

'Pull yourself together, men. It's not over yet.'

'Well... there aren't many fat ladies round here to sing, is that it?' joked another, trying to make light of the nightmare they were in.

As the supply parachutes rained down through the sky, Les sat, intently watching.

'You know, Major, I don't think they could see the one that fell to the left of those trees over there.'

'Yes, you're right Les,' the joker added, 'they were too busy celebrating with the other three that landed right into their laps!'

'Give it a break, Jonesy.' Les quipped. 'But seriously, watch! No-one's gone to get that one.'

'Fat lot of good it is to us though.' The joker had lost his humour.

'You never know,' Les said with a spark in his eye.

'Les, haven't you noticed something? Like -it's the other side of the bridge for starters.'

Major Carper looked at Les. He recognised that look, the look Les got when he was up to something. 'What's on your mind Les?' the major asked.

'Well, I don't mean to go on about it; but that drop is ours, sir!'

'I admire your fair reasoning, but there's not a lot we can do about it.'

'I don't tend to believe that, Sir. I need to think something through.'

'Well, go right ahead. It's not like we're pressed for time! I'll even give you my last cigarette if it would help you think...'

'Would you save that offer, Sir. I wouldn't want to waste it.' Les, not taking his eye off of the area where the drop had fallen, sat, thinking everything through, over and over.

'Well, there's no doubt about it, we're going to have to get that -otherwise we're done for. If we can get it, we could blow the bridge. Our lives are on the line here, and not just ours, but all the rest of the lot out here.' Then he took a deep breath and added, 'I've got to risk it.'

'Risk what exactly, Holmes?' The major was concerned, 'Don't just put yourself to slaughter for no apparent reason. You won't make it to the bridge. They'll shoot you the moment they see you.'

'Yes, but they don't shoot everyone do they!'

'Explain.'

'That Dutch boy just strolled over, no problem, no questions asked, nor nothing, Sir.'

'He's Dutch!'

'Who's to say I'm not!'

'Blimey, Les! Do you really think you could pull that off?'

'I have to try.' Les said the words with a cool determination in his voice.

In the barn, Les had found a set of old, worn-out, dirty working clothes and a pair of clogs. He took off his military uniform and boots then changed into the field worker's outfit. He paid meticulous attention making sure it all looked authentic, down to the tatty bit of rope around his waist and particularly the muddy old clogs. He then took up the wheelbarrow that was also in the corner and loaded it with as much of the pile of manure near them that he could and stuck the spade and sackcloth in as well. Messing up his hair and rubbing some of the muck all over him, then treading his clogs into it he turned to the major,

'What do you think?'

'Stinking good luck to you!' The major said with reserve in his voice, not wanting to show his concern for what Les was about to do.

Les slipped out of the barn, unseen, crossed the field and joined the road. There he was, wheeling the wheelbarrow full of manure, whistling that Dutch tune he'd heard everyone hum, and walked jauntily, as if nothing was untoward. He'd become totally inconspicuous, having made himself almost invisible.

The last thing these rather precious, poncy Panzer officers in their fancy uniform wanted to have to deal with was a dirty, smelly, peasant farm worker. As he approached the bridge his heart was going crazy. However, he slowed down and became as if bored with his work, dropping his shoulders down, letting the wheelbarrow lead the way and carried on whistling. One of the officers looked up, but they barely paid any attention to him, engrossed as they were with an approaching convoy of army trucks about to cross, slowly chuffing their fumes while checking paperwork, so he simply waltzed across.

The major was speechless, he couldn't even breathe; he got into position, behind some trees so he could see this incredible feat of fearless bravery for himself. He couldn't believe the heroics of this man. Over the bridge one way, was hard enough, but back over the bridge, with the wheelbarrow laden with ammunition was another thing entirely.

Les made it to the supply box. He was right: the Germans hadn't found it yet. The box was blocked out of their vision by a few large old oak trees among others. He acted swiftly, undoing the box. Once opened, his spirit leapt. He kissed the box, realising how lucky he was: it was full of ammunition -it could have been full of plasters for all he'd known.

'Oh Lord! The men are going to love this!' He thought.

Les loaded what he could. Wrapping the bombs, grenades, fuses and ammunition in the cloth sack and placing them in the wheelbarrow, covering them with manure, then he buried the rest of the box with leaves and earth and prepared to return.

Les had to shake out his joy and try to suppress any excitement within his being by losing the massive grin on his face, dropping his shoulders and his expression to become that bored starving stinking Dutch peasant again.

'They know no different; give them what they want to see,' he kept telling himself as he put one step in front of the other and walked back. It seemed that the wheelbarrow was squeaking louder than before,

'That's all I need,' he thought. He started whistling again to counteract it. Somehow, it all worked. Step by step, squeak by squeak, he approached the bridge.

The Panzers were lounging around, laughing about something. The smell of fine cigars wafted to Les's nose.

'I'll be having one of those myself, one fine day soon,' he decided.

Then, towards the far end of the bridge, one of the younger officers was staring at him. Looking him up and down, he beckoned Les over. Les slowed as he approached the officer, giving himself a second to prepare. His adrenalin pumping as he considered his options: jump the bridge or be shot. He needn't have worried, as the officer looked at the muck in the wheelbarrow. The smell of the manure was so intense the officer waved him away, disgusted. The young man turned to his others, making some remark about the dirty, smelly peasant and they looked at Les as he carried on and laughed at him.

'I'll have the last laugh!' Les thought to himself as he strolled nonchalantly down the road, round the bend and out of sight. He made it through the woods and headed for the barn. Once in sight Les started to softly change his tune and whistle Rule Britannia as he approached. The men waiting for him were jubilant.

'All present and correct, sir!' he saluted.

They all lifted him up on their shoulders and patting him, did a turn round the barn, laughing and boisterous. It was as if he'd just won a home goal, and in a way he had.

'I do believe, Major, I'll have that cigarette now!'

'I promise you this act of bravery will not go unnoticed Les. HQ will get to hear of this; when we get our radio up and running.'

'Anything to get us out of this hole, Sir.'

Unfortunately, as he was of low rank, he never did get any acclaim for his actions. It was just another one of the many brave manoeuvres that went on by so many, during such difficult times.

They did blow the bridge that night; but they never made it to meet up with the 1st Parachute Division.

Chapter Thirty-Three

South of France,
Winter, 1936.

Wallis and the now, Duke of Windsor, had to wait their time at other ends of Europe until the Decree Absolute came through; enduring months of enforced separation - for Wallis it felt like enforced incarceration.

This waiting game was hard on them both. Due to the serious threats on Wallis's life, she had continual surveillance. Armed guards, both British and French Police surrounding the house, along with press reporters; but still she felt threatened. She wrote pained letters to the Duke: "the world is against me and me alone." She, who'd always sought to be the most popular and envied of women, was now the most hated.

Edward escaped, by invitation, to Schloss Enzesfeld (the Rothschild's castle outside Vienna), to sit this waiting game out. He found it impossible to be without his Wallis, mounting up massive phone bills and mooning over her photographs, as he was hit again and again by the political and financial problems caused by their actions. Edward panicked, furious and fretting for many an hour on how they could afford to live in the way they'd become accustomed: now that he knew he was not going to make a penny other than the rents of Balmoral and Sandringham, as he'd been 'struck' from the Civil List.

Wallis, blaming soon to be King George and Queen Elizabeth, wanted Edward to make the new King, Queen, Prime Minister, Archbishop etc...

stop treating them like social pariahs, and to give her the title she believed she so deserved. She expressed her loathing of the thought of becoming: "undignified and of joining the countless titles that roam around Europe meaning nothing..."

At the beginning of March, Wallis finally ventured out to a spring fashion show in Cannes. She bought thirteen outfits in all: dresses with matching jackets, a stunning evening gown of blue-grey crepe satin and an extravagant silver fox fur made of 10 skins.

Finally, it was time to make her way, sweeping up the impressive drive with her friends the Rodgers, to the Chateau De Cande, and await the arrival of the Duke. The chateau was owned by a naturalized American tycoon, Charles Bedaux, a fellow Nazi sympathiser.

Wallis was relieved to be back in the lap of luxury, appreciating the way Fern Bedaux ran her house. She noted the linens, the monogrammed china, the chandeliers, the impeccable staff in livery, the top chefs, the flowers and the overall opulence of the whole place.

During this time Wallis was seen to be wearing a large sapphire ring and not the famed engagement Mogul Emerald. She'd apparently tired of the stone, so, had sought something more flattering to the colour of her violet eyes. Wallis busied herself with designs and fittings for her wedding dress and trousseau, along with ordering a staggering 66 other outfits.

There were a few problems. Firstly, due to the fact that Wallis had no birth certificate as she was illegitimate, there was no certification of baptism required for the marriage; secondly, the problem of the 6-month rule that was to have passed after the final Decree Absolute, before entering into another marriage. They forged ahead regardless, dismissing these as insignificant.

Finally, what they'd been waiting for did come through: the Decree Absolute was granted on the 3rd of May. Edward couldn't make his way to Wallis fast enough. He and his seventeen cases were aboard the 4.45 Salzburg express train to Paris, that very same day, all crammed into his private car.

The crowd awaiting the Duke of Windsor at the Chateau de Cande cheered as he raced by, eager to be reunited with his Wallis there on the steps of the Chateau, in a public embrace. Wallis, her cold guard down, actually glad to see him for once, obliged him with a kiss.

From that moment on they were together again, back to their extravagant lifestyle. The Bedaux were the most entertaining of hosts and they all hit it off. Wallis admired Fern's elegant personal style and strict attitude to the staff, and the Duke appreciated how Charles had risen from nothing by sheer hard labour, particularly admiring his attitude to industrial growth.

'They really are so charming! Don't you think?' Wallis's remark was unusual for her, to compliment anyone.

'Yes, I think they've made quite an effort for us. Touching really!'

'I know! I mean for Fern to give up her own bedroom for me! That's rather generous,' she said, as she stroked the sumptuous ivory silk and satin bedspread, 'I doubt I'd do the same!' She lay languidly across the bed, 'We've so much to arrange. I mean, we do need to set a date, and you've not even made this marriage official yet!' Almost scolding him in a matronly way. He loved it when she took control; happy as a sand boy, to be back under her watchful spell.

'David, Please!' she shouted, as she pulled her angular body up off of the bed and flounced over to the window, half mad at him. 'Concentrate!' She looked out at the woods, to the pine trees swaying in the strong wind and started to despair, 'It's just that we've come this far and I need to arrange all the details.'

He approached her and slipped his hand round her waist. As he watched the trees swaying in the wind with her, he wondered how he could also sway his government - and his brother at that - to accommodate his wishes.

'I just want the day to be the best for you, Darling,' he said, wistfully. 'It seems whichever way we turn, we're up against it.'

Wallis knew what he was referring to.

'Ok,' she sighed, 'What date for the actual wedding? How about the 3rd of June?'

'Well, we've some things to...' Edward stopped mid flow, his head dropped suddenly remembering the face of his father: the face he'd aspired to and been afraid of all his life. 'Damn it, Darling! I can't do that day; it's my father's birthday.'

Wallis looked at him with distain,

'What has that got to do with it? If I remember rightly -and don't take offence- he's dead!'

Edward recoiled from her words.

'Don't I know it!' Referring to the situation he'd been thrown into.

'Well then, this is just one other way to show them that we stand apart. They are the ones that forced us into this predicament; it will show them 'W.E.' are more important than their silly protocol.'

'I don't know. There are my sisters to think of as well; they'd take this quite badly.'

'So what, David! Grow some balls and stand on your own two feet.'

'What about the day after?' he muttered meekly.

'No! I'm sticking to it. I've had enough of them dictating what we can and can't do. I mean, for Christ's sake: you had to abdicate!'

'Oh Wallis,' he sighed, placing his head on her shoulder, 'you don't know the half of it.'

'What?' she said disturbed, 'I knew it! You've been moping around all day. What have they done now?'

'It's been discussed, and it seems it's decided.'

'What? Tell me!'

'Well... they've finally decided you're not to be allowed any of the rights of HRH.'

'You mean, definitely?'

'It seems so, my darling.'

'Don't darling me! What is this persecution against me?' Wallis was furious.

'I don't understand it either,' he was distraught.

'Well, that's absurd! You are His Royal Highness, I am to be your wife, so that makes me Her Royal Highness, and I won't have it otherwise.'

'Between us you always will be,' he said, apologetically.

'Well. That's that! We will announce our engagement on the 11th of May, and we marry on the 3rd of June.'

Wallis walked over to the servant's cord and yanked hard on it, at the same time, turning, announcing,

'I won't hear any more about it. I'm going to order some champagne. We will celebrate this, just you and I. Then you may leave me while I dress for dinner.'

The next day the Duke was sulking, not amused.

'What is it?' Wallis snapped.

'Well, it's just that I go to all that effort, and you don't even appreciate it.'

'What are you talking about?' Wallis started to get agitated and looked at him, 'What?'

'It was embarrassing last night. Announcing the dates at dinner and you weren't even wearing the emerald engagement ring.'

'Oh, for God's sake! I was wearing blue, and this sapphire obviously went so much better with the dress.'

'But I've not given you that ring.'

'Yes, you have -in a way- you paid for it. I ordered it from your jewellers. Doesn't it match my eyes?' holding her hand up near her face and fluttering her eyelids, teasingly. Edward huffed, and thought about it,

'You wanted that Mogul Emerald. I had such a lot of hassle getting it for you! You've no idea.'

'And I do appreciate it! You know I do. I simply wanted something more wearable on a daily basis.'

'Well, you should have thought about that before you chose the Mogul for your engagement ring!' He lit a cigarette and paced around the room. 'It had better be back on your finger by dinner tonight!'

'It will. Do calm down, but, while we are on the subject, there's the matter of our wedding. You see, Manbocher has designed me this glorious dress suit, and it's in the most delicate of blues, he's even named the colour Wallis Blue! Can you imagine anything more adorable!'

'What's this got to do with the emerald?' he retorted.

'Well, the sapphire goes beautifully with the dress. I mean, stunning; and you know what they say about wearing blue and green together...'

Edward spun round, in a rare temper.

'Absolutely NOT! It's out of the question. The emerald is the one I proposed to you with and so it shall be what you wear to be married in.'

Wallis looked at him in shock. She was usually the one with the upper hand. He would bow to her every need and kiss the very ground she walked on, but on this matter he put his foot down. Edward suddenly became the powerful man he had been born and bred to be, dictating like a king. Horrified, she knew to give in on this one.

They greeted the press, on the eve of the 11th of May 1937, relaxed and happy, displaying the emerald for the world to see. From that time on it was a countdown to the big day.

There was the problem of the guest list. London had forbidden any of the Royal Family to attend the wedding. Edward was mortified, not wanting to believe his brothers or sisters wouldn't show. There was also the blow of the announcement in the 'London Gazette' on the 29th of May stating that: "The Duke of Windsor shall... be entitled to hold and enjoy for himself the title, style, or attribute of Royal Highness, however, that his wife and descendants if any, shall not hold said title, style or attribute." This was really affecting him. They also had the problem of who would perform the religious ceremony. The Archbishop of York had put a stop to anyone obliging the Duke, but at the last minute, a clergyman, Reverend Jardine, bravely offered to help, at the demise of his position in England. By the time Cecil Beaton arrived for the wedding photo's everything was sorted and the scene was set: it was simple and elegant, very stylish.

Edward had still been contacting his brother, pleading with him to change his mind: firstly, to allow Wallis the prestige of HRH, and secondly, to let his brothers, the Dukes of Kent and Gloucester join him for his wedding day.

The couple were posing, for Cecil Beaton's famous shots of them looking out of the long French turret windows, when Fruity Metcalfe came and whispered the bad news,

'Sorry old chap. Bertie just won't give in. He's as stubborn as you, it seems.'

Edward was struck hard, he'd been counting on his brother seeing reason and changing his mind, but it seemed that would not happen. He could hardly hide his emotion, gripped with grief at the reality of the situation. Devastated, he retreated for a moment, but then in the true British style of 'stiff upper lip', he pulled himself together and carried on with the photo shoot.

They went back into lunch, then coffees. The butler entered the room carrying the silver trays laden with the days post.

'How many are there today?' Wallis asked.

'Only four hundred and fifty,' Hale, the butler answered.

The telephone wouldn't stop ringing with well wishes and presents were arriving thick and fast.

'How sweet, there's something here from Alberto,' Wallis said, while eying the present from her past lover, Da Zara. 'Oh, and one from Mussolini! How thoughtful!'

Edward approached the table where all the gifts were gathered, picking up the present from Hitler. They opened it to reveal a stunning personally inscribed gold box.

'Well, that's adorable!' Wallis announced, her eyes gleaming.

'That reminds me, Van Clef and Arpels are arriving this afternoon with some presents for you. They're also bringing loose gems for you to have made how you wish.'

'How wonderful, we were starting to tire of that ruby set I've been wearing, weren't we?' She was referring to her huge ruby and diamond feather brooch, her ruby and diamond earrings, bracelets and the ruby ring. She'd worn the set only the other night making every woman's eye's green with envy.

'Well, I thought we needed to mark the occasion with something special.'

The Parisian jewellers arrived with the wedding jewels. They had designed a 'one of a kind' marriage contract bracelet in the shape of a garter, with invisible settings of diamonds and sapphires. Not forgetting the pièce de résistance, the Duke of Windsor's wedding present to her: a diamond encrusted tiara. More importantly, they had the wedding ring; it was a simple band of Welsh gold, the tradition among the royal family for centuries.

'David, I adore the tiara, what do you think?' Turning round to him with the tiara firmly on her head. He'd so wanted to say, 'Fit for a queen', but he couldn't bring himself to do so. He opted with saying diplomatically,

'You are the queen of my heart'.

That night, on the eve of the big day they had a sumptuous supper. Their guests all gathered in their finest as they began the celebrations.

Wallis was bedecked with jewels, including the Mogul ring and the tiara. It was possibly one of the few times she wore the tiara in public as she was soon to be banned from wearing a tiara by the Royal Family: fuelling her hatred for them even more. The atmosphere that night was animated, and the couple excitedly went over their honeymoon plans.

'It'll be thrilling to meet with Hitler!' Wallis gleamed.

'Yes! I must say that will be the highlight of the trip for me. I find what he's doing with the working class quite revolutionary,' the Duke explained excitedly.

'It seems Germany is on the turn; industrially they're really shifting up a gear,' Charles Bedaux added, admiring the German factory policies.

'Exactly! There's so much scope for change,' Edward agreed.

Edward eagerly started to launch into a conversation of his favourite topic, fascinated by the conditions of the working class. On addressing this situation alone, he thought he could win back his country. Charles, a month later, at a press meeting accidentally made a faux pas, explaining how the Duke was touring Europe on his honeymoon with an added desire: "to make a complete study of working conditions in various countries", but then letting it slip, "with a view to returning to England at a later date as the champion of the working class."

This was a loaded bomb: giving London the knowledge that Edward was looking to upstage his brother King George VI and 'take' the country in a political game of chess.

The next day, the wedding day, went according to plan. As they were getting ready in the morning, it's known that Edward, after seeing his mother's handwriting in his prayer book, shed a few tears for the sadness of the situation, he really hadn't wished for it to turn out this way.

Whereas, Wallis, dressed in her 'Wallis Blue' dress, with matching sapphire and diamond jewellery (along with the emerald ring), was said to have looked hard, cold and quietly triumphant.

Chapter Thirty-Four

Sunningdale,
Autumn, 1944.

It had been well over a month since the fateful evening when Sam had been caught 'in flagrante delicto' at the cottage, but Sam couldn't stop thinking of Gwen. They'd moved him, changed his base and posted him further away from her. Sam had promised he wouldn't see her; but he felt he had to, just once, to explain. He knew Gwen would find it difficult to understand otherwise and didn't want her to get hurt in all of this.

Sam had a day's leave so risking it all he went to see her. Arriving at the cottage, with no answer at the door he walked in and was shocked as to what he saw. It was midday but all the curtains were still closed, the gramophone was spinning round, and round, with the record finished, crockery was all over the floor. Pattie was pretending to have a midnight feast, sitting on the floor in the middle of this chaos, and Dickie was asleep in the cot. Gwen was limp, laid out on the sofa. She'd not dressed or washed: she'd not the heart, nor the energy. She'd lost more weight, even though she had nothing to lose, and was smoking cigarettes incessantly, lying there in a haze of smoke.

'Oh, it's you! The one who jumps through windows and walks through doors!' she exclaimed, laughing hysterically.

'Gwen!' Sam approached her.

'I know, you can't be with me, ect, ect, bla bla bla...' She took another drag of her cigarette, then carried on erratically, 'You don't need to explain, though you never did, not one to do as you're told, are you!' she declared as she waved him away.

Sam was distraught. What had he done! She'd taken all this very badly and he felt it was his fault she was suffering so. He drew back the curtains, letting the daylight filter into the room, hoping the sun would change the atmosphere, then went to put the kettle on. Looking in the cupboards he noticed there was nothing in the house to eat but for apples and potatoes, then he remembered he had brought her some chocolate, 'If only I could get some food into her,' he thought. Returning to her he said,

'Angel, we're going to drink this and have some of this chocolate,' as he handed her a cup of tea and placed a piece of chocolate on her tongue.

'Ooh lovely,' she muttered. The medicinal effects of the chocolate melted into her bloodstream. Pattie took a piece and ran out to the garden to see her rabbit.

'Ok, you beautiful thing! We're going to get you washed and dressed.' He couldn't stand to see her like this, so unkempt, for a minute longer.

'Anything you say, Sam!' she said, giggling while giving him a salute. 'Wouldn't like to disobey orders.' Her mood was all over the place, erratic and ecstatic all at the same time.

He took her into the bathroom. He was floundering, wondering the best way to help, reckoning a bath was as good a place to start as any. Hopefully, he thought, it would instantly make her feel better.

The water splashed loudly into the tub and the steam started to do its magic and infuse clarity back into her. He helped her into the bath, pouring in her favourite rose bath oil and washed her beautiful body with all the caring love he had for her. He talked gently, reassuring and letting her know how he would love her forever, how his heart was broken, how he'd had to promise never to see her. Sam described how Les had made it plain Sam could never be part of her life, but how Sam thought of her, always. She wept while he washed her. By the end, she stood up, rising out of the water, her body glistening like a goddess, arms outstretched towards him and said,

'Please, take me to paradise, just once more,' she said as he wrapped a towel around her nakedness. 'I can't bear to be without arms around me,' she whispered.

He couldn't resist the one he loved as she wrapped herself around him, they made their way to the bedroom. He gently caressed her body, and they lay there together, savouring every moment till ecstasy took hold of them for the last time as they shuddered with orgasm, climaxing, locked together.

By the time he had to go she already had that distant look in her eyes again.

'I deserve this,' she whispered sadly, 'I deserve to be left all alone. It's my come-uppance you know. I was told so. I'm a wanton woman.' A tear rolled down.

She was acting strangely and it scared him, she was so fragile and this overloading emotions of guilt, ecstasy, loss, and especially the loneliness, was finally pushing her over the edge.

He was distraught, what could he do? He had to return to base, to report for the next day's operations, but he couldn't leave her alone like this. He remembered Pieter. Pieter would know what to do, so he left a message for him to come as soon as possible.

When Pieter arrived the next day, Gwen was naked on the floor, rambling senselessly, muttering about her being a 'wanton woman', over, and over again. He made her a special herbal tea of valerian and passionflower he had collected, then dressed her like a mother dresses a sick child. He then held her tight, rocking her back and forth as he had done the night her father had died; remembering how she'd explained her father had always done so when she felt 'poorly'.

After a while she came round enough to say, 'Pieter, what have I done! What am I to do?'

'My dear Gwen, you are the loveliest, and your gift to the world is your love. You are so precious; don't forget that. Things are difficult, but that's life I'm afraid.'

'Oh Pieter!' she cried, burying her face into his chest, 'don't stop holding me.'

He cradled her for hours, finally the body had calmed from shaking, and her breathing was less erratic.

'I love them both you know.'

'I know.'

'And, I think, in a way, I love you too.' She placed her lips on his and kissed him gently. 'That's a thank you kiss.'

'I know.' He didn't dare respond, he could hardly speak. His love for her would pour out otherwise and he knew he had to look after this flower in his life, not harm her with more confusion. But she took his hand, holding his gaze, and placed it under her shirt and onto her breast, over her heart.

'Can you feel the love?'

He could feel her pert nipple transmitting the electricity of her body, the energy pulsating through his hands.

'Gwen... Don't!

'You've been so good to me. I'm so lonely without Les now for so long, not heard anything, he probably will never come back after what happened. I even feel he may be dead." Her body trembling again as tears fell. 'I don't know where I'd be without my guardian Pieter. Let me repay you with the only gift I have -as you said- my love.'

She started to undo her shirt that he had so caringly done up for her, to bare her breasts.

'You don't need to do that, Gwen. You're confused... tired,' he said as he tried to do back up the shirt. 'I do love you though...' he said sadly.

'I know,' she uttered, kissing him till he kissed back.

Knowing it was wrong, but only love seemed to keep her sane. Her schizophrenia had turned sexual, the only thing that kept the dark scary thoughts in her head from tormenting her.

By the time Les made his way back home from the traumatic experience at Arnhem, he was a different man. He had seen so many die; whole families and their homes had been destroyed right in front of his eyes. It had been so hard to survive. He was just glad to be alive and that his family, Gwen, Pattie and Dickie were safe.

When Les saw Gwen, it was months later from the 'Sam saga'. Gwen was well into her pregnancy. He had to stop and work this one out. It definitely wasn't his. After everything he'd been through, this was a final blow.

'You left me,' Gwen muttered, distraught. 'You never even came to say goodbye. I didn't know if you were dead or alive...' She finally looked into his eyes, 'You've no idea how much I missed you. Nights were so dark, dawn so scary. I'd hear the worst things on the radio not knowing anything of your where-abouts. All I'd hear about Arnhem was almost everyone was dead: Thousands dead. It seems I've worried for years now.' Her whole-body trembling. 'I get so frightened alone, Les, you know that. You don't even know the worst. Sometimes I feel I'll go mad... seriously mad.'

'Yes, but Gwen, you can't expect me to...' looking at her protruding belly.

She interrupted him, 'I know this is going to be hard for you to comprehend but comfort was the only way I could cope. I don't ever expect you to forgive me; but we do still love each other, don't we?' Shaking so, she grabbed hold of the chair for support, then continued, 'You're my husband. I've wanted to be with you for so long. I would get so worried, go nearly out of my mind,' she said, tears streaming down her face, 'worried you'd been tortured. I saw it in a vision... oh it's so hard to explain...' she said, trying to speak through trembling lip. 'This,' rubbing her belly, her head low with shame, 'is yet another blow the war has thrown at us! Don't think I've not tried to get rid of it because I have. Please don't make me feel any more guilty than I already do or I'll literally burst.'

It was harrowing to see the tortured soul in front of him, no sign of the beautiful effervescent woman he'd married, but he knew she was in there somewhere if he could just look past the neurotic delicate bird trembling with paranoia. She still loved him, he could see it in her eyes, in the blushing way she looked at him. He could also see how fragile she'd become, with her face tormented with worry.

'I warned you I was delicate. You promised me you'd always be there for me...' Gwen said through her sobs.

'I know. I'm sorry; but I'm home now.'

'Please don't hate me. I needed you so much.' Her tears falling like rain she smoothed her face, then looked back at him, imploringly, 'Could you ever love this child like your own, or maybe you'd rather leave? I'd understand. I wouldn't want to be with me, either.'

'How could I ever leave you?' Les said, pacing about, trying to work it out, then stopped, lit a cigarette and turned to face her. 'Gwen, I must ask this, just once - whose is it? I need to know.' He needed the facts but dreaded to hear the name Sam; she replied truthfully,

'I'm not really sure,'

Her trembles turned into shakes as she started to rock back and forth, already very pale and hyperventilating.

'Ok,' he said, realising there was more to this. So, in a regimental manner continued, 'We can get over this. Our love is stronger than any setback and you're right, we certainly don't need any more casualties of war.' He paused, coming to grips with the situation, he lit a cigarette, took a deep drag, exhaled slowly, then said, 'On the condition that from now on we are back together - just you and I. As it should have been, as it will be from now on.'

'Oh, thank God,' Gwen said, crumbling, crying into the floor, 'If only this war hadn't confused everything. I can't stand it anymore, I just can't. If only you knew...' as she hit at her head at the memories, torturing herself. 'Where have you been Les, where? I tried... I can't tell you how much I missed you. I would think of you all the time. I prayed and prayed for you to come home, even used to sing to you at night, imagining you curled around me; but then the cold reality scared me. They said they would come for me you see...at night...' she muttered, shaking and sobbing into her hands.

He knew then that this had been her war, her private battle. She'd had her own fight for survival, be it mental and physical. Nevertheless, they were together now, things could only get better. He'd been lucky enough to somehow survive the war, and he was going to keep his promise he made to her when they married, to be there for her, and look after his queenie, whatever it took.

The war had a lot to answer for.

Chapter Thirty-Five

Europe,
Summer, 1937.

The Duke and Duchess of Windsor set off on their honeymoon. They, and their 266 pieces of luggage headed for the train, the Simplon-Orient Express, touring through Europe whilst waiting for the finalities of the German invitation. The Duke famously greeted the crowds in Venice with a fascist salute, then in Vienna, was known to pass on top secret information to the Italians. English and American intelligence were watching him like a hawk, knowing what a risk he was becoming. They were fully aware he wanted to spark unrest in America, and doing so, hoped to strengthen his semi-fascist 'comeback' in England.

He was also disobeying rules concerning how he was meant to conduct himself whilst visiting these countries, placing the embassies in difficult positions as they didn't wish to upset the Duke, but they also had to comply with their orders. Sir Vanisttart had sent a dossier to every British minister and ambassador in the world, forbidding them to accommodate the Windsor's. They were told not to give them dinner or officially present them to anyone, and certainly not to be met at the train station by no more than a third secretary. Vanisttart had decided that they were playing way too dangerously with the Italians and were too deeply embroiled with Nazi Germany to be swanning around gathering information at the courtesy of the British crown.

The Duke, it's true, just couldn't wait to visit Germany. He wanted an official visit, in particular, a meeting with Hitler. It was finally arranged that they would stay 12 days, visiting 9 cities. The German government generously laid on 2 airplanes and 8 cars for them to use. In reality, the whole time spent in Germany was basically a Hitler-funded-Honeymoon, as special funds were made available for the couple, from the Reichsbank, controlled by the Fuhrer himself.

So, on the 11th of October they entered Germany, only weeks after Hitler had joined with Mussolini and taken Berlin. The couple dined with the Goebbels, Himmler, Hess, Goerlitzer, and their good friend Ribbentrop.

Edward visited one of the modern German factories; three thousand workers, working under the flying flag of the Swastika. The factory had an assembly, concert hall, swimming pool, gardens and fancy restaurant. He then visited the headquarters of the training school of the Death's Head Division of the Elite Squad of the SS. The cream of Hitler's youth. The Windsor's even visited a concentration camp together. When they enquired as to what this seemingly deserted building was, they were given the chilling reply: "It is where they store the cold meat".

Eventually the day came that they'd both been waiting for, the 22nd of October; the day they were to meet Adolf Hitler.

There he was, awaiting them on the steps of his hunting lodge, dressed famously in his brown Nazi party jacket, black trousers and black patent shoes. Hitler had also been looking forward to this day, having watched videos of Wallis over and over again. He found Wallis fascinating and attractive, she was his idea of a real beauty. Interestingly, he could make an exception for her being of Jewish descent. Wallis agreed with his anti-Semitic ideas; but she was for mass exodus from the country rather than mass annihilation.

They all hit it off. Wallis and Edward were entranced by Hitler's strong beady stare. Hitler took them on an extensive tour of his gardens, then Hitler and Edward withdrew into a separate room for about half an hour having a private political conversation. It's known that Edward tried to keep it mainly on the topic of National Socialism, but the real gist of the conversation was Hitler wanting Edward to approve of Germany attacking communism and Russia; claiming it was a threat to both of their countries.

The Duke, then belittling his brother by strategically exclaiming to the Fuhrer: "my brother is weak," hinting that he didn't see King George as a major threat to their plans.

From this moment on the Windsor's were naive to continue believing they were a powerful force in their own right and not -as they really were - a pawn in Hitler's European game of chess.

Wallis and Edward returned to France, from their 'almost' state visit of Germany and carried on making one blunder after another. These were dangerous times approaching and they were playing every card they had badly, with one wrong decision after another. Their choice of acquaintances was as if pulled off the secret intelligence list of the most volatile characters in Europe. They were becoming a political liability and an embarrassment to Britain, let alone a threat to themselves.

Wallis then upped the stakes (sexually unsatisfied in the matrimonial bed) by starting an affair with William Christian Bullitt. She couldn't resist this attractive and wealthy US ambassador to France. When exactly the affair had started isn't sure, but what was sure was this was a dangerous liaison. He was an American pro-Nazi with many connections to German Royal collaborators and had friends high up in the Fascist movement. He was an incredibly engaging person and could have had anyone, but his bisexuality and fear of impotence with women affected his belief in himself. Wallis knew just how to handle this problem. They would meet, as she used to with Trundle, at her dressmakers, at the Place Vendôme, in Paris.

It wasn't long before Sir Robert Vansittart was aware of what she was up to and as in the past, they had to make sure the Duke didn't find out; more importantly, they had to keep an eye on the situation as they knew she would give over any information she could to her lovers. London had to find a suitable spy to keep tabs on her and came up with Lady Jane Williams Taylor; someone who mixed in similar circles.

War broke out, and the Windsor's were placed in a predicament. If they stayed in France there was the chance Germany may kidnap them as accomplices in a plan for the Duke to take the throne. If they went to America, they would look like cowards. They had to return to England and show willing. This was all such fake sentiment as they cared little for helping Britain: planning on taking it for themselves. Intelligence knew this, having to be strategic with the handling of the double-crossing couple. The Duke had met with Hess, this time declaring how he thought of himself: "more German than British", giving comfort to Hitler that they would sway to his side when needed.

They landed back to the misty green lands of England, nevertheless his mother, Queen Mary, refused to see them. The government needed to find a suitable post for Edward, but it wasn't an easy task to find a position that seemed to be worthy of the Duke's stature, with no linked risk. So, they set him up, back in Paris with a dummy post. Churchill had already done the intelligence required for the job, and made sure Edward wasn't entrusted with any confidential information.

No one was happier than Wallis; back in Paris, able to resume her sordid affair with Bullitt and relaying any relevant information she could get on the Maginot line to the Germans.

Within a year King George had to go to the extreme of issuing an order restricting the Duke from even entering British occupied territory. In an offence worthy of a court-marshal, the Duke, fuming, disobeyed this order and travelled north, 'inspecting the troops' close to the German border. He came across information useful to the Germans and immediately wrote a letter directly to Hitler telling him the file was on its way, being carried personally by Charles Bedaux. Edward wrote: "I am hardly able to stress the importance of the information": this was a treasonous act.

Wallis's dressmaker, Anna Wolkoff, was arrested in London for leaking information to the Nazis. Soon, Sir and Lady Mosley were also to be imprisoned; her lawyer Armande Gregoire was proved to be a Nazi agent, tried and imprisoned; Charles Bedaux, imprisoned for treason, would take his own life; her old lovers, Alberto da Zara would hand over his fleet to the allies; Count Ciano would face the firing squad; and their faithful friend Pierre Laval would also be shot for betraying France. Wallis's world was falling apart.

Churchill, unable to forget emotional ties he had with Edward, believing Edward could be nothing but loyal to his motherland, mistakenly decided to include him 'in the loop' when it came to discussing strategic details if Germany invaded England. The best plan now finalised, involving what and where, was then conveyed to Edward, then suspiciously, the information immediately ended up in German hands. Churchill was furious. This was the most devastating leak yet. Whether it was Edward or Wallis who'd initiated the leak was irrelevant. They were ordered to leave Paris as they presented serious security risks; there was even talk they should be brought to England for interrogation, but in a moment of weakness Churchill decided against it.

The couple headed for Antibes. Ribbentrop, continually in touch with Wallis, was still obtaining detailed accounts of their itinerary. It was then reported by the secret service that: "the contacts of the Duchess with Ribbentrop at the Villa (Antibes) became so serious it was necessary for the British government to compel them to move. The Duchess was obtaining a variety of information concerning the British and French Government official activities which she was passing on to the Germans".

Due to the facts outlined in the report, they were ordered by the SIS to leave for Spain at once. The couple then had the audacity to threaten England with non-compliance of orders to return to England or travel on to the Bahamas, unless Wallis was given her title of HRH. Churchill, run ragged, realised the full extent of Wallis's malicious intentions, writing on the 9th of July: "as I told you once before, this is not the first time that this lady has come under suspicion for her anti-British activities, and as long as we never forget the power she has exerted over the Duke in her efforts to avenge herself on this country, we shall be alright".

Once on the boat, the Windsor's were filled with ungracious and bitter resentment, feeling they'd been shoved out of the way to Nassau.

There were still the usual blunders; the Duke announcing how he thought: "Hitler is a very great man", and Wallis still relaying information, even hiding messages in her clothes sent to New York for dry cleaning.

It came to the point they had to be chastised by London due to the senseless, extreme spending of the couple; the clothes and jewellery being so extravagant the British newspapers were picking up on it. England, so deep in the grips of rations and hard times, could find this nothing but insulting.

Edward, it seemed, concentrated his anger by focusing it all on his determination to obtain the title for his wife. This sadly became his 'raison d'être' and spent his time rallying for this. He decided that once the war was ended the plan was to make a visit back to England and appeal against the HRH decision.

Chapter Thirty-Six

Wormwood Scrubs,
February 28th, 1947,
The night of the storm.

Les had been playing it all out as he stared at the prison walls, running through the past looking for clues as to why he'd acted as he had: shell shock, post-traumatic stress, his brother's actions, Gwen's insecurities; they all added to it, and could have been used as an excuse if one was weak.

He was drenched in sweat. The night had gone well below freezing and Les, normally so tough had a fever, maybe brought on by the mental unrest -history tormenting him- or maybe as he felt so powerless yet again to save Gwen and his children: with his defences down the fever took over. He'd become so tough, cold to emotion within himself, but deep down he was still that gentle, kind sensitive man.

More newspaper headlines swirled round his head in his delirium; The Evening Telegraph's: "World Probe for Windsor Jewels ... Investigations are also being made by the Belgian and American Police...". He remembered reading The Press and Journal on Saturday 19th October, they wrote: "£2000 Reward In Windsor Jewels Theft Case... With Scotland Yard as chief headquarters, the detective forces of Paris, Brussels, Amsterdam and Copenhagen are combining to hunt down the cat-burglars who stole the Duchess of Windsor's jewels...That the jewels might be on their way to America has not been over-looked... Full details have been radioed to the Federal Investigation Bureau, whose G-men at once went into action."

Les remembered his disbelief at the extent of the search, knowing at that point it had spiralled way out of control. The press and media had pounced on the story, making it world-wide, larger than he felt it deserved. He'd realised there was no way he'd ever be able to get rid of any of the jewels now.

The Western Morning News followed with more information: "European Manhunt... Ports watched for any attempt to take jewels out of the country. Continental Police watching all incoming boats. Suspicion is growing however, that the thieves may be British. American La Guardia Airfield's guards put to any attempt to smuggle into US – Extra care was being placed on inspection of all jewellery brought into the United States by transatlantic planes."

The Courier and Advertiser had clues to the military car, believing it was Canadian: "It contained three men and witnesses have been taken to Scotland Yard and shown the 'Rogues Gallery', in the possibility of recognising any of the men."

Les had thought about this one and really couldn't remember any large military car lurking around; he probably would have passed it as he worked late a few of those nights and would surely have remembered such a distinctive car; but then, he thought, who knows what Wallis was capable of getting up to.

The fact that the papers had said: "The gang had known exactly what articles they wanted and discarded those which could not be disposed of, among them was a necklace of pearls," led Les to think the press had lost it completely. The famous opera length string of Queen Alexandra's pearls -as they turned out to be- that were left at the scene would have probably been the easiest thing to have 'dismantled' and dealt with individually, making countless pairs of untraceable pearl earrings -except for their size. He'd had his own reasons for not touching them.

France had thought they'd had a lead in the week after the robbery, making everyone excited that the jewels had been found, as a Brittany farmer had declared he'd seen a suspicious parcel being dropped by parachute onto his land. The Courier and Advertiser explained: "A parachute container which a Brittany farmer saw dropped yesterday, and which some reports said might have contained jewels stolen from the Duchess of Windsor, belonged to the French Meteorological Bureau. The bureau, announcing this last night, said the operation was just part of a routine weather check."

The next memory of the press saga that Les remembered was the couple of waiters, this story had made him belly laugh till he cried, he'd seen it in the Evening Telegraph and also the Echo, which explained: "Waiters' False Story of Jewel Robbery- They'd given false information 'worth a fiver or a tenner', explaining how they'd been in the military car and met with American officers. The Detective Inspector said: "it was a colourful story". Adcock told the court: "We had been drinking rather heavily -in fact very hard- at the time, and we were drinking at the time we met with the gentleman of the press...It was done more in a spirit of bravado. We are not criminally minded people!"

The whole thing was becoming fantastical, next was the Sunday Post on November 10$^{th:}$ "Windsor Jewel Search Centres On New York. Mr Ivring Shumbord, a 'private jewel-tracer' said in New York yesterday he believes the £25,000 stolen jewels are in the U.S. He also expects an American seaman will shortly contact him to claim the £2500 reward for their recovery which Lloyds have placed with him. Mr Shambord said: "My secretary has described to me a man of seafaring type who called here a few days ago, fidgeted uneasily on a waiting-bench, then left without giving his name or business." Not only this visit, but a series of other events which he did not specify led Mr Shumbord to believe the jewels were in the U.S. The New York Daily Mirror reported that Lloyds world-wide search was now concentrated in New York, following a tipster's telephone call to Lloyds London office. The tipster advised Lloyds to get the reward money into Shumbord's hands quickly so he can talk money with a Yankee who will get in touch with him."

This was the most farcical of stories yet, but then on Tuesday November 12th Les had gone to get the papers, thinking things must start to calm down soon, when the next lead was spread across all the papers: "Windsor Jewels on Plane. A large quantity of jewels of great value which is thought may have formed part of the proceeds ...were discovered when the Rome-Rio constellation plane arrived at Recife, Pernambuco, Brazil, yesterday."

Les remembered feeling sorry for the Italian gentleman, as he was sure to have had quite a grilling, along with his luggage having been confiscated; it took a few days for him to be released from police custody. As the Bristol Mirror explained: "The Italian had bought the jewels as presents for his family."

On Friday November 15th the attention was turned back to Mr Shumbord in New York, papers including the Courier and Advertiser printed that Shumbord said: "I got contact at my home this morning. I have reason to believe the whole thing will be broken before the week is over. That is all I can say."

Les didn't know what to think about this bluffer -how exactly would it soon be over when the man couldn't have a clue as to the whereabouts of the jewels? Les, now aware how jewellery turned everyone irrational, desperate for a piece of the action; there really was no way he could give them up without a world-wide story to go with it.

The next elaborate tale was a bag full of jewels found on the roadside at Secondigny, near Poitiers, France. How this bag of incredible jewels made of diamonds, pearls and gold had been left, discarded, he never quite understood: it seemed a widow had run off with a Moroccan, but forgotten her booty!

Then finally, there was a suitcase left on a train, found to contain what was again believed to be Wallis' jewels: the train had arrived in Italy and jewellery found aboard. Les was bemused as to why people could forget such wealth, but he also knew there were reasons to things one would never understand; as his reasons had been.

He was exhausted and still shaking, it was still only about three o'clock in the morning and his mind would not relent from going over everything. He felt desperately sad for Gwen and the little ones, not knowing quite the extent of how hard life had become without him. He then put his thoughts back to when he'd returned from the war, scrutinising his movements, hoping to understand, to find a way for peace of mind, for the mental torture to abate.

CHAPTER THIRTY-SEVEN

Sunningdale,
May 1945.

Les, finally back from Arnhem, was visiting his old friend Ronald the farmer, when the news came, as ever those days, over the radio. There he was, sitting at the long sturdy table in Ronald's kitchen. The familiarity of the surroundings was of great comfort to him. Nothing had changed, it was as if time hadn't passed and he'd never gone to war. The only evidence of years gone by were the deeper creases on the face of his friend, as if holding the documentation of hard years had by all, and of course the torment of horrendous memories forever on Les's mind.

'Oh, it's good to be here,' Les declared, looking around.

'Yes, good to see you,' Ronald said, as if checking over one of his cows, 'I suppose I gave you the odd thought every now and then!'

'This isn't a display of sentimentality, is it?' Les laughed.

'Oh, get on with you! But it couldn't have been easy out there,' Ronald added, matter-of-factly.

'No, but it doesn't seem to be all that easy here either.' Les was finding adjusting to home-life difficult. He knew he'd changed: he'd had to harden up or he'd not have survived; but what he'd seen and done had affected him deeply, haunted him continually.

'It's been rough,' Ronald said flatly. 'I wish I could offer you work but I'm barely making by.'

The burley farmer stood up and went to turn on the radio, the news came across loud and clear. He froze, then put his hand up signalling for Les to be quiet, muttering, 'Shhh! Wait... shhhh!' They locked eyes as they listened with every ounce of their being, their full concentration on the words emanating from the little wooden box on the sideboard.

'I don't believe it!' exclaimed Ronald. Les tilted his head, concentrating. As the words came forward, they knew it was for real. Before they knew what they were doing, they were both up on their feet, hugging and patting each other on the back, then Les broke into a jig, on the spot, jumping into the air,

'It's over!'

It was May 8th, 1945, and peace had been declared throughout Europe.

'It's over, IT'S OVER!'

They shouted and whooped, collapsing back into their chairs, in a fit of hysterics.

'Good riddance to them Gerry's,' Les spoke with all his might.

'I know,' softly and seriously, shaking his head Ronald continued, 'There were moments when I wondered if this day was ever going to come.'

'Good will always out evil,' Les stated, so surely, as if fact.

'I agree; but it just doesn't seem that way sometimes, and Hitler... I hate to think of all he's done...all the people he's massacred.'

'He was surely the evillest of all evils.' Les added, 'To think he had the luxury of taking his own life!'

'Hey!' Ronald jumped up out of his seat nearly knocking it to the ground, 'I'd almost forgotten...' as he turned his back to Les, stood on a stool and started rummaging in the back of the cupboard.

'What are you doing?' Les asked, inquisitively.

'Da Daaaaaaaa!' Ronald turned back with a look of glee on his face, 'How could I have almost forgotten this?'

He produced a dusty bottle of port and two cigars from, it seemed, nowhere.

'Where did you get that?'

'Well,' with a grin from ear to ear, 'do you remember that Christmas... with 'that' pig?' throwing a wink at Les.

'How could I forget! I can still taste it!'

'I swapped a bit of that, for this! And I decided there and then I'd put it by, stashed for this very day, hoping and praying it'd come, I really was...' He paused, putting his hands together as if praying to the Lord, 'so I could drink this beautiful bottle of port!' They fell roaring with laughter as he pulled the cork.

The two friends sat and talked, confiding with one another about the hard times, the woes and the jubilations of the last few years. It was cathartic for Les to talk.

'Oh goodness,' darkness had fallen, 'I must get back to my Gwen.'

'She does love you so much. You do know that don't you?'

Ronald looked directly into Les's eyes. How he must have known Les's fear, he didn't know, but it reassured him down to his very soul.

'I love her too, and the little ones,' he said referring to the children and the newcomer, the beautiful, bouncing baby boy, Peter.

'Yes, get back home with you! I've got to get to bed. Up early in the morn!'

Les walked back that starry night, and his feet were as if walking on air. He hoped things would be different now; the war was over, he was home with Gwen and he prayed that the haunting nightmares of death and destruction would leave him alone.

Les wasn't to have known then, quite how hard things were going to get. The initial jubilation of the ending of the war passed. This unfortunately led to even harder times. Les was de-mobilised from the KRRC, and he couldn't find work anywhere. There was just no money available for building work as the Government hadn't yet released needed funds for building; so, no work, no money, and rationing stricter than ever. It was as if the whole country was starving. Les was distraught, he desperately wanted work, money, to provide for his family. He'd dreamt of spoiling them once he got back from the war, to make up for the times he hadn't been there, and now, finally back home, he could do nothing. He felt so helpless, and angry it had come to this.

Gwen had become more withdrawn into her world than ever, dancing and singing on a rare, good day, or just silently staring out at the garden, so thoughtful, on others. He'd noticed she wasn't able to cope with the little ones, let alone a newborn baby. It wasn't that she didn't always have endless love and affection for them, for she did, but it was the upkeep, the mundane -keeping an eye on them, looking after them, their clothes and food- was often forgotten as her mind drifted elsewhere.

Les took it upon himself to look after the children. He bathed, fed and watched over them, doing all he could. He hoped that by taking the strain off Gwen, and the reassurance of him being home again, would help her to get better: he couldn't bear the thought of her being taken away.

His amazing survival skills, honed to perfection in the war, were now needed here, at home. He decided he'd have to resort to foraging at night, once the little ones were safe asleep in bed. He knew he couldn't risk leaving them under Gwen's care in the day and he didn't want anything to happen to any of them, her included. So, he started to steal out into the night, looking for firewood, food, or anything that would help their poverty-stricken situation. His moral code had become blurred throughout the war. In the KRRC, out in the field, he'd been ordered to rummage through sheds and garages, looking for anything edible, anything that could help them to survive. Now, under the siege of poverty and starvation he slipped back into survival mode.

Eva came by and over a cup of tea, opened up about the goings on at Fort Belvedere, explaining how the Duke and Duchess of Windsor were planning on coming to England.

'What! But they're traitors! I didn't think they would be welcome.' Les exclaimed, shocked. He knew that Wallis and Edward were barred from entering this country after all their actions of espionage during the war.

'I know. Crazy isn't it! Well, it seems that Simpson woman wants her title!'

'I'll give her a title, but I don't think she'll like it,' Les said, his words dangerously laden with hatred.

'Well, they won't rest till she's allowed to be Her Royal Highness, and they're coming over to do battle for it.'

'They'll never get it,' he said, spitting his contempt for the couple.

'No! Surely not after all that fraternizing with their Nazi friends?' she questioned, looking at her brother.

'She doesn't deserve to breathe, not after what she's done.' Les had never forgotten all the rumours he'd heard over the years, not only from Eva but also in the army, while at war. Things filtered through, his Major had been warned against the Duke and Duchess of Windsor.

'Well, it seems, as you'd imagine, The Family isn't too pleased,' Eva said.

'I'll bet!'

'Imagine! The ex-King thought he could just waltz back over here and open up Fort Belvedere, now the war is over.'

'Don't kid me!' Les couldn't believe what he was hearing.

'Anyhow, the officials won't allow them to stay in any royal establishment. So, Earl Dudley was asked to offer them his house. Couldn't really refuse, so 'They' are going to be staying up at Ednam Lodge, right here in Sunningdale, while the Earl and his Countess clear out to Claridge's!'

'Ednam Lodge?' Les's ears picked up and his eyes went bright.

'Exactly! Just round the corner from you! Well, there's lots to be done before they come,' she said sarcastically, 'to prepare the house to the 'ex-King and his mistress's' standards. There's probably some work for you, Les.'

'Get me it, Sis. Could you?' He couldn't hide the desperation in his voice. Ednam Lodge was just across the back of the golf course, literally a stone's throw away from the cottage. He could even walk to work if he wanted; it would be perfect.

'I'll see what I can do, then let you know dates and times ect... OK?'

'You've no idea how I'd appreciate that. It really would be a godsend. We had to eat Pattie's pet rabbit last week. I don't think she'll ever get over that!'

'Oh, the poor dear! She just loved Joey, carried him everywhere with her, she did.'

'I know. I felt so rotten doing it, but what else could I do? We'd not had any meat to eat for ages. I admit, Sis, I needed it, I'm still starving hungry from no food at the front, but I'm not just worried about me, the kids are so thin and Gwen -well she doesn't eat anyway- but her feet are becoming less and less on the ground; if you know what I mean.'

'Oh Les,' she said, putting her hand over his, 'my dear brother, you are carrying all this alone, aren't you. I wish I could do more. And you thought the war had ended!' she said, seeing the dark pain in her brother's eyes.

'Eva, if you could just get me a job up at the lodge I could sleep at night,' Les pleaded.

Little did she know he meant what he said, not only metaphorically, but literally.

Eva did come through, finding Les a position in the grounds at Ednam Lodge. He started working doing gardening, and after a while, once they realised what a good craftsman he was, they had him restoring one of the stone statues outside. Les, in his usual friendly manner, had got to know most of the staff, and the Earl's dogs just adored him, following him around as he worked.

So, there he was, working away in the garden on the statue, when the Duke and Duchess of Windsor arrived on that fateful visit. They and their entourage piled up the drive and poured out of their fancy cars. Les stood there, invisible to them as he watched this facade unveil before his eyes. The couple, immaculately dressed, descended from their car, approaching the Earl and Countess Dudley with their staff all lined up, as if for inspection, to greet the infamous couple. He could see from where he stood, the straight back of the frozen woman, and then as she turned, the look of distain on her face as she surveyed the scenario she was placed in.

It was obviously not to her liking. He could feel her anger and was surprised at himself when he realised how glad he was to see her dismay. Les didn't wish to judge anyone, everybody had a right to live in this world, but something deep down just kept surfacing when he thought about her.

Wallis' words for England's bombed: "I can't feel sorry for them," and Edward's: "I feel more German than English," kept swirling around in his brain, welling up, becoming stronger and stronger. Shaking his head, 'Let it drop!' he said to himself, picking up his tools he carried on working as they entered the lodge.

Then, to his absolute shock and horror, the deep rattling noise of army trucks startled him out of his concentration as they rolled up the drive. The sound of the trucks instantly took him back in his mind as suddenly there he was, in the field at Arnhem, with flashbacks of Dutch pleading with them to help as the Germans massacred everyone: tears of loss, fearful pained screams, gruesome disfigured bodies lining the roads as the unforgettable stench of death permeated his conscience. He tried to shake out of it, but seeing the trucks made him angrier than ever.

'How dare they!' He noticed his hands shaking, and a cold sweat came upon him, he'd frozen in his flashback.

He'd not seen an army truck since the front, he'd not been prepared for this, never in his wildest dreams had he imagined army lads would have to carry the Windsor's luggage. The smell and sound of the trucks triggered horrific memories he'd desperately been trying to suppress. Realising he was still so raw from the atrocities of Arnhem,

'How could they have the audacity to use our Army for protection when they were spilling secret information of our whereabouts, betraying our boys every chance they had. They are so blatantly hypocritical. How can people not see this!'

Les stood as if witness to a crime, watching the three army trucks being unloaded: piece after piece of their expensive luggage, matching trunks and suitcases, carried inside. He clocked how they were all fussing over one particular case, a padlocked leather suitcase handed over to the Royal Guards.

He worked the rest of the day in a fury, knocking the rage out of his fists onto the statue, non-stop, as if in a trance. He couldn't even eat, unable to swallow he threw his sandwich to the dogs running about while he ignored everything else around him. He felt violated: that this memory of a threat could come so close to his home sent him reeling for his defences. He'd not been prepared for this strong a reaction, but he felt as if the Nazi's themselves had arrived at the bottom of his garden, on his home territory. Threatened; but also fuming, for all the innocent lives he'd seen blown away, in order to protect king and country; something this royal couple had relished plotting against.

Les made his way home, deadbeat, almost too tired to walk; only to find Gwen in pieces that night. She was in a bad way: the delusions, a part of her schizophrenia, were getting stronger as she drifted further from 'normal' daily life. As he walked through the door she clung to him, her eyes dazed,

'I had to hide...I didn't know where you were! It's so late and I had this terrible feeling you weren't coming home tonight.' Panic stricken eyes searched his for reassurance.

'It's ok. I'm here now,' he said calming her down. He looked around only to notice that the room was dark, the kitchen was a mess, the fire wasn't lit, and the children still hadn't been fed; but at least they were curled up asleep in their beds.

'But really... is it all ok? Les, what's happening to me?' After he hugged her and sat her down, she calmed a bit. 'I don't remember much of today. I think I drift off but I'm not sure what's real. These horrible men in uniform came and told me you wouldn't ever be coming back.'

'Don't worry, Queenie, I'm here, no-one came.'

'I saw them, as bright as day standing there, in our living room, oh Les!' She fell to the floor, crying, 'I'm afraid without you.'

'I'm not going anywhere. I'm here for you, forever, my dearest petal. The war is over and I will be here, every day, for you. For it's us, together for the rest of our lives: remember that.' He lifted her face and kissed away her tears. 'Don't you worry, those guys were just your fears, just acting out the nightmares in your head. They were as real as a dream.'

'Are you sure? Are you? Maybe they were a premonition? I have had premonitions before,' she asked, searching his eyes for the peace of mind she needed.

'I promise you, now come here,' he said with his arms outstretched, 'No more talk now, come and give me a cuddle, then we'll have something to eat and go to bed. I've brought you a bit of cake back from the 'big house'.

At the thought of cake, he saw her face light up to a smile for the first time in ages, her woes quickly dismissed, and his anguish numbed for a moment.

'Cake?' she questioned delightedly, with her innocent champagne smile.

Chapter Thirty-Eight

Ednam Lodge,
October 1946.

The Duke and Duchess of Windsor were settling in at Ednam Lodge, having returned to England with the intention of persuading the King to allow the Duke some menial duties, but mainly, to sort Wallis's HRH situation once and for all. However, things were not going to plan.

Wallis was in another foul brooding mood that October night. While getting ready to go out to their dinner engagement at Claridge's she ferociously attacked Edward with her vicious tongue,

'What on earth are we doing here? Will you tell me that?' lashing out at him in their private room at the lodge. 'What did you think would be accomplished?' she spat, flailing her arms around the place as she stormed the room, 'Other than wasting my time by dragging me over here, to this godforsaken country, to deal with 'your family'.' She hadn't finished on this yet, 'Have you any consideration to how humiliating all this is? Have you?' She took a breath and screeching, carried on, 'And what do you mean they won't see us? That's just absurd. They can't deny my existence forever: I am your wife! They should be grateful to me - I have to put up with you every damn day; day in, day out: They don't!'

'I know,' Edward said humbly.

'Oh, shut up you stupid little man, don't you realise the insult you are allowing them to hurl at me?' Her paranoid reasoning was becoming malicious. 'You've no backbone! Otherwise, we'd have the titles we deserve. You pathetically handed everything over.'

'We will win this one, Wally, but please just appease them a bit.'

'What did you say? Appease *them*! That's just dandy that is! Ha!' She moved over to the bar and poured herself a gin, 'You bring me all the way to make me beg with my tail between my legs, for something that is rightfully mine... I find this whole thing outrageous. I mean who do they think they are?' she said, taking another sip, 'You'd better find a way to sort this out with 'your family'. I'm finding you all rather pathetic and this whole charade is boring me beyond belief. Exactly who will want to invite us to dinner while we're here?'

Chapter Thirty-Nine

Sunningdale,
October 1946.

Les went to bed that night but couldn't sleep a wink. Restless, and in a lucid state, he tossed and turned. It was as if he had a warrior within, dancing and chanting: preparing for war. His mind was as restless as the wind bashing branches of the tree at the window, tormenting him, blowing his fears into his mind. Anger rising at seeing the army trucks; harrowing images of war flashing back, being under siege, faces of dead comrades haunting him; and then, to top it all, the worry of Gwen's deteriorating state of mind. He felt so helpless and there was nothing he could do.

Dawn arrived and he was exhausted, enveloped in deep sadness. Depression had hit, feeling how life could have been so different. Glad he'd survived; but wracked with guilt for those that hadn't made it home from the war. Finally, questioning why, he made his way back to the lodge, ashamed after all he'd been through he was now working for traitors.

He didn't know what was happening to him; but he knew something was about to happen. For days this feeling of anger and anticipation -almost as if being under attack- continued brewing, like a storm approaching. He couldn't put his finger on it or express in words; it was pure emotion, like a gut feeling. He'd always known to follow his gut instincts. These instincts of his were what had helped keep him and others alive during the war.

Then after days working flat out, keeping his head down, and suppressing his boiling hatred towards the mistress of the ex-King, it came to be the fateful Wednesday October 16th, 1946. The day had carried on, like any other. He'd worked hard, taken his breaks and listened to the staff chattering; they were alive with gossip. It seemed that Wallis was absolutely livid at not being received by Buckingham Palace and she was taking it out on Edward once again.

Les couldn't bear to hear any more, it made his belly curdle, and so he walked back across the grounds to get on with the statue. Hours passed as he lost track of time, so engrossed in his work. The dogs still played around him, so he talked out his mind to them; he felt dogs were great listeners, probably because he'd been giving them titbits of his sandwiches for the last week; but he loved dogs, and what with working away and chatting to the dogs he was oblivious as to how late it had become.

The sound of the Duke and Duchess's car descending the gravel drive pulled him out of his concentration. He saw them pass by in their fancy clothes, all dressed up, on their way to a social engagement. Then soon after, a second car followed on, the royal bodyguards were leaving the estate; stood down as there was no longer any need for them as no royalty on the premises, though still leaving an in-house detective on guard.

He looked around; something had changed. The wind that had been blowing for days had abated. It was as still and silent as if the earth itself had stopped spinning. That was how it felt, as if time had stopped ticking. Delicate wisps of high cirrus danced a delicate shade of apricot across the twilight sky and at that magical moment he knew what he was to do. It reminded him of the night just before he and the rest of his troop entered the chateau on his first mission; there in the caves, preparing to enter, seek what they were looking for and leave. And maybe he did feel at war, under siege: these known Nazi sympathizers on his territory, literally yards from his own home. His adrenalin rose and he knew what he had to do, and to act quickly. He'd been given this window of opportunity and if he didn't take it and follow his gut instinct, the door of chance would never open again. What was life, but moments of chance? he thought.

He picked up his wheelbarrow and loaded it with a bit of white sashcord rope he'd found in the store, a cloth, a small jemmy, an axe and his gardening gloves, then jauntily, whistling once more passed most of the groundsmen huddled together, gathering in the outer shed as there was to be a big horse race on the radio, he made his way inconspicuously to the lodge. He had his excuses ready:

'a faulty window-frame the housekeeper has requested he mends before he goes home'. The rest of the staff were at supper, sitting round the staff table in the basement kitchens far away in the east wing of the house, even the detective had gone to eat with the staff.

It was easy for Les; no Germans to fool with a disguise this time, and he had rights to be on the premises, or at least in the grounds. His years being a roofer came into play as he surveyed the way forward: how to make it to Wallis's bedroom window. He knew which window as he'd seen her silhouetted there once or twice with Miss Martin, her personal maid, in tow. Like a game of snakes and ladders he positioned the wheelbarrow below Wallis's window, slung the coiled rope around his torso, with the gemmy and axe wrapped in cloth tied to him, put on his gloves, placed his strong hands around the drainpipe and with a hoist and a push from the lower windowsill he was up and over to the first-floor window ledge.

A bird flew overhead, squawking and looking with its beady eyes right at him as if to say, 'get on with it'. He needed to concentrate, shuffling along. The ledge was narrow, but he was agile and with his hands almost glued to the walls he made his way, till he was outside Wallis's secretary, Elsa Blaisdell's room. He was aiming for Wallis's bedroom, but he realised the secretary's window was already cracked open, the sash window had not been locked closed. He couldn't believe his luck. Relieved he wouldn't need the gemmy, he lifted the window further and manoeuvred his first leg over, ducking his head and twisting his body inside, and he was in. This was second nature to him, all the times he'd had to do it for 'King and Country'.

Assessing the situation, he made his way to the Duchess's dressing room, the room adjoining her bedroom, noting the trunks piled up with some still in a state of being unpacked, when he heard someone approaching. Hiding behind the heavy silk curtains, as he had at the chateau, he could see the Duchess's maid enter the bedroom through the open adjoining doors. Crossing to the wardrobe, Miss Martin placed a gown that she'd obviously pressed ready for Her Grace within it, turned and left.

Once safe, with his keen eyes surveying the luggage Les couldn't see what he was looking for, so went straight through to the Duchess's bedroom. He walked in, her perfume still lingering in the air, unnervingly, as if her presence. The dogs on the bed looked up and started wagging their tails excitedly, they recognised him immediately as they'd been sniffing and playing round him for days out in the garden, so luckily were no hassle. He went over to them, speaking softly,

'Shh, it's our secret!' He stroked them down and they curled up and went back to sleep.

Les glanced to the dressing table, staring in disbelief at a signed photograph of Ribbentrop in German uniform, in prized position, also noting a solid gold vanity set. He was looking for anything, not sure what, but something. But deep-down, he knew what he was after: the padlocked suitcase with what he knew to contain the leather-bound reinforced case holding the famous jewel boxes he'd seen handed over to the Royal Guards on arrival - embedded in his memory.

Then as he turned, he saw it. There on the stool by the fireplace was a strongly locked leather suitcase. He went to assess it, feeling its weight and strong sides knew it to be reinforced. He couldn't comprehend how it was left lying around like this, but there was no doubt: This was it, looked the same as her other cases, thought this was different. Les knew he didn't have long, he had to break the lock and retrieve the jewellery case within. Using the gemmy to prize the lock, and the axe to force it away from the leather case, it was swiftly accomplished. Upon opening, he picked out a particular jewellery case among others, noticeable as weighted, steel lined for security. It was the size of a small overnight suitcase, hard leather with buckle straps and padlocked. There were others, but this one especially held his attention.

'That's the one,' he whispered to himself, as he immediately took the sash rope from around his chest, tied the end to the handle on the case, opened the window and lowered it down into the waiting wheelbarrow beneath.

This was the riskiest part of it all; if he was caught at this point, he was done for. He had to get out and down to the ground as fast as he could. Time was of the essence as he had to get back to the hut, to join the groundsmen in the shed before the end of the race, for an alibi. It was as if he'd shape-shifted into a cat as he sprung down, with a jump, slide and jump he was back on the ground. As he landed, he made no sound, thinking how eerie it was; almost surreal. No time for questions as he covered the case with the cloth, hiding it in the wheelbarrow and wheeled it all away.

'Here I am again. Me and my faithful wheelbarrow. Not under Nazi fire this time, and at least this wheelbarrow doesn't squeak!' Les joked to himself.

Les made his way to the statue, leaving it all there -wouldn't be for long. He entered the hut, the men were too engrossed listening to the race to have noticed exactly how long he'd been with them. They all shared their jubilations and commiserations on the outcome of the horses, then made their way home.

Les then took the wheelbarrow to the back of the shed, wrapped the case and tools up tightly in the sack cloth and left the empty wheelbarrow propped up and ready for the morning. Clutching the bundle, he made his way through the grounds, along the boundary of Ednam Lodge and towards Sunningdale Golf Course.

Les knew the grounds well by now and knew exactly where he could make it through the boundaries, so arriving onto the golf course. The wind suddenly whipped back up, out of nowhere, blowing him home. The window of opportunity had closed and he felt he had to disappear fast.

There was no-one around. It was late, and the golf course was closed. He found a safe place among the trees and laid the parcel down, unwrapping his weighted package. He picked up the axe and made four swift accurate swipes, breaking the padlock and buckles from the case.

Looking around once more, knowing his time was running out, he lifted the lid. He was still not totally sure he'd chosen the right case, they all looked identical, but the large padlock on this one made him almost certain it had to be.

There before his eyes was what it had all been for: her jewels! Wallis's prize possessions: her absolute raison d'être and Achilles's Heel, all in one. He hadn't been sure what he was doing or why, but now he knew as the overwhelming hatred poured out of him. It was so out of character for Les, never one to judge, but it was a release of sorts. He'd resented hearing about her for years and years: the gossip of her affairs behind the Prince's back, of her Nazi liaisons, of her being the reason for the abdication, for her spying antics during the war and her absolute and total insensitivity to the extreme hardships normal people were facing, that he, Les, was facing with his family, with the nation starving, and all she cared about was her title and her jewellery. It all welled up and burst.

'Ha! Gotcha! Wallis, you traitorous, evil Nazi lover!'

He started to rant, like never before, releasing all his pent-up anger in one fail swoop, 'Who do you think you are! You think you're so superior to everyone else; but I know you are the lowliest of humans: You have no heart. You are a calculated avaricious whore. You adorn yourself with rocks stolen from our Royal Family, just to try and prove your worth. Well, you're worth nothing without your 'symbols of stature.' My Gwen is more of a queen than you'll ever be, and she needs nothing to display her finest qualities.' He swore over the box, spitting almost, as if speaking to Wallis herself as he lifted her jewels. 'You deserve to be punished for all the atrocities you deliberately carried out, with no remorse whatsoever -against our country: Traitors are executed!' Trembling still, some pieces fell through his hands onto the grass.

Taking a few deep breaths, he tried to calm down and pull himself together: he'd never lost it like that, never, not even with his brother; he needed to get a check on his emotions. He had to be a rock for his dear queenie, she couldn't pick up on this anger, it would disturb her greatly, being so sensitive.

His hands moved swiftly, not really looking at each piece, just gathering the contents and placing them into the cloth, wrapping and rolling them up as he went. There was an opera length string of the finest natural pearls, but as he touched them he shuddered, let them slip through his fingers and drop onto the grass. He remembered how Gwen hated pearls, stating how unlucky she believed them to be; 'wife's tears' she would call them, so he left them there on the ground, along with other jewels he'd dropped in his haste. He wrapped up his booty and headed for home, across the golf course. He didn't exactly know what to do next, but he knew he didn't have long.

Les arrived home to a quiet house, the children were fast asleep, and Gwen was preparing something in the scullery. He said hello then went through to the kitchen table. Lighting the candle so able to see, he heard footsteps, Gwen came to find out what he was up to.

'Oh, my lord! Look at your face!' she exclaimed, laughing teasingly, and approaching him for a kiss, 'What have you been up to?' As she did so know her husband.

He held the cloth wrapped bundle close to his chest, hugging it to him like his life depended on it, his eyes wide, sparked with adrenalin, now not quite sure what to do.

'Gwen, I...' He suddenly felt the extremity of his actions. The bundle seemed incredibly heavy, weighed with trepidation. What had he done? Disbelief settling on his conscience. He stood there a second, wondering whether to tell her or not -best not- but he trusted her more than life itself and she was already onto him.

She came and put her arms around him and the parcel. She had a feeling something serious had occurred, and she was sure it was something to do with the bundle he was clinging onto.

'Don't question me! I know what I've done is wrong. I don't know what is happening, but I just had to do it. It's so unfair! The way the ex-King and his mistress flaunt their wealth when the whole country is starving! I really...' he said, losing his breath, 'I've done wrong, I know, but I don't care. NO!' With that he stood up straight, as if saluting his senior officer and said, 'I'm glad!'

'Right... enough of the speech! What on earth are you going on about?' Gwen asked impatiently.

'Queenie, you've got to promise me, on our children's lives, on our life, on our love, on the stability of the future of this family, that this is never to be talked about.'

'If I knew what I was promising I would, but I don't!' She was becoming slightly infuriated with all this. He put the parcel down onto the kitchen table, took her firmly in his arms, looked right at her and said,

'I know you, and I believe you will never tell, whatever happens... They could hurt you too though.'

'Les, you're frightening me now! Let go, this instant!'

'Sorry, Queenie, I don't really want to involve you. I had to make sure you realise I'm serious. But... Lord forgive me...I darn well think I've gone and stolen that Simpson woman's jewels!'

'Bugger!' Gwen exclaimed, almost taking an in-breath, and covering her mouth as her eyes widened in disbelief, 'You're kidding!'

'No. Seriously,' he said flatly, paused, then said, 'Make sure the curtains are all closed, turn the lights off, light the candles, and pour me a drink.' He went to splash some cold water on his face while she did as he asked. The parcel sat wrapped on the table awaiting them.

They gathered back round, both taking a sip of the fine elixir of strength as he slowly started to unwrap the bundle. Unravelled, before their eyes, glittering and sparkling in the candlelight, were piece after piece of the most incredible jewellery: brooches, earrings, bracelets, rings and necklaces all glistening with precious stones of the finest hues.

Some items included in the bundle were:

A starburst sapphire brooch with sapphires of deep blues of the night sky,

A gem-beaded lily flower brooch with iridescent pearl petals,

A contemporary circle brooch set with spiralling diamonds of grading sizes and incredible brilliance, shooting sparks of colour all-round the room,

An art-deco baguette buckle-shaped diamond brooch, with diamonds of the cleanest clarity and purest colour,

A diamond and ruby flower brooch,

A fashionable ruby bow brooch of the time,

A chain and ruby brooch,

A crowned ruby thistle pin,

A large ruby ring,

A fantastically pavé set ruby heart with two arrows piercing through and a crown resting on top of the heart,

A fine baguette set, precious stone 'cross' pendant,

A stunning ruby and diamond necklace, with matching earrings,

A diamond and aquamarine brooch,

A platinum and diamond bracelet,

An aquamarine and diamond bracelet, with 6 large aquamarines as clear and vibrant as the sparkling Caribbean Sea,

An intense large aquamarine and diamond ring,

A gold ring with a golden sapphire shining its warmth like the sun,

An emerald square–cut solitaire ring, resonating deepest Muso perfection.

A sapphire and diamond paradise bird brooch.

These are just to describe a few, and most came with matching earrings, sapphire and diamond, or ruby and diamond clusters, and of course, there were gold cuff bracelets, intricately woven metals, heavy gold chains with sapphires, rings piled high with as many gems as the talented jewellers could mount onto one ring; all sourced from the most exquisite quality gems using the best craftsmanship in the world. The pièce de résistance of the jewellery artwork was the famous diamond and sapphire 'paradise bird' brooch.

Awestruck by the beauty lying in front of them, they gently laid all the pieces out onto the table to really appreciate the wonder of nature and craftsmanship combined in these pieces of jewellery; humbled to be in the presence of these majestic stones as the gems glowed all their glory in the candlelight.

Les picked up the diamond and ruby flower brooch, the stones took the light from the candle as its petals became brilliant refractions of every colour under the rainbow, almost hypnotising him and speaking to him of the wonder of the powers of the earth, the strength of ultimate design, as blinded by beauty he turned and pinned it onto Gwen's dress, as if to shield her heart; the diamonds alighting her with their magical reflections of light. He leant forward, kissed her and said,

'I love you, my delicate flower.'

She looked at him, mesmerised by the diamonds and Les's declaration of love. He then picked up one of the beautiful ruby cluster rings; the rubies looking like frozen droplets of blood, shining the colour of love and life; he gently lifted her hand and slid the stunning ring onto her finger, it fitted like a glove, and he leant forward and kissed her again.

'I will always love you, Queenie,' he said, so purposefully; weighed heavy with his love. She was taken aback, something resonated deep within her, and she would remember this particular moment all her life.

Les then took the heavy gold chain bracelet with an exquisite sapphire, the stone so pure and the cut so perfect the light was shining as if reflecting from a moonlit lake. He wrapped the chain around her delicately fine wrist and fumbled with the clasp. This time he looked at her and said,

'I want you to understand how my heart is chained to yours: I am a slave, bound to your love.' He kissed her lips. She still sat so still, staring deep into his eyes, sending him back all her love for him. He then reached for the elaborate ruby and diamond necklace and placed it round her elegant neck.

'I wish I had been able to bestow these gifts upon you, my beautiful queenie, so I could describe in gems how I feel for you; how you are the most precious thing in my world.' Again, he kissed her gently on the lips. Gwen loved him so much and this absolutely extreme display of his feeling was bringing tears to her eyes; but still she just looked deep into his eyes, telling him all he needed to know.

Les took hold of the finest pair of earrings; the diamonds and coloured gems so beautifully crafted to resonate perfectly next to each other; and clipped them onto Gwen's ears and each time he brushed her cheek with a kiss. He took her hand and explained,

'Just for this special moment in our lives, you really are my queen. I only wish I could have been more like a king for you, but my love is of the same worth -whoever we may be.'

Tears were rolling down her cheeks, so touched by his vulnerable confessions of love. She leant forward and kissed him back, and as she leant towards him the image of her in the candlelight, so mesmerizingly beautiful with the jewels complementing the power of her soul, the colours of the gems playing with her own colours in her hair, and the diamonds competing with the spark of her eye, he saw how she had become a majestical vision, and this vision ingrained deep into his memory. They held the kiss for, it seemed, eternity; both of them taken to another world, where he was king and she the queen.

Les came round from the trance the stones had placed on them, came back to reality. He started to pack them up, wrapping them so delicately back into the cloth and hiding them away from the magic of the light, until they were safely packed.

'I'd best get these hidden. I'll be back soon I promise,' Les said, as he took the bundle and left through the back door. Gwen remained seated, there at the table, in the candlelight. She was still mesmerised, hypnotised by the jewels. She hadn't even noticed he'd forgotten to take the ruby ring from her finger. It felt like ages that she waited for his safe return, but it couldn't have been more than an hour or so.

Chapter Forty

Ednam Lodge,
October 16th, 1946.

All was in a state of total chaos at Ednam Lodge. Later that evening, Miss Martin, Wallis's maid had taken more pressed clothes up to Wallis's room and upon entering noticed that the main suitcase had been broken into and the jewellery case was not where it should be, there in the suitcase, on the stool in front of the fire. She searched the room frantically, then her own, and then the secretary's. Immediately seeing the opened window in the secretary's room, she panicked and ran downstairs alerting the rest of the staff, who then, in turn, alerted the detective. Due to the high profile of the situation, the royal connection and the value of the jewels, both the Surrey Police and the Metropolitan Police were contacted. Meanwhile, the Earl's butler, together with the Duke's valet, searched all the nearby rooms while the staff swept the lodge looking for anything untoward.

Assistant Commissioner R.M. Howe arrived at Ednam Lodge along with Detective Inspector John Capstick of Scotland Yard, and soon police were crawling all over the house. The Windsor's were called back from their dinner engagement with Earl and Countess Dudley, also informed to return to the lodge.

Wallis was absolutely livid; her mood turned most foul.

'I want every one of these despicable servants to be searched. Everybody is to be interrogated, do you hear me?' she screeched at the sergeant, 'They know what's happened here, one of them knows for sure!'

Countess Dudley was taken aback that Wallis could be so disdainful towards her loyal staff. Wallis was shooting insults at staff that had served at the house for most of their lives. The Countess had never had a problem with theft of any kind before and was not to be insulted on the calibre of her staff now.

'This is my house, and I will order what goes on here. You may interrogate, as you must.' Countess Dudley said, addressing Detective Inspector Capstick directly, 'The staff here at Ednam Lodge are incredibly loyal. I pride myself that I have never had an untoward incident here in my home. Not once. This is all so shocking,' she said shaking her head. 'Yes, interview them, but please, I just ask one favour - don't harass my cook! She is the kindest and most faithful of ladies, she has been with us for over 50 years, and I don't want her upset. She won't know anything about this. Leave her alone; that's all I ask.'

'We will take that into consideration Ma'am.'

Wallis, fuming at being up staged by Countess Dudley, flounced around Ednam Lodge, spitting curses as she went. The Earl of Dudley was not amused either, and when Wallis passed him in the corridor, he had to get it off his chest and say,

'If you remember, I had recommended that you placed your jewels in our vaulted, burglar-proof strong room we have here at Ednam. I even had it strengthened for your stay, for Gods-sake,' he uttered, incensed, shaking his head. 'If you'd only done as I'd requested before you'd left for your engagement, we'd all have been spared this major embarrassment!' And with that he stormed off, muttering, 'So much for keeping this visit a 'low key affair!' as he headed for his study and the solace of a large brandy, aware they were in for a long night.

'Oh, I just hate this god-damn place,' Wallis spat at Edward, 'What were we thinking of -coming back to England! It's all your family's fault: it's always your family's fault. God! I bet they even arranged for this to happen. They were complaining about our spending only the other day.'

'Really, Darling, that's a bit rough,' he replied, insulted as to how she'd been putting his family down all the time. He was at a loss; the jewels were his livelihood too, he'd poured a lot of his finances into them, but more than that, he couldn't bear to see Wallis like this.

That night the Surrey Police carried out a "careful examination of the premises", while the Metropolitan Police "made thorough search both inside and outside the premises for finger impressions." The sixteen staff, eight of Earl Dudley's, eight of the Duke's, were interrogated way into the early hours, till around 4am. The next day the lodge was turned upside down, not a stone left unturned: cupboards, linens, beds, cutlery, even the coal and wood stacks were emptied and checked. The staff were interrogated again, and again. One of the newest members of staff, a young scullery maid, was heavily grilled, only for her to break down, tears flooding from her eyes, scared, pleading her innocence.

Even police methods were brought into question as another point of entry may have been found, that morning staff suspiciously found the Duke's strongbox left broken on the floor in a near bathroom, along with a Faberge box on the windowsill leading to a flat roof. How this had been missed the night before, by not only the butler, the valet, and the Surry Police but also by the Metropolitan Police was a mystery in itself.

By 8am they'd found the broken leatherbound jewellery case abandoned in the scruff on Sunningdale Golf Course. Four inner velvet trays strewn over the grass, four single earrings dropped in haste, and Queen Alexandra's string of pearls mysteriously left behind. A white sashcord was near the case, but other than that, no other clues. The police still had nothing on who carried out this brazen heist.

The situation was serious. Immediately a high publicity case, the police were under intense scrutiny as the press were already having a feeding frenzy. The Assistant Commissioner and Detective Inspector had their hands full with theories:

- Was it an inside job?

The staff was best positioned to have been able to enter Wallis's room and take the case out of the house without raising suspicion, knowing the exact timing of the Windsor's movements.

-Was it professional jewel thieves?

It was done so meticulously, with no trace of evidence, leaving or entering. There had been a spat of high-end jewel thefts at large properties in the last year.

- Why was a Canadian armoured car said to have been seen near the house, pulled up, waiting suspiciously in a lay-by?

- What happened to the madman sighted on the golf course, ranting about the Royals?

- Was it the Windsor's themselves, and why didn't they place the valuable jewels in the strong room as requested?

It all seemed so easy, as if left deliberately available, arrogantly dismissing security advice. The Windsor's were spending way beyond their means; known to be in debt their situation would undoubtedly benefit from a handsome insurance claim. Wallis, however, explained she always had her jewel cases in her rooms with her, believing by never making any special fuss over any particular case she avoided suspicion of its contents.

- Or there's the idea that Wallis herself put around; that maybe it was even the Royal Family that had arranged for the theft. In so doing, reclaiming the many stones they knew Edward had plundered; stones meant only to be worn by the monarch of the throne. If so, why leave one of the most prized string of pearls in the whole world, Queen Alexandra's opera length pearl necklace, strewn on the golf-course.

The only hard evidence the police had was that they had very little to go on. The thieves had left no evidence except for two open windows; the jewellery case and the sashcord found on the golf course.

So, why was the secretary's window left open, disobeying security regulations, and was it definitely the point of entry?

Why did nobody see anything when there was a full complement of staff on hand at the house that night?

How did the thieves know the exact layout of the lodge, and the timing of the Windsor's movements?

How did they know among all the trunks and suitcases which suitcase, when there were so many, all so similar, and some also padlocked?

Why did they not take anything else?

Wallis' solid gold vanity set was on her table, and Countess Dudley's jewels had been left out for all to see.

Why did they escape across the golf course?

It wasn't the easiest route at all, leading nowhere, and surely the thieves would have come in a get-away car and had it waiting ready to whisk them away.

Why on earth did they leave the case to be found, broken open on the golf course rather than taking and disposing of it further afield?

Why had they carelessly left pieces strewn around, particularly the priceless string of pearls?

And the main one, puzzling everyone...

Why hadn't the dogs barked at the sight of a stranger entering Wallis's rooms, so alerting the staff to an intruder? And if not the Duchess's dogs, then not at least arousing those of the Earl's?

After intense interrogation, Countess Dudley's head-housemaid, Miss Jones, was exonerated. She'd explained she had done her usual evening security checks, closing all windows, however, had left that particular window to the secretary's bedroom cracked open as the room had been so warm due to the central heating. This was verified. Miss Martin, the Duchess's maid, after grilling was also released from suspicion. Even the Dudley's handyman- Dunster, after initial suspicion due to a past criminal record was cleared, claiming many years a changed man, along with a tight alibi. All sixteen staff were finally unable to be considered, none had any idea Wallis had such an amount of jewellery with her, even the butler wasn't aware her jewels were carried in such a nondescript suitcase left lying around her room.

The secretary's window-ledge had definite markings of entry, along with the secondary discovery of the bathroom window-ledge, but to use two ways in and out did not add up. The police decided the found white sashcord would not have had the strength to have held any weight, probably used to lower a case, so leaving hands free to descend.

The madman was found and arrested, honouring Edward's ridiculous theory. The man was then released, as it was obvious he hadn't a clue, nor the wits to carry out such a highly skilled operation.

The Canadian armoured car was a mystery, no one had seen it. Had Wallis been up to her old tricks of selling secret information, but why to the Canadians? And what information would she have, now kept at bay to anything sensitive.

The press had a field day, the story was as mystifying and glamorous as an unsolved Agatha Christie. However, the poverty stricken public -although concerned for the couple- couldn't quite find it in their hearts to feel sorry for the Duke and Duchess; not once the information unfolded as to how much they'd been spending on jewels during hard years of rationing. Wallis only made matters worse by snapping at a reporter when asking about the jewels, "A fool would know that with tweeds or other daytime clothes one wears gold, and with evening clothes one wears platinum." This insensitive comment didn't go down well.

Losing public sympathy to their plight, Wallis claimed she felt victimised, and "not taken seriously in this country", while she continued taking it out on Edward in yet more vicious torrents of emotional abuse.

Chapter Forty-One

Sunningdale,
Autumn/winter 1946,

It was weeks later when there was a knock at the door. It had gone nine o'clock in the evening and the police were outside. They had come round to question Les. He'd been expecting it, knowing their initial questioning on the night proved futile, the police were on the warpath for anyone.

'Answer it, Queenie, we've nothing to hide,' Les said, aiming his voice at the door. The police came in, and after the initial questions, started to search the house. They were thorough, turning furniture over and ripping at pillows, they even woke and moved the children out of their beds as they searched the mattresses. Little Pattie, firecracker as she was, started kicking and screaming and ran over to protect her brothers, Dickie and Peter.

'Stop that! Do you really have to disturb my children? They were sleeping!' Les said firmly, seeing his children frightened. 'Do you have a search warrant?'

'Right! You -Leslie Holmes, you're coming with us for questioning!'

'On what charge?'

'Don't get clever! We can carry out the interrogation here if you wish.'

Les was bundled into the back of the police car, and they roared off into the night.

Sitting there in the interrogation room, Les felt safe in the knowledge that they had nothing on him, nor any reason to suspect him. He calmly smoked a cigarette while they fussed around him, until they finally got down to business.

'So, tell me your memory of events of the day in question, October 16th, 1946.'

'Look, Detective Inspector Capstick, I have nothing to tell you to help your inquiry; therefore, nothing to say,' Les said in his evasive manner, but still looking the chief right in the eyes, 'I will answer any questions you have, to my best abilities, but nothing I say will bring you any closer to finding those jewels.'

Capstick looked at him, long and hard. 'Oh my,' he thought, 'this is a hard one to crack, this man's soul is steel,' trying to get an overall picture of this character, Les. They talked about Les's role in the war, and how he'd had to forage for survival at times and had a reputation on record for being able to crack safes, but other than that, he had a clean criminal record and had never done anything wrong.

'Admittedly I had to do things that made me feel morally uncomfortable, but they were always upon orders of my senior officer, and let me remind you...' he leant right into the chief, looking deep into his eyes, saying, 'we were at war.'

Capstick changed tack, 'It says here that you were a renowned safe cracker for the army.'

'I don't know about renowned!' Les chuckled raucously.

Capstick couldn't help but laugh with him. This guy was such an amiable fellow, but somehow, deep down, Capstick felt this may be the one, after all. Les did have a reputation in the underworld. Les had the gall, the guts and the wits to seize such an opportunity. Nevertheless, how could Capstick prove it. He knew he'd have a hard time getting this nut to crack out a confession, and Capstick had many other leads he had to follow up before he could know for sure.

The searches and inquisitions continued for a few more months, but to no avail. Due to suspicion Les lost his job and found it impossible to find work with the country still in extreme poverty and tight rationings. Gwen's mental state wasn't easing either. Things couldn't get any worse, and now even his rational state of mind was slipping. In desperation, he resorted to risking it once more, going out scrounging at night again: they were in such dire straits what else could he do. He'd so wanted to provide for his family once he got back from the war, but now felt so inadequate, so helpless seeing them suffer so. He'd not fought for this.

'Les, please don't. They're on your back. Be careful,' Gwen worried.

'I'm the invincible magician, remember!' Les winked a knowing glance. He was going to provide for them, come what may. He'd still not decided what to do with the jewellery and just left them well hidden for the meanwhile. So, he admittedly did a spat of other cat-burglaries, just sheds and garages, bits and bobs, anything he could exchange, until, one night, he overdid it again.

He couldn't resist it, got carried away wanting to spoil Pattie and took a rather special elaborate Victorian doll's house. Extremely expensive, it must have come from one of the wealthy spreads around Sunningdale: the sort of doll's house only ever seen in palaces or rather grand stately homes. It was coming up to Christmas and he'd so wanted to give his daughter something special. Pattie had been such a good girl, invaluable round the house, helping with the chores and always had an eye on her little brother Peter, looking after him like a mother.

Gwen, upon seeing the doll's house was livid, and put her foot down,

'What on earth!' she exclaimed.

'It's a bit special isn't it!' he said excitedly.

'Special! Special Branch locking you up, more like!' she threw back at him.

'But Pattie would just love it!'A childish look of glee appeared on his face as he thought about spoiling his little girl.

'She'd also love her daddy to be around every day; not behind bars! It's way too obvious!' she said, matter-of-factly.

'I know,' he said sheepishly.

'It's also too big, we couldn't even hide it!' she added, looking at it.

'No, I suppose not,' he muttered, his balloon deflated.

'It's got to go, and I mean NOW!'

All the noise had woken Pattie, she staggered along the hall and into the room, standing there in her nightie and rubbing the sleepy dust out of her eyes; she couldn't quite believe what was in front of her.

'WOW! For me?' Her face lighting up further than it ever had before. She ran towards this fantasy of a dolls house, opened the tiny door and peeked inside: there before her was a perfect miniature world, immaculately laid out, from matching cushion covers to curtains, mahogany tables and chairs, all utensils needed for fine dining and sumptuous silk bedspreads in the bedrooms. This was the real deal.

'Daddy! For me? Thank you!' she exclaimed, excitedly jumping up and down. It was too late, there was only one way to deal with this and that was sternly.

'No! It's not for you. It's none of your business, and you have NEVER seen it, or you are in deep trouble, do you hear me? Go! Get to bed!' Gwen boomed.

Pattie's little feet ran as fast as she could, back to the safety of her bedroom,

'Oh Mummy, I'm sorry,' she said, crying a little as she was in shock. It was so rare that her mother ever raised her voice to any of them, 'I'm so sorry.'

The doll's house disappeared as swiftly as it had arrived to the house; but it had been that one step too far.

Oh heck – they're here, Les thought to himself, as his heart skipped a beat to the sound of what was definitely policemen walking up the gravel path towards the front door. It had to be policemen: three different sets of heavy purpose-laden steps. They were back, and Les just had a feeling by the sound of the intent in their stride they were back - for him.

Les stood still for a split second, fight or flight mode took over, adrenalin coursed through his veins. *This was it*. Rationally he worked out his options: 'I could run, right now. I'd probably make it too, considering they don't know the heath like I do; nevertheless, running away will only sign my death warrant: prove I'm guilty. Anyhow...' he thought, trying to take deep breaths like he did when he was at war, 'They can't have anything on me. It's just not possible. I'm sure of it.' With that he decided to remain calm and collected, confront them with charm. He quickly ran into the scullery, Gwen was preparing potatoes for the pot,

'Queenie, I need you to be calm: the police are back. Just remember what we talked about. Don't worry, Petal, we'll be OK.' Her eyes widened with fear, but then his calming hypnotic voice soothed her worries, looking deep into his trusting loving eyes.

And with that, there was the hard insistent knocking at the front door. This time it seemed to echo its doom around the house, a pivotal moment in time as with the opening of that door life would never be the same again. Les smoothed down his ruffled hair as he walked towards it. As soon as he opened it, he saw the hard faces of these policemen that meant business. They didn't waste time,

'Lesley Arthur Charles Holmes, you are under arrest. We are arresting you on suspicion of attempted housebreaking and larceny...' Les didn't really hear the rest of what the police had to say: it was his children and his queenie he was thinking of as they took him away.

Back at the cottage, the police continued their search, this time they were brutal. Gwen watched in horror as they ransacked her home, her garden, even ripped her children's teddies to bits as the children screamed in horror. Gathering the kids close, she said nothing; for she didn't know where Les had hidden the royal jewels. She just stared out the window while watching them digging up the garden, then the vegetable patch, even the chicken coop was turned upside down.

Les was thrown in prison, as he'd not the means to pay his bail. He'd been caught for petty burglary. All he could do was sit tight and await his fate.

Les came in front of the court on that cold and miserably wet day in January 1947; unluckily in front of the toughest of judges, known as 'Judge D'; renowned for his harsh sentencing. Les stood in the dock at the Surrey Quarter Sessions Court waiting to hear his fate. He stood tall and proud as his life was judged and signed away. They had him on 26 minor cases of house-breaking and larceny, things like a screwdriver here, lawnmower there; nothing major; but it all added up. He'd not done all of them, but there was no proof, not a lot he could do or say, the judge's steely mind was already made up about him: three full years to be served in Wakefield prison, West Yorkshire. Family visits would be impossible. He couldn't have been placed further away from his family if they'd tried.

The chaplain believed Les had been given an overly harsh sentence, particularly as it was his first offence, and considering Les had worked so hard and been so brave in the war, so persuaded Les to go to appeal over his sentence, telling him to explain the hardship he'd been under at home: no money, no work, an ill and unstable wife, three young children to look after; let alone no help financially or emotionally, in any form, after having come back from the front, recovering from the horrific battle at Arnhem where he'd showed incredible bravery for his fellow men. It was to no avail: Judge 'D' was not famous for leniency. Threatening Les:

'If you don't own up to your involvement in the Royal Robbery, we will extend your sentence from 3 to 5 years.'

Les, realising he was strapped well over a barrel, made no reply. Fine - if that's the way you want it, he thought to himself, that's the way you'll get it. Something snapped and he knew not to trust anyone, anymore.

The courts actions were unusual, underhand, as they had nothing on him: no evidence whatsoever linking Les to the royal theft. The chaplain of the prison took this on as a personal cause against the judge, to put right the wrong. But to no avail. The judge was personally infuriated at Les's stubbornness.

Meanwhile Detective Inspector Capstick still had no leads on the jewels. There had been many fantastical stories, but none had any substance once they'd looked into them. They'd tried leaning on Les, threatening him, taunting him with how Gwen wasn't coping without him, trying to sway him emotionally, but this wouldn't wash with Les, and what could he do from inside the slammer anyway? He only hoped they didn't realise Eva was his sister and worked at Fort Belvedere, otherwise that connection could complicate things further. He didn't want her threatened for something she had nothing to do with. These things made it harder for him, realising the delicate pack of cards he was juggling, but only made his resilience stronger.

They even tried interrogating Gwen, but her information wouldn't stand up in court due to her mental instability, even if they did get anything out of her. She would just clam up under pressure and retreat into her inner world, staring out the window, not uttering one single word.

At Detective Inspector Capstick's request Les was eventually moved from Wakefield Prison in West Yorkshire to Wormwood Scrubs in London: he wanted Les closer so he could see him regularly. He believed he may eventually be able to persuade Les to confess. Capstick never stopped believing Les was behind it all. So, Les was transferred and stayed at Wormwood Scrubs for the full duration of his sentence, plus the two extra years, not given even one day off the sentence for good behaviour. Even though he was closer to his family and siblings, he never had one visit in the whole five years - other than Capstick, of course.

A chapter of Les's life closed. The extremity of what he'd done sunk in. He saw how he'd got carried away with the burglaries - to the point of almost getting a reputation within the underworld of London. What was he meant to have done? He wondered, hour after hour, staring out of that tiny, barred prison window. There really had been no work for him anywhere, and Gwen had been so delicate. Through his remorse, Les started to fret about his beautiful family again...

Gwen, at first, had been ok, but soon, the stress of other's gossip and snide comments started playing on her mind. She was never one to care what people said, nevertheless, the cruel words started to go round and round, in her head, haunting her, like those of Victor's.

Their German friend, Pieter, still hadn't been sent back to Germany and came to visit Gwen, giving her a hand looking after the children for the day and trying to make her smile.

'It's so hard without Les keeping it all together,' she said sadly, she wasn't dealing with Les gone once more at all well.

'I can imagine, but you must keep strong. Time will pass quickly, and he'll be home before you know it.' Pieter tried to reassure her with his words.

'It's not going to be that easy this time though, is it?' her voice quivering. She had gone to pieces with the thought of Les inside, gone for another five years. The war had been one thing; but this was too much.

'Oh Gwen,' he sighed, and placed his kindly arms around her, just comforting her in this frightening time. Suddenly the doorbell rang, she sat up with a start.

'I bet it's the police. I can't face them again. Will you go to the door for me?' Her eyes wide and sad. Pieter went to the door, opened it, and was greeted by a look of pure hatred. Gwen came to the door. It was the gossiping nosey neighbour of a few doors down. She was saying how she was worried as the kids were still out, playing so late across on the heath. Pattie had gone with her friend, Elsie, to play on the common, 'and that's the last time I let my Elsie play with your daughter!'

'There's nothing I can do; they could be anywhere over there.' Gwen said, 'And if I remember rightly, it was your Elsie that called for my Pattie. They love it over there. They're probably engrossed in their game of cowboys and Indians and lost the track of time. I wouldn't worry... they'll be back home when they're hungry.'

The woman just stood there, in the doorway, disgust emanating from her eyes, staring at Gwen and the German. She'd heard all the gossip, about Germans always calling at the house, she'd even started some of the gossip herself, had seen the uniformed men walking past her gate but... being here, actually seeing

Gwen so relaxed with this German Prisoner of War was all the fuel she needed for her next fire of evil, shallow gossip.

This was taken to the hilt, before the accusation was ever able to be rightly addressed. They'd been looking for an excuse to get at her, the word spread and by the next day people gathered outside Gwen's house. It was to be another horrific afternoon that Gwen had to endure during her life. People stood taunting her, spitting at her, then pushed her around, gained access to the cottage and started to throw all the family's belongings onto the common heath land opposite. They accused her of being a "Nazi lover", shouting how they wouldn't have Nazi lovers in their village. The golf club had been looking for a reason to evict them from the property since the possible involvement with the 'grand theft' and had now found it as Gwen hadn't been able to pay the rents now demanded. It was by the by, that they were throwing an innocent, vulnerable, unstable woman and three children out into the cold winter's evening air with nowhere to go.

All their belongings; not that they had many; but the lovely bohemian curtains, the African statue, the children's few precious toys, their clothes and bedding, were all strewn, with contempt, over the common opposite the cottage.

Gwen, at first, was shrieking and pleading her innocence, explaining how Pieter was just a dear friend. This fell on deaf ears, so she fell silent, stood proud and took it: her spirit would not let her fall. She stood there with the grace of a queen, whilst these small-minded, ugly spirited women taunted her.

'You may knock me down, but still I'll rise,' she said to herself, echoing it over, and over, as if a mantra. It was at this point, due to the extreme shock and stress of the situation that her schizophrenia really kicked in and took a turn for the worse.

They huddled together that icy evening, Gwen and her children, trying to keep warm. Night was fast approaching, and they had no shelter. They couldn't leave their belongings either, as there'd be nothing left. Gwen was so knocked by the fast turn of events of that day that she wasn't able to work out a way forward, so just sat, cradling her children while humming to them, pretending it wasn't really happening.

Out of nowhere, when it was very late, one of the villagers (who wasn't among the pack of wolves and who still had some compassion) came to their rescue, bringing them a large tarpaulin. He helped Gwen and the kids pull it over their belongings, making a shelter of sorts for the family to huddle under that night, a layer of protection from the cold, damp winter's night. The children thought it was an adventure, camping with Mummy, not really understanding; just confused Mummy was upset.

The press had been alerted, and there they were, in position awaiting the first signs of life. So, when Pattie opened up the tarpaulin at dawn and poked her head out to see the new day before her, she was clocked by a press photographer and made the front page. The story line was pitching something like: 'This is what happens to a war hero's family, accused without proof.'

Gwen was moved into a Nissan hut, near Sunningdale. Without the familiarity of the surroundings of the cottage, without the comfort of her happy memories around her, without her privacy, she started to break down, deteriorating quickly. She'd only just been able to keep herself together until Les came back from the war, but now she found it harder than ever: almost impossible. The slightest thing totally threw her. Not knowing how to survive in the camp: the noises, the bustle, her way round, even going to get basic essentials was too much; having to face so many people, so many different faces everywhere; all confused her. Breaking down over the children, not being able to harbour them from the turmoil anymore, Dickie was sent to stay with his grandma, leaving Gwen with Pattie and the youngest, Peter, who was still an adorable but vulnerable toddler. Pattie would do all she could to help her mummy.

Gwen didn't know what she could do. How could she get herself out of this terrible predicament? She had nowhere to go and no-one to turn to. Understandably, Eva had to distance herself from them. Gwen wasn't even able to visit her husband, nor see her friend Pieter. She had nothing; she was so thin and incredibly nervous. The days when she'd just coast through life like a sparkling glass of champagne, always bubbly and fun, were far gone; now she was so fraught, nervously smoking with her hand trembling once more, talking to herself and becoming more paranoid that 'they' were against her, they were coming for her too: She broke down.

The voices and taunts in her head were becoming stronger and louder, until one night, she lost it. She couldn't work out where she was, where Les was, where even the toilet was, where her lovely cottage was; everything had gone blank, her mind was on a black-out. She screamed: she couldn't take it anymore. Screaming and screaming; high-pitched, pained screams emanating like the sound of a pig being slaughtered as it squealed for its life. Her piercing calls of despair haunted the camp that night, disturbing everyone. Gwen couldn't take the snide comments and evil glances anymore. She shouted, wanting her lovely life back, with her Les, her children and cottage, as it had been before he'd had to go to war. She threw whatever she could get her hands on, picking up the few bits of crockery she had there with her and smashing them at the walls; venting her anger at it all: smashing up the last pieces of her already broken life.

It wasn't long before the wardens arrived, along with the police, and assessing the situation they realised they were going to have to get this crazed banshee of a redhead to calm down. That wasn't going to be easy, and the more they tried to calm her down, the wilder she became, kicking and scratching, screams piercing ear breaking howls. Gwen was like a wild animal. It was a terribly sad sight that night: Gwen, in pieces; amongst her broken china.

It took six men to get hold of her, holding her down long enough so they could get the straight jacket on her and carry her into the white van. She fought even stronger when she realised where they were taking her, to one of 'those' institutions. Gwen had no-one to defend her; she feared she'd not be released, lost forever in an asylum, if she had no one on her side on the outside. Pattie and Peter screamed and cried their little hearts out to go with their mummy, screaming as they ran alongside, following the van; but were taken into the hands of strangers. Pattie, gripping Peter with all her might, wouldn't let go of her little brother's hand, not allowing any separation to happen that night.

All Gwen remembered was arriving outside the austere building, and a nasty looking woman in a white coat opening up the door. They came at her with a long needle, injecting her with some tranquilizer, and she, totally unable to defend herself, strapped up in her jacket, could do nothing but pass out almost immediately. They took her limp body, stripped off her clothing, replacing them with just a straight-jacket and threw her in a padded cell. Gwen came round, hours later, to find herself naked but for the jacket, screaming for her life and her children.

'What's going to happen to my little ones? You must let me go! I need to look after my children; my baby needs me!' The more she screamed the more they drugged her, but the drugs would soon wear off and she would start all over again. A couple of wardens came to check on her, this time she just threw herself at them, biting and kicking at them.

'You've got to let me out! You don't understand. My children need me!'

They grabbed hold of her and dragging her by her jacket straps they pulled her along the ground, into a different room, where there were a few other wardens waiting for her, it seemed. They lifted her up onto a trolley, strapping down her arms and legs into thick leather buckles. They pulled really tight, securing her in, then placing a leather 'biter' into her mouth, leaned over her and told her, 'It's for your own good,' as they secured a head strap onto her.

Gwen was screaming and contorting but could do nothing. She was absolutely scared shitless. What were they going to do? She felt like they were going to cut her up into little pieces. She'd heard terrible rumours of things they do in these places. They'd been known to take organs for medical research. She'd seen people that had been 'given' a frontal lobotomy, leaving the patient totally docile and without any character. She'd also known her grandmother was abused sexually. Her mind was racing, her eyes wild with fear as the warden took a shaving razor and shaved off her hair from the sides of her head. Beautiful red tendrils fell to the floor as they finished their work, then dabbed a little water on her temples and secured the most hideous cold metal contraption onto her head. It looked like a torture implement from the medieval centuries. Screaming through her eyes, she thought, 'No! NO! NO!' But what could she do?

'They can break my spirit, but they can't have my soul.' Gwen thought as they prepared her. Suddenly, with no anaesthetic -these were very early trials- and not ever even knowing anything like it, a whirring kinetic sound started up. The shrill pitch enhanced its force until the electric volts shot through her brain; coming at her from both sides at once (in these times, they were using high doses of electricity, on both sides, at the same time, for longer periods of time: not ever allowed to be practiced now), as the electricity seared through her brain and down through her veins, her body was sent into a state of extreme contraction, arching and raising up as if demon possessed. They held her there, in this horrific state for a good few seconds, then abruptly stopped the charge. Her body fell limp onto the table; but her eyes, still lucid, staring directly into theirs with volumes of strength.

They decided to give her another go; angry she'd bit them. Again, the horrendous sound started as the machine whirred up its power. The body contorting out of control, every cell was maxed out with the ecstatic overload of kinetic energy. This time it took her deep within, far away, and she was gone: Out cold. They released the voltage rapidly. Her body dropped like a dead weight onto the trolley, and her eyes were out: she wasn't in there anymore.

'That'll teach her for biting me!' said the first warden.

'Yes, we've got to watch this one!' said another.

'Pretty though, isn't she!' added the foul first warden as he looked her up and down.

A few days later a mysterious dark suited man went into the consultation room with the doctor, discussing Gwen. He explained to the doctor about Gwen's husband possibly being the royal jewel thief. He wanted to make sure that if she mentioned anything at all in her ramblings, anything about jewellery or hiding places, or the robbery, or if they could get her to talk, even for a moment, they were to notify him straight away. He then disappeared out of the building –invisible- as his job required.

Gwen was left strapped to a bed. When she came round deep confusion had set in; her head was pounding with the most excruciating headache and her muscles ached painfully. She felt as if she was floating on a cloud, in a mentally muggy cloud, there was no rhyme or reason to anything, just the energy of life buzzing around. She swore she could see energy, in balls of beautiful colours swirling round the room. The sense of how precious life was overwhelmed her, but then, it wasn't long before the extreme sadness for her children came back to haunt her, she'd become upset, then be moved back, naked, to the padded cell.

This was to become a vicious circle she was to enter for a long while, sadly, for many years. She'd amass the energy to beg to see her children, only to be hit down with electric shocks. The shocks were administered on a regular basis; at some points it was almost daily; but still her spirit would not lie down. Nor did she give anything away, not even in her worst moments.

When Les found out that his wife had been sectioned, he went white, and for the first time in his life he broke down, alone in his cell. He fell to his knees, guilt and remorse so deep, praying to God to watch over his precious, magical wife. He'd never wanted her to pay for his dues.

He was haunted: understanding how delicate she was and how vile they could be in mental asylums. The thought of his children, his boys and spunky little Pattie being passed around from home to home, broke him again and tears of grief welled in his eyes. The heavy burden of guilt rode him hard. He looked up, out to the blue sky beyond the bars at his cell window, to the treetops he could see wafting in the wind he couldn't feel against his skin and begged God to help him. The shape-shifting cat had turned into a caged bird. How could he turn this around? He had to bide his time, be strong, and get out of this hell hole as quickly as possible to piece his family together.

Les was exhausted after having tried to keep it together for so long. The feeling of disaster, failure and defeat stayed with him for weeks: he'd hit rock bottom. Doom had set in.

One day as he watched the rain pour down onto the rooftops, remembering the wonderful smell of fresh rain falling, the warden came to his cell, tapping on the bars with his truncheon,

'Holmes. Visitor. Now! Capstick here to see you -again.'

'Ok,' Les said, as he dragged himself together and stood waiting as the bar doors clunked open and he shuffled along behind, making his way to the interview room.

Detective Inspector Capstick still came to visit him regularly. By now they had quite a rapport going between them. The Detective Inspector always hoped that Les might open up about the theft and decide to confide in him and tell him where they were hidden.

'Hello Mr H,' as he called Les.

'Hello Chapstick,'

They had their nicknames for each other: Capstick's 'Mr H' showed his underlying respect for Les, where-as, Les's 'Chapsick' (the name of a lipsalve) was a slight reference to the fact Les would never 'grease' his lips and tell.

'How are you doing?' Capstick asked sincerely.

'Well, funnily enough, I can't be doing that well as I think I'm almost glad to see your sorry face!' The men laughed at ease with each other; their camaraderie had bonded them into an unexpected friendship.

'I've some bad news,' Capstick said, looking concerned.

'If it's about my wife...I already know.' Les's face was frozen with grief.

'I really am so sorry,' replied the Inspector.

'Just as long as it wasn't you lot that masterminded the whole situation and pushed her over the edge.' As Les said this his eyes pierced into those of the Inspector's. 'It would be just dandy if you could use her to get to me -wouldn't it.'

'Honest to God, Mr H! We're not that bad.'

'Hmmm, just like I'm not a thief!' Les said slowly.

'I really am sorry for you. I can't imagine how it must be cutting you up - not being able to help her. Maybe there's something I could do? From the outside?'

'That really is thoughtful,' Les said, touched at his display of sincerity. 'Look, I know you had nothing to do with it really, I'm just feeling a bit helpless today.'

He paused, looking at the barred window in the corner and added, 'Being in here.'

'Well, you know if ever you were to change your mind and help me solve the Royal Robbery, I'd personally see to it the courts were as lenient as possible with you.'

'Is that after they hang me for treason!' Les joked.

'Well, it would mean a promotion at my end, so I'd be in a strong position of power to help you sway the judge.'

'Yeh, but you couldn't promise me that,' Les said flatly, then head back down added, 'Nothing can help me, Chapstick, nothing. Thanks for the thought, though.'

'Well, at least...' Capstick paused uneasily, 'I want you to know I'm standing by, if and when you change your mind.'

'Yes, yes! But enough of all that,' Les said, wanting to change the subject, 'What's going on out there?' pointing with his thumb beyond the prison walls. They fell into a conversation about the football, and the news that day, then Capstick came back to the subject of Gwen,

'I could visit your wife, if you like, Mr H? I could take her a letter from you?' Capstick said this as he turned round, getting up ready to leave, 'I could check she's in good hands and all?'

'No, I won't have you doing that. It'd only worry her more. You're a good man though. We could have been friends, in another life!' Les said, thoughtfully.

'Yes, I believe we still could, Mr H... that is if you tell me what you've done with those damn jewels!' They both laughed, knowingly, a deep long laugh, and then he was gone. Les was taken back to his cell.

Detective Inspector Capstick would visit, every now and then, on the off-chance Les would change his mind and spill. But he never did. Nevertheless, the Inspector never gave up hope, even sent Les a Christmas card with well wishes and his personal telephone number every year, without fail, till the day he died.

That night, once back in Les's cell, on the night of the storm, February 28th, as the thunderstorm gradually passed overhead and the rain stopped lashing down and playing tricks with Les's mind, stopped falling in rhythm to the soldier's quick march, Les's fever gradually started to lift and the wind whistled words of wisdom. He lay there, huddled up, and watched the moon-lit clouds being blown away, racing against the night sky. His mind was also clearing from the fog of tormented memories. He suddenly felt his dead father's presence pervading the cell, could almost smell him and feel his strength and unending love for him envelope around his body. Les finally cried: for all he'd done, for all he'd tried to do, for loving his queenie and kids but failing them at the last hurdle, for having judged Wallis -a woman he'd not even met: for everything. He prayed for forgiveness: there in that hard bed, wet with sweat, the feeling of intense love filled his heart. Staring out of his tiny window the stars came out; calling to his conscience and Queenie's face calling to his heart, he weighed up the best way forward.

If he gave-in to Capstick and told him what he so wanted to hear, confessing everything, what exactly would be the outcome?

He would be accused of stealing the 'Royal Jewels'. This would not be taken lightly by any judge, let alone what Judge D would do to him. Whatever position Capstick was promoted to wouldn't be high enough to look after him, he couldn't promise to protect Les, even if Capstick meant it, the others involved played to their own tune. The 'hierarchy' as it were, would see to it that Les was in for life, or worse. It would definitely be longer than the five years he was already serving – that was for sure. He would kiss goodbye to ever gathering his family back together. He'd never be free to look after Gwen and his family. Even when he was 'freed' the stigma of 'the royal jewel thief' would stick. Life would be even harder than before: he'd be unemployable.

Ok, so the Windsor's would get their jewellery back. Jewellery made from certain gems taken without consent from the royal vaults. With which, Wallis would be able to adorn herself once more and flaunt her avarice and self-adoration, inflicting it onto others. Was this necessary for the world situation at that time? Was Wallis suffering without them? It wasn't as if what Les had taken was all of Wallis's collection as most of her jewellery had been waiting in the bank's stronghold in Paris for her return. And as for *her* traitorous actions, they would still go unpunished, in a time when treason was an executable offence.

Giving in to Capstick certainly wouldn't help Gwen. It wouldn't mean she'd recover any quicker. If anything, it would exacerbate her mental state, already unable to deal with the persecution would only lead to more extreme paranoia. He certainly would be longer inside, regretting not able to see her for years as it was. Confessing wouldn't help his children - aside from the fact that they'd probably be all grown up by the time he'd be released - if ever; they'd have to carry the burden of being labelled 'the jewel thief's kids': this would probably destroy their chances of ever making a fair start in life.

'No, the jewels are staying where they are,' he decided, 'for good'.

He found some ironic sense of strength, of satisfaction, in his decision. He knew he'd come to the right conclusion, given the circumstances. He lay back and finally, after the long hours of mental torment that night, after his guilt, his running through of every event that they'd had to live through in the last 10 years, of the elaborate stories in the papers that had made him realise he just couldn't risk getting rid of the gems anymore; after looking back at all of it, a feeling of total peace came over him, his fever abated and his muscles relaxed. He was now at peace with it all, as much as he could be.

He stared out through his tiny window as the stars sparkled in the night sky, the stars glistening so brightly that they suddenly reminded him of the incredible diamonds he'd held, and how breathtakingly beautiful Gwen had looked, adorned 'that night' as his very own queen. He felt how life is nothing but 'swings and roundabouts', and ironically the jewels were now back where they came from. It felt right, to leave them back where they belong, deep in the earth as an offering of forgiveness to God for his actions; a gift of the bounty of beauty to appease the spirits, for the enjoyment of no-one but mother-nature.

"Good and buried."

Chapter Forty-Two

Mental Asylum,
1950.

'Les...Les?' Gwen called out, coming out of a groggy, drug-induced sleep. Someone was running their hands up along the inside of her leg and she realised it wasn't Les. Her mind was playing tricks on her. It was becoming harder and harder to keep the pieces of her mind, and memory, together. The continual shock treatments were taking their toll. She didn't remember how she'd got to be in here, sometimes she hardly even remembered who she was, but she never forgot her children. She could feel them, their love for her deep within, and this then, instead of calming her, led to screaming panic attacks. Anxiety wracked, she'd wear herself out, and retreat into her fantasy world. Hallucinations were becoming more prominent, another hangover of the 'treatment'. Gwen was losing her sense of reality; she imagined she was living in a beautiful world where she was someone special: 'Queenie' was her name.

The man touching her was blurred to her sight. There was nothing she could do, her body was limp with poison searing through her veins. She felt that even breathing was a struggle, sure she was suffocating. The institution had been experimenting with muscle relaxants during the shock treatment to hinder the damage done to the bones and had injected her with a deadly South American poison, small doses froze the muscles, making the person unable to move but totally coherent. They were preparing her for another dose of shocks.

'Hey, don't touch her up too much!' said the other warden as he entered the room

'Yeh, yeh! We all know what you're like!' said the vile warden, 'Jealous!'

Once again, they attached the helmet contraption to her head and started the procedure. They'd decided to 'up' the electric volts, as it didn't ever have an immediate effect on her. They weren't to know then that redheads felt pain more, needing more anaesthesia, higher dosages of pain killers. This time as the electric volts seared through both sides of her brain and down into her body she constricted further than ever, as if her bones bent back on themselves; the joints doubled up, and they left her with such high volts coursing through her body for well over a minute, contorting like crazy as the force of the electricity had control over her being.

She flopped back down onto the trolley, once they'd reduced the volts. She was out cold, but her arm still looked odd; it had dislocated itself in the extremity of the contortion and snapped out.

Gwen came too, after a long while. It took days before she could piece things together. Her memory was so hazy, her speech was blurred, and her mind just wanted to stay in her fantasy world where, with the help of the hallucinations, she was safe, loved and with her husband.

But then, as the mind-fog cleared, the feeling of persecution, that they were deliberately doing this to her, punishing her, became overwhelming. With the panic, once again came the desperation for her children and she became the wild banshee again, screaming and hitting herself till they put her back in the straight jacket.

With her situation getting worse the institution were at a loss, deciding to try and bring one of the children in for her to see. The thought being that by letting her see her children, and know for herself they were Ok, she may be able to calm down and start to stabilize.

Pattie, being the eldest, was sent for. She was taken into the doctor's room and explained that, 'Mummy is very sick, and we are trying to help her.'

Nothing could have prepared that little girl for the harrowing sight waiting for her.

They opened the heavy metal door, to reveal the padded cell, marked with old blood stains and body fluids. There in the corner, like a wild, beautiful, caged animal was her mummy, huddled on the floor, hugging her knees to her body. Gwen was wide-eyed and naked, with her long red hair loose, wild and tangled. She snatched her child from the hand of the doctor, pulling her close to her body. They sat on the ground, cradling each other, rocking back and forth as Gwen hummed a melody through her tears; comforting her child as she hugged as tight as possible. There descended a moment of peace, a calm fell over the room as Gwen's love for her daughter was finally able to be channelled.

But the torture had only just started, as it was soon time for Pattie to go back. As they told Gwen Pattie had to leave, Pattie started to cry,

'But I want to stay with my mummy.'

This was the worst possible experience for Gwen to see her little girl crying so she pulled her even closer, and tighter, promising they wouldn't be separated, not ever again. The wardens had to come in and prize the child away, gently at first, but Gwen held her so tightly, they had to start pulling at Pattie till it hurt, tugging her apart from her mummy. Gwen's screams became intense, she was the tiger looking after her cub, roaring, threatened, she became extremely violent shouting, sobbing, and begging,

'Don't take my baby! ...She's MY baby girl!' she roared. 'Please don't take her from me.'

Gwen had become totally distraught. She tried to hit and scratch the arm of the warden; to make her release little Pattie. At this, in rushed the other wardens with an injection: Gwen fell to the floor, like an animal tranquilised, as they strapped her back into the straight jacket. For Pattie, the memory of her mother, naked, in that padded cell, tied up in the straitjacket, haunts her to this day.

Gwen stayed in institutions, on and off, for the rest of her life. There were periods she'd be able to be 'out,' but only with guidance and in the hands of a guardian. She'd become afraid, paranoid everyone was accusing her and may do her harm. In disturbed moments she was known to ask the where-abouts of her ruby ring; this only confused the family as Les had never been known to have given her a ruby ring.

Gwen had electric shocks for almost thirty years of her life; it obviously didn't help her case, blurred her mental capacity and shortened her life span, so in a way they succeeded in dampening a part of her: her spirit.

Chapter Forty-Three

Paris,
Winter, 1946.

Furious, Wallis and Edward returned to Paris. They'd not achieved their objective, if anything far from it. They'd lost all public sympathy, once siding with the couple's abdication the public now turned away, shocked by their extreme spending in times of rationing. The Royal Family, ever more exasperated by the Duke and Duchess's actions were less likely than ever to offer Edward any duties, let alone sway to the demands for Wallis's title, HRH.

The Duke and Duchess tried to forget the incident and forge on, but the relationship between them had been tainted by the theft. However, there's no doubt it had been extremely advantageous for the couple, as they consequently received a timely and generous insurance claim of £400,000 (22 million in today's money). There is good reason the Duke and Duchess may have exaggerated their claim. Desperate for funds at the time, they may have seen their opportunity in defrauding the insurers by adding many jewels to the list that were still in Paris.

Wallis would have felt little remorse over this, feeling nothing but animosity towards Britain. Her deep hatred for the Royal Family, and even Britain itself pushed a painful wedge between herself and the Duke, as she now resented everything he stood for.

Not only did Edward have to accept the idea that Wallis would never be Her Royal Highness but also come to terms with the fact that the bonds between themselves and his family were more strained than ever: even irreconcilable. Sadly, he desperately missed the company of his brothers and sisters most of all and would try to secretly meet them from time to time.

Wallis and Edward settled on a house in the outskirts of Paris and resumed their decadent but empty lifestyle of shopping, decorating, and entertaining. It was during one of these soirées they entered into their messiest affair with a bisexual to date. Nevertheless, even the pleasure of parties began to wane for Edward, often retiring early and alone.

They lived in this grandiose world they'd built around themselves, with no real purpose, never having achieved any of Edward's original dreams or charities. Wallis wasn't interested in charity, unless it was to her advantage. The hope of what they could have achieved faded, along with the curtains. The butler in later years was to describe them as:

"Just two lonely old people."

The only thing that didn't fade was Edward's devotion to Wallis, and his only known request upon his death was that the jewels he'd had personally created for Wallis were never to be worn by anyone else.

Chapter Forty-Four

Surrey,
1952.

The years passed, and Les was finally released. Over the years, Chief Inspector Capstick, having formed a surprising admiration for Les, famously took him out for dinner and even bought him a suit, hoping to help him find work. He even offered Les £4000 for a confession. There was a knowing between them that Capstick only hoped would be able to be proved one day. As adamant as he was, Capstick had met his match in Les, knowing only too well that Les had his reasons for his silence.

Gwen was still institutionalised. The doctors explained to Les that Gwen's condition was permanent, and for her to be released and live with him would cause a probable relapse. Les was told in no uncertain terms he couldn't risk this possibility and should consider re-marrying. Les was utterly distraught, the thought of reuniting the family had been the only thing that had got him through those harrowing nights inside. He had hoped Gwen had merely had a breakdown or severe post-natal depression, and that she'd be able to recover. He'd prayed that once back together, back in his company, she'd be fine and he'd be able to make it all up to her and protect her once again. Les was never allowed this chance. He privately thought the real damage might have been all the trauma they'd inflicted on her, let alone what they'd pumped through her veins.

Les's life was shattered by this heart-wrenching diagnosis. His heart broke, his guilt immeasurable as the last hope of gathering the family was torn apart. His children were scattered between the children's home, Dr Barnardo's, extended family and foster care. He did everything in his power to bring them back together, back into his company once released, but that was beyond his control and never became a reality.

Being hounded everywhere, all the time, with his home searched and always accused, he realised he couldn't inflict this upon his loved ones. Breaking his heart further he gave Pattie to be raised by another family, hoping for a chance of a good life. He also knew deep down he had to divorce Gwen, even though he'd never stop loving her he needed to release her from any connection with the theft, as continued persecution of the police and press did her paranoia no good whatsoever. The family, now broken into pieces, never rejoined.

In 1951, Chief Inspector Capstick wrote, in Scotland Yard's Secret Police Files, to the FBI: "There is little doubt that he has buried the jewellery, and I am convinced that he is afraid to dispose of it." Capstick had looked into every possibility and knew deep down who he believed had done it. He sent Les a Christmas card with his contact details every year till he died, just on the off chance.

Chapter Forty-Five

2004

Many years later, on the 27th December 2003, Pattie (now known as Tricia), was reading The Times newspaper, when to her horror, as she turned the page her father's face stared back at her, emblazoned in print under the heading: "The Duchess and the Thief who would not Confess". The in-depth article almost took the whole page, including a black and white photo of Les alongside one of the Duke. She was in shock.

Upon seeing her father's face, dark distant flashes flooded back. Flashes she'd tried to forget all her life. Flashes of German POW's, policemen roughly handling her in her nightie, her mother's champagne laugh and her father in uniform. Grief stricken, with hands shaking she rang her estranged father. She'd not spoken in a long time, having been given away, however she needed to speak to Les, to clear her clouded memories. She'd never known about any connection to the royal theft. Les, it turned out had no idea it was all in the news, or that his photo was in the papers, and became very distressed.

After these revelations, Tricia braved it and went to visit her father. Finally, the two of them were alone for the first time in many many years. It was one of those moments when one's able to put some of the pieces of life's puzzle together, and to say those things left unsaid for so long. She shared Les's joy in his later hard-earned achievements, against all odds.

Of course, the 'so did you do it?' question was flying around the room. During Tricia's childhood she remembers her aunts sometimes asking her, 'What did your dad do with the jewels?' however, she'd never any idea what they were talking about. Now, with a greater understanding, everything was falling into place and finally start to make sense. To piece her fragmented memories together, she knew she had to broach the subject. The moment she did, Les sat up, wide-eyed and alert, looked right at her and said, slow and sure,

"They never found them, though, did they!" said with an inner knowing. He took her hand and squeezed it, as if verifying her thoughts through touch, and with eyes glistening, looked deep into hers. They held each other's hands and gazed for what seemed a long while, during which an unsaid transference of knowledge, of truth passed between them, as his eyes danced distant memories with hers. Then he explained, adamantly, "There's only one way to keep a secret..." His eyes glimmered, sparkling truth and secrets once more, saying everything in his silence. Nevertheless, as dark memories of war flooded back, as his reasoning returned, his eyes pained deep, and face turned full of rage at the thought of the Duke and Duchess of Windsor arriving at Ednam Lodge.

"The Windsor's rolled up using army trucks - Army Trucks! The utter audacity made me so mad!" He turned his face away, haunted in memories, "The trucks triggered ALL the horrors of war, of Arnhem."

His breathing erratic and hands shaking, he explained, repeating, "*Her* luggage in *our* trucks," continually. He was livid, "Using *our* men to carry *their* luggage, men they'd betrayed..."

She tried to calm him down, this obviously wasn't good for him, so changed the subject. However, Les reached out for her hand once more, and looking deep into her eyes tried to explain his actions,

"What was I to do? I had no help. I couldn't leave you little ones with Gwen, she just couldn't cope." A tear formed and his lip trembled slightly, remembering, "Gwen was too ill. I had to be there in the day to look after all of you, and remember, Peter was still a baby. So, you see, I could only go out at night once I knew you kiddies were safely tucked up in bed. I'd then go out scrumping for anything I could find. I'd been doing it for years in the army: we'd be dumped in the fields with absolutely nothing, but I always found a way to keep the men alive. God knows how we survived, most didn't..." his voice drifted as he looked away.

Tricia realised how the war hounded him still, and how brave he must have been. They talked about the many other sides to events, explaining he'd been watched all his life. That glimmer of fear still lingered in Les's eyes at the thought of being 'sent back inside'. He was sure his phone was always bugged, and whenever anything went missing on the building site, even with the slightest excuse, his house would be raided; totally turned over. He'd never been able to trust anyone, never risked having friends, as early on, they'd turned out to be policemen 'undercover'. Les explained he'd even come to like Chief Inspector Capstick.

With this, she had a glimpse of the torment that had always been with him, finally understanding why he'd had to make the difficult decision to give her away, knowing he could never confess.

Tricia's pervading memory of the visit that day is of Les, incredibly determined in his decision, with that glimmer of something unsaid dancing in his eyes: the only way one can be when one has a great secret. She can tell a lie a mile away and is adamant he took them. Les didn't actually say: 'Yes, I stole Wallis's jewels,' but explained all he needed without incriminating himself. Nevertheless, it's interesting he never denied it, never once said he *didn't* do it. Sometimes it's the words left unsaid that hold more power.

If it hadn't been for Wallis's avaricious nature, her incessant need for blatant displays of wealth and prestige, let-alone her infatuation with Nazi men and politics, Les may not have done what he did. The enforced poverty of Les's situation, undoubted PTSD from Arnhem, along with fury at the Windsor's wartime actions, drove him to take judgement wrongly into his own hands; hoping to fund his starving family and abate his anger at the same time. He went too far, admittedly, and the repercussions of his actions still greatly affect everyone concerned, as Les and his family lost everything that fateful night. All Les had left was the memory of his queenie in the candlelight, and of course, not forgetting -Wallis's jewels somewhere...

Interestingly, years later in 1987, Wallis went against the Duke's dying wish, and upon her death bequeathed almost their entire estate, including her personal jewellery, to be auctioned off at Sotheby's Geneva and (possibly blackmailed by her lawyer over her Nazi movements) donated to France's Pasteur Institute. Roughly £39 million in all.

Included in the Lot were a certain 30 items later believed to also have been included in the list of stolen jewellery on their insurance claim. It turned out the pieces had been secretly stored in the Duke and Duchess's Paris strong vaults ever since the robbery; however, identical as they were, this has never been proved.

Known information in the jewellery world was that the Duke and Duchess of Windsor never paid for any of the jewellery made for them in later years. At one point both Cartier and Van Clef Arpels were driven to make a pact not to make the couple another piece until they settled all their debts. The jewellers would only lend on promise of return. Neither of these ever happened: not the Duke and Duchess ever paying their dues, nor returning borrowed items. Famous jewellery houses were left seriously out of pocket. It is well known receipts were burnt by the Duchess throughout her life, and then famously, by her maid upon her death.

The skilled craftsmanship, high-quality sourcing of the finest materials, and the unspoken trust so very important in this business, were greatly abused. Let alone the gems stolen from the Royal Vaults, exquisite irreplaceable gems meant solely for the monarch. It makes one wonder if the Windsor's weren't really the thieves in question, and Les, the man.

Les and his family paid their dues a thousandfold for that moment of furious *Retribution Royale*, for the Royal Robbery. Nevertheless, the traitorous Duchess was never brought to justice for her even greater treasonous crimes of espionage against Great Britain during a time of war.

The End.

References

I searched all over for snippets of information relevant to the story: from newspaper archives to radio, royal interest sites, European Royal History Journal, particularly volume 9.4 2006 by Tori V Martinez, television dramas, The life and Legends of Wallis Simpson, by Elizabeth Proud, Wallis & Edward, by Sarah Williams and many other documentaries, Wikipedia, Tatler, and the wonderful books on the subject, particularly Charles Higham's, 'Mrs Simpson', Churchill, by Ashley Jackson, and also recommended reading, published since writing, Traitor King, by Andrew Lownie, and That Woman, by Anne Sebba.

Quotes from papers of the time came from The Courier and Advertiser, The Daily Mail, The Western Morning News, The Western Daily Press and Bristol Mirror, The Derby Evening Telegraph, The Press and Journal, and the Sunday Post. The more recent, The Sunday Times, The Telegraph, The Daily Mail.

About the Author

HL Leavey: writer, linguist, adventurer and alchemist: jewellery designer, goldsmith and gemmologist (FGA, DGA).

Taking the path less travelled, she has lived and worked from Europe to the Amazonas. Fuelled by an insatiable curiosity for life, she explores its beauty and the paradox of wonders so often wrapped in danger: the fragile vulnerability not only of our human gifts, but of the natural world itself.

Returning to her passions for writing and jewellery, she now weaves the entrancing magic of gemstones into suspenseful tales of fate and transformation. She began with the true story *Retribution Royale*, and follows with her mystical suspense novels *Rubies of Resilience*, *Mystique of the Muisca Emerald*, and *Diamond Deception*. Through her writing, she hopes to support Dartmoor Preservation and help the Amazonian Yanomami people protect their sacred lands.

HL Leavey's work is original, evocative and adventurous; passionately exploring human nature while immersing readers in faraway worlds, each laced with intrigue and danger. Her stories transport you to places you long to visit, gripping you with wonder until the final page.

Find also find HLLeavey_Author on Instagram.

Printed in Dunstable, United Kingdom

79907653R10163